the cinema of KRZYSZTOF KIEŚLOWSKI

DIRECTORS' CUTS

the cinema of
KRZYSZTOF KIEŚLOWSKI

variations on destiny and chance

marek haltof

 **WALLFLOWER PRESS** LONDON & NEW YORK

First published in Great Britain in 2004 by
Wallflower Press
4th Floor, 26 Shacklewell Lane, London E8 2EZ
www.wallflowerpress.co.uk

A catalogue for this book is available from the British Library

ISBN 1-903364-91-4 (paperback)
      1-903364-92-2 (hardback)

Book design by Rob Bowden Design

Printed in Great Britain by Antony Rowe, Chippenham, Wiltshire

CONTENTS

ACKNOWLEDGEMENTS

I would like to thank Northern Michigan University in Marquette for supporting this work with a generous grant. In the course of writing this book, I also received help from a number of individuals. I wish to thank Dr Anton Kozlovic (Flinders University of South Australia), Adam Cichorski ('Polimark' in Calgary), Marek Domaradzki (Calgary), Prof. Alicja Helman (Jagiellonian University), Dr Mikołaj Jazdon (University of Poznań), Dr Jan F. Lewandowski ('Silesia Film' in Katowice), Prof. Wacław Osadnik (University of Alberta), Dr Elżbieta Ostrowska (University of Łódź/University of Pittsburgh), Prof. Mirosław Przylipiak (University of Gdańsk), Irena Strzałkowska and Krzysztof Zanussi (Tor film studio in Warsaw) and Dr Piotr Zwierzchowski (University of Bydgoszcz) for assisting in the preparation of this book in various ways.

Special thanks go to Adam Wyżyński at the National Film Archives in Warsaw for his help with researching Kieślowski's documentary films. I am also grateful to other members of staff of the National Film Archives, Grzegorz Balski and Robert Mazurkiewicz in particular, for their generous assistance, as well as for providing the majority of the illustrations reproduced within this book. Other still photographs come from the Tor film studio headed by Krzysztof Zanussi.

I am also very grateful to Dr Bohdan Y. Nebesio (University of Alberta) and my colleagues in the Department of English at Northern Michigan University: Dr David Boe, Dr Russell Prather and Emily Walter, for their insightful comments on evolving versions of the manuscript. Similar words of gratitude go to two anonymous readers commissioned by Wallflower Press.

As always, I would like also to thank my wife Margaret Haltof for her unfailing support. This book is dedicated to the memory of my mother, Danuta Haltof (1924–2002).

Fragments of Chapter 5 appeared as 'Krzysztof Kieślowski: European Art Film and National Context' in *A World of Slavic Literatures: Essays in Comparative Slavic Studies in Honor of Edward Możejko*, edited by Paul D. Morris (Bloomington, Indiana: Slavica, 2002), 79–89; part of Chapter 2 was published as 'Screening the Unrepresented World: Kieślowski's Early Film-Essays (*Personnel, The Scar* and *The Calm*)' in *The Polish Review* 48, 4 (2003), 463–79.

PREFACE

Born on 27 June 1941 in Warsaw, Krzysztof Kieślowski became the best-known contemporary Polish film-maker of the 1990s. His fame spread beyond national borders toward the end of the 1980s. *Dekalog* (*Decalogue*, 1988), a ten-part series of contemporary television films loosely inspired by the Ten Commandments, was hailed by Western European film critics as a great achievement and incontestably placed its director among the ranks of renowned European auteurs. In particular, extended feature versions of two parts of *Decalogue*, *Krótki film o zabijaniu* (*A Short Film About Killing*, 1988) and *Krótki film o miłości* (*A Short Film About Love*, 1988), were exceptionally well received in Europe. Kieślowski's international co-productions, *Podwójne życie Weroniki* (*La Double Vie de Véronique*, *The Double Life of Véronique*, 1991) and his filmic trilogy, *Trois couleurs: bleu, blanc, rouge* (*Three Colours: Blue, Red, White*, 1993–94), consolidated his position as a household name in European art cinema. His subsequent unexpected decision to give up film-making, for health reasons, was treated with disbelief by a number of critics. On 13 March 1996, Kieślowski died in Warsaw following heart bypass surgery. His premature death at the age of 54, and at the peak of his artistic powers, came as a profound shock for the world film-making community.

Scholars and critics often discuss Kieślowski's road to film-making. They stress his nomadic childhood that placed him in a succession of schools due to his father's tuberculosis which required treatment in different sanatoria. The same motif of unsettled childhood returns powerfully in interviews with Kieślowski including the best-known work in English, *Kieślowski on Kieślowski*, edited by Danusia Stok.[1] In 1962 Kieślowski graduated from the Warsaw College for Theatre Technicians (*Państwowe Liceum Techniki Teatralnej*) and worked for one year as a tailor at the Warsaw Contemporary Theatre (*Teatr Współczesny*). On his third attempt, in 1964, he was admitted to the famous Łódź Film School (*Państwowa Wyższa Szkoła Filmowa, Telewizyjna i Teatralna*), completing his studies there in 1968. After a series of documentary films, such as *Z miasta Łodzi* (*From the City of Łódź*, 1969) and *Pierwsza miłość* (*First Love*, 1974), Kieślowski established himself by the mid-1970s as a leading Polish documentary film-maker. A modest television drama, but a breakthrough film for Kieślowski, *Personel* (*Personnel*, 1975), marked his shift toward narrative cinema and a long-term working association with the Tor film studio in Warsaw. By the late 1970s and at the beginning of the 1980s, Kieślowski became one of the best-known representatives of the movement in Polish cinema known as the Cinema of Distrust, which explored the corrupted aspects of communism. (Like several scholars and film-makers, I object to the ill-fitted Polish term *Kino moralnego niepokoju*, which refers to realistic films made between 1976 and 1981. The term is translated by various English authors as the Cinema of Moral Concern, the Cinema of Moral Anxiety, the Cinema of Moral Unrest and the Cinema of Moral Dissent. Following Polish scholar Mariola Jankun-Dopartowa, I prefer the new label, which will be used throughout this book, the Cinema of Distrust – *Kino nieufności* – to describe films characterized by contemporary theme, realism and the social initiation of a young protagonist.)[2]

A closer look at Kieślowski's oeuvre and his artistic persona reveals that he does not fit the traditional image of a 'great Central European *auteur*', obsessed with politics and history. His films are also unique in the context of Polish cinema; for critics used to Polish film functioning for the most part as an expression of Polish history and political tensions, Kieślowski's films (especially his 1990s international co-productions) can be puzzling. His last films embrace several stylistic and thematic obsessions characteristic of European art cinema and, therefore, should be examined beyond their national context.

Given the complexity of Polish history, cinema (and, for that matter, all Polish art) has generally been regarded as more than just entertainment. The artist's 'mission' was that of a prophet and teacher bringing a message to society. During the communist period, film and other art forms performed the role of safety valves in the controlled, corrupt political system. Film-making was a platform, on which political debates were carried out sometimes openly, sometimes in Aesopian language. Politically active film-makers such as Andrzej Wajda were always at the foreground of Polish life. Artists felt an immense responsibility; they were also accustomed to a situation in which their voices were heard and analysed by the people and by the authorities.[3]

As opposed to some internationally known Polish film-makers, such as Wajda or Krzysztof Zanussi, Kieślowski was never directly involved in politics nor was he ever explicitly political in his films or in public appearances. Although persistently subjected to an Aesopian reading by Polish critics and filmgoers alike, his early, still under-appreciated films, such as *Spokój* (*The Calm*, 1976), *Amator* (*Camera Buff*, 1979) and *Przypadek* (*Blind Chance*, 1981), do not demonise the communist system. Rather, they show the system as an obstacle to achieving happiness and, to use the title of Kieślowski's 1976 film, calm. Discussing Kieślowski's career, Tadeusz Sobolewski describes the problem that Kieślowski's 'apolitical' stand generated in Poland: 'None of the critics in Poland had the foresight to perceive the uniqueness and specificity of Kieślowski's films, except in terms of their being a function of social, political or religious aspirations. The Polish critic persistently forces the artist to answer the questions concerning social issues.'[4]

Unlike several internationally recognised Polish film-makers, Kieślowski never made a historical film or an adaptation of a well-known Polish novel. Almost all his works, with the exception of *Krótki dzień pracy* (*Short Working Day*, 1981) which deals with the workers' strikes of 1976, are set in the present, although they may have segments that venture into the past. Kieślowski's interest in the everyday aspect of Polish reality and commitment to uncover the 'unrepresented reality' makes him the leading proponent of the Cinema of Distrust. Although the Polish authorities shelved several of Kieślowski's films (*The Calm, Blind Chance, Short Working Day* and some documentaries), Kieślowski never used this fact to create an image of himself as an oppositional film-maker (as did, for example, Andrzej Wajda). Perpetually independent, Kieślowski operated outside mainstream Central European aesthetics. Within this highly politicised culture, where political choices were of greater importance than aesthetic ones, Kieślowski was clearly an outsider, not afraid of expressing unpopular views concerning, amongst other issues, religion and political commitment. Kieślowski frequently stressed his disillusionment with politics; in 1994, explaining his surprising decision to retire from film-making, he claimed that 'one of the reasons for my departure from the cinema is my dislike for fulfilling public roles, and a longing for privacy'.[5]

In film criticism, Kieślowski is not associated with one particular form of authorial expression. Critics, particularly Polish film critics, usually debate the distinction between the 'early' realist and 'mature' metaphysical Kieślowski, and the majority of them clearly favour 'Kieślowski the realist'. At the beginning of his career Kieślowski operated on a smaller scale ('In Depth Rather than Breadth', as he put it in the title of his 1981 statement),[6] believing in the power of faithful and detailed representation of reality. Later, Kieślowski moved from realistic, documentary-like observations of people and places to films grouped in series: ten films in *Decalogue*, three in his *Three Colours* trilogy, two films in one in *The Double Life of Véronique*, and three films in one in *Blind Chance*. He began to infuse his films with false tropes, episodic plots, and often-enigmatic scenes of little consequence for the storyline.

Some Polish critics considered Kieślowski's move to international co-productions and his growing critical recognition as suspicious.[7] Kieślowski achieved his international *auteur* status without relying on the Polish romantic tradition, which, as Bolesław Michałek says, is characterized by its 'battle for social justice, and its preoccupation with gaining independence, the tradition in which dilemmas are solved by a single gesture. Kieślowski indicates that a dilemma is something you live with.'[8] Michałek's statement closely resembles Paul Schrader's distinction between American movies which are 'based on the assumption that life presents you with problems' and European films 'based on the conviction that life confronts you with dilemmas – and while problems are something you solve, dilemmas cannot be solved, they're merely probed or investigated'.[9] Kieślowski's films certainly deal with dilemmas.

In the manner of other great European *auteurs*, Kieślowski was in full control of every stage of the cinematic process; he not only directed but was also the scriptwriter or co-scriptwriter of all his films, and he worked closely with his editors in the cutting room. He usually worked with a small circle of collaborators; they included cinematographers such as Sławomir Idziak (since 1973), Jacek Petrycki (since 1971) and Witold Stok (since 1972), editors Lidia Zonn (early documentary films), Ewa Smal (*Decalogue*) and Jacques Witta (since *The Double Life of Véronique*), sound editor Michał Żarnecki, and scriptwiter Krzysztof Piesiewicz and composer Zbigniew Preisner since *Bez końca* (*No End*, 1985). Kieślowski also favoured certain actors, for example Jerzy Stuhr, who acted lead roles in *The Calm*, *Camera Buff*, *Decalogue 10*, and supporting roles in *Blizna* (*The Scar*, 1976), *Three Colours: White* and an episode in *Blind Chance*. 'Kieślowski's actors' also include Aleksander Bardini (lawyer Labrador in *No End*, medical doctor in *Decalogue 2*, choir and orchestra conductor in *The Double Life of Véronique*), Bogusław Linda (leading roles in *Blind Chance* and *Decalogue 7*), Zbigniew Zamachowski (leading roles in *Decalogue 10*, *Three Colours: White* and an episode in *Three Colours: Red*), Irène Jacob (main roles in *The Double Life of Véronique* and *Three Colours: Red*), Grażyna Szapołowska (leading roles in *No End* and *A Short Film About Love*), Artur Barciś (supporting role in *No End* and the supporting role of a mysterious young man in *Decalogue*) and Janusz Gajos (*Decalogue 4* and *Three Colours: White*), among others.

It is important to note, although this lies beyond the scope of this book, that Kieślowski also worked as a film lecturer in Poland at the Katowice Film School (1979–82) and Łódź Film School (1994–96), as well as abroad, in West Berlin (1984), Helsinki (1988) and Lausanne (1985, 1988). Despite his often-voiced love for theatre (originally he wanted to become a theatre director), Kieślowski produced only a small number of theatrical plays. In 1978 he directed *Życiorys* (*Curriculum Vitae*, based on his 1975 film under the same title) at the prestigious *Teatr Stary* (Old Theatre) in Kraków. Kieślowski also produced two television theatrical plays for the popular and respected Polish Television Theatre: *Two for the Seesaw* (William Gibson) in 1977 and *Kartoteka* (*The Card Index*, Tadeusz Różewicz) in 1979. The latter, an absurdist social satire often described as 'Poland's *Waiting for Godot*', belongs to the classic repertoire of Polish television theatre.[10] Unlike several important Polish directors who often alternated between film and theatre (including television theatre – popular in Poland) such as Andrzej Wajda, Kazimierz Kutz and Krzysztof Zanussi, Kieślowski devoted himself primarily to cinema.

My approach to Kieślowski's films draws mostly on the critical concept of auteurism. Despite its shortcomings, and after years of being marginalised, this interpretative strategy is once again at the centre of Film Studies and in practice governs the way films are received and analysed. In my discussion on Kieślowski's cinema I am not so much preoccupied with the director's biography but with Kieślowski as a figure emerging from films authored by him. While I remain cognisant of the important contributions of Kieślowski's collaborators, I share an opinion that Kieślowski's work as a director combines various contributions into a structural whole and determines the final form of the film.

This book focuses exclusively on Kieślowski's film-making career in the context of Polish documentary and narrative cinema. In this burgeoning field – studies of Kieślowski's cinema published outside of Poland – there is sometimes little awareness of the relationship between his films and the Polish political, cultural and cinematic contexts. Therefore, chapter one, 'Documenting the Unrepresented World', situates Kieślowski's documentary films within the context of Polish documentary cinema. Chapter two, 'Film-Essays: Kieślowski and Polish Cinema in the 1970s and During the Solidarity Period', looks at Kieślowski's early narrative films in the context of the Cinema of Distrust and its attempts to look at the underside of communism, to portray the mechanisms of manipulation, corruption and other social maladies. Chapter three, 'Choices, Chances and Politics', discusses the implications of the imposition of martial law for Polish cinema and for Kieślowski's career. Chapter four, 'Entomological Observations and Metaphysics in *Decalogue*', looks at Kieślowski's epic ten-part series through the prism of the last years of communist rule in Poland. The final chapter, 'The Double Life of Kieślowski: European Art Film and the Polish Context', discusses not only the 'art cinema' qualities of Kieślowski's international co-productions but also provides 'the Polish perspective', and acquaints non-Polish readers with some representative comments voiced by Polish film critics. The 'Afterword' briefly discusses films made in Poland and abroad after Kieślowski's death that are either based on, or referring to, his film-making ideas.

CHAPTER ONE

Documenting the Unrepresented World

As I saw it, the artist's fundamental obligation in the seventies was to describe. Life operated on a number of planes: the same people or events took on different appearances depending on whether they were viewed from an official or private angle; inequities that were common knowledge but not to be ventilated in public abounded; a variety of languages gained currency. These were the things we had to pinpoint.
 – Krzysztof Kieślowski[1]

Like the majority of Polish film-makers, Kieślowski started his career with a series of documentary films. Documentary cinema in Poland was by no means only a training ground for the future mainstream film-makers – it was a well-established art form generously sponsored by government funding bodies and prudently analysed by local critics. Despite being financed by the communist government, documentary films (similar to fictional films) often contested the political system by providing thinly veiled messages regarding political and social issues. In the 1960s and 1970s several Polish directors specialised in documentary cinema. At the beginning of his career, Kieślowski clearly wanted to belong to this group.

Documentary films in Poland have been made primarily at the *Wytwórnia Filmów Dokumentalnych* (Documentary Film Studio) in Warsaw,[2] which was established in 1949. Starting in 1958, Polish movie theatres were obliged to screen short films (animated, documentary or educational) before the main feature, a factor of great consequence for the makers of short films (this practice lasted until the 1980s). Documentary films also featured prominently on Polish Television. The importance of documentary cinema in Poland is also evidenced by the annual Festival of Short Films in Kraków (*Krakowski Festiwal Filmów Krótkometrażowych*) inaugurated in 1961. Kazimierz Karabasz's celebrated documentary *Muzykanci* (*Sunday Musicians*, 1960) became its first winner.[3]

During the Polish School period (1956–65) a number of documentary films portrayed the negative aspects of everyday life, breaking the silence imposed by the poetics of socialist realism that was reigning after the war. The political changes introduced after the 'Polish October' of 1956 – the symbolic end of the Stalinist period in Poland and an eruption of patriotic feelings that were quickly suppressed by the Communist Party, were reflected in the so-called 'black series' of documentary films. The forerunner of the series, Jerzy Hoffman and Edward Skórzewski's *Uwaga, chuligani* (*Attention, Hooligans*), deals with topics also discussed in Polish periodicals at that time – juvenile delinquency, alcoholism and hooliganism. Particularly known are documentaries by Kazimierz Karabasz and Władysław Ślesicki: *Gdzie diabeł mówi dobranoc* (*Where the Devil Says Good Night*, 1957) and *Ludzie z pustego obszaru* (*People From Nowhere*, 1957). The title of the latter became a description of the criminal sphere of life. Jadwiga Głowa writes that 'The message of the "black documentaries" was stated right at the beginning of an off-screen commentary … Authorial commentaries, emotional in tone, revealed the film-makers sincere commitment to the mission of discovering the truth about a society exposed to communist propaganda.'[4] Due to strict communist censorship, however, the 'black series' film-makers were unable to go beyond the description of some obvious social maladies. Their depiction of reality remains fragmentary and sketchy; it mirrors more the political struggle within the Communist Party than life as it was in the late 1950s.[5]

The best-known examples of documentary cinema made at the beginning of the 1960s in Poland dealt with World War Two. *Powszedni dzień gestapowca Szmidta* (*An Ordinary Day of Szmidt, the Gestapo Man*, 1963) by Jerzy Ziarnik, and *Requiem dla 500 000* (*Requiem for 500,000*, 1963) by Jerzy Bossak and Wacław Kaźmierczak are included in the canon of Polish documentary film.

A scene from Kazimierz Karabasz's celebrated documentary, *Sunday Musicians* (1960)

Jerzy Bossak (1910–89) and Kazimierz Karabasz (b. 1930), the two giants of Polish documentary cinema, taught at the Łódź Film School when Kieślowski studied there between 1964 and 1968. As he later recalls, 'Jerzy Bossak and Kazimierz Karabasz made the biggest impression on me. As well as Jerzy Toeplitz.[6] Karabasz was a kind of signpost that shows where one has to go ... I was under his influence. I think to this day that nowhere in the world were documentary films so magnificent and precisely constructed as in Poland from 1959 to 1968.'[7] In 1968 Kieślowski wrote his diploma thesis, 'Film dokumentalny a rzeczywistość' (Documentary Cinema and Reality), under the supervision of Bossak.[8] The Łódź Film School granted Kieślowski his Master of Arts degree in February 1970 on the basis of his diploma thesis and two films, *Zdjęcie* (*The Photograph*, 1968) and *Z miasta Łodzi* (*From the City of Łódź*, 1969), the latter made under the artistic supervision of Kazimierz Karabasz.[9]

Bossak's vision of documentary cinema, very much in line with John Grierson's concepts, certainly had an impact on the young Kieślowski. In his text published in 1965 by *Kwartalnik Filmowy* (*Film Quarterly*), Bossak postulated the production of films with a 'national character' and a 'polemic passion'.[10] Kieślowski, however, did not share Bossak's interest in historical affairs, his sweeping generalisations about the past and the didactic tone of some of his documentaries. More influential became the classic examples of sociological documentary produced by Karabasz: *Sunday Musicians* and *Rok Franka W.* (*The Year of Franek W.*, 1967). In his first films, Kieślowski shows the same interest in typical, undistinguished individual characters, in an observation of a small portion of reality portrayed 'in depth rather than breadth' – to use the title of one of his later statements.[11] Like Karabasz in *Sunday Musicians*, the classic study portraying the rehearsals of an amateur brass-band established by older male tram-workers, Kieślowski favours simplicity and meticulous observation of the subject and avoids obvious authorial intervention. The camera only reveals reality, which has to speak for itself; it never interferes, alters or arranges reality. Faces in close-up, characters' dialogue and diegetic music tell the whole story without the need for voice-over commentary.

In his book, *Bez fikcji – z notatek filmowego dokumentalisty* (*Without Fiction – From the Notes of a Documentary Film-maker*), Karabasz writes that

> One of the most difficult tasks is photographing people's feelings. Not in the 'easy' circumstances (disaster, sharp conflict, sickness…), but in those that are 'ordinary' in the stream of life (happiness, indecision, meditation, tiredness, hope). Such a task requires discretion on the part of the cameraman (no easy effects in framing or camera movement), and then simplicity in editing and the adding of a soundtrack. The restraint, however, pays off: the viewer remembers such takes as these longer than scenes of the most frantic parachute jumping or car chases.[12]

A scene from Kazimierz Karabasz's sociological documentary, *The Year of Franek W.* (1967)

Kieślowski expresses his documentary credo in a similar manner:

> Regardless of the subject of my films ... I am looking for a way of evoking in audiences feelings similar to my own: the physically painful impotence and sorrow that assail me when I see a man weeping at the bus stop, when I observe people struggling vainly to get close to others, when I see someone eating up the left-overs in a cheap restaurant, when I see the first blotches on a woman's hand and know that she too is bitterly aware of them, when I see the kind of appalling and irreparable injustice that so visibly scars the human face. I want this pain to come across to my audience, to see this physical agony, which I think I am beginning to fathom, to seep into my work.[13]

In Kieślowski's striving for directness and authenticity, sometimes resulting in 'the poetics of talking heads', one can also discern the influences of American Direct Cinema, Richard Leacock and Robert Drew in particular. Leacock and Drew are quoted in Kieślowski's diploma dissertation, although at the time of writing Kieślowski had not seen their films (he was only familiar with their statements published in *Film Culture*).[14] Like Leacock and Drew, Kieślowski makes films to record because, in his own words, 'what exists is wiser and richer than my visions and myself, and to register that existence satisfies me completely'.[15]

In his early films Kieślowski deals with several individual cases representing a universal meaning; they are, *pars pro toto*, studies of the communist system. Unable to criticise the system openly, he focuses on its several micro-aspects in the hope of presenting its unveiled, true nature. In Krzysztof Wierzbicki's film, *I'm So-So*, Kieślowski states that 'perhaps we were the first post-war generation – and I say "we" because there were so many of us – who tried to describe the world as it was. We show only micro-worlds. The titles suggest this: *The School*, *The Factory*, *The Hospital* or *The Office*. If these mini-observations were pierced together, they would describe life in Poland.'[16] The need to describe, to uncover what is hidden and rarely mentioned, is also forcefully postulated by Kieślowski in a statement published in the turbulent year of 1981 in Poland, the year of Solidarity: 'If a particular aspect of reality is to be opposed and an alternative put forward, it must first be delineated ... You cannot dissent unless you have a clear idea of what you are dissenting from.'[17]

When Kieślowski started his education at the Łódź Film School in 1964, film-makers such as Jerzy Skolimowski (b. 1936), Edward Żebrowski (b. 1935) and Krzysztof Zanussi (b. 1939) were finishing its programme. Often labelled by some Polish critics as belonging to the Third Polish Cinema,[18] they were preoccupied with the present rather than history, personal rather than political problems. Unlike Wajda and some members of the Polish School generation, Skolimowski, Zanussi and their colleagues were suspicious of the national romantic tradition, sceptical about the world, and focused on detailed and personal realistic observation. The films that they produced in the late 1960s greatly influenced the course of Polish cinema.[19]

Kieślowski, like some of the members of his class at Łódź, among them Andrzej Titkow (b. 1946), Krzysztof Wojciechowski (b. 1939) and Tomasz Zygadło (b. 1947), was chiefly interested in documenting reality. They appeared as a group at the Documentary Film-makers' Forum during the 1971 Festival of Short Films in Kraków. Together with Grzegorz Królikiewicz (b. 1939), Marcel Łoziński (b. 1940) and Marek Piwowski (b. 1935), to name just a few, they developed and shaped documentary film in Poland in the years to come. According to Mirosław Przylipiak, their concept of documentary film stressed: (1) the need to describe reality, to present its truthful picture; (2) the call to contest the political system (although their films were produced within this system); (3) the necessity to 'activate reality' in order to 'expose the hidden truth'; (4) the urge to speak metaphorically (due to political censorship) about reality.[20]

The year 1971 saw the production of such classic Polish documentaries as Zygadło's, *Szkoła podstawowa* (*Elementary School*, 1971) and *Ziemia* (*The Land*, 1971), Wojciechowski's *Wyszedł w jasny, pogodny dzień* (*He Left on a Bright, Sunny Day*, 1971), Titkow's *W takim niedużym mieście* (*In Such a Small Town*, 1971) and Piwowski's *Korkociąg* (*Cork-Screw*, 1971) and *Hair* (1971). Not all the members of Kieślowski's circle of friends adhered to the earlier mentioned program, for example Piwowski, whose *Pożar, pożar, coś nareszcie dzieje się* (*Fire, Fire, Finally Something Is Going On*, 1967) and *Psychodrama* (1969) exhibit some surrealist touches.

Since he wanted documentary film to humbly record reality, Kieślowski showed no interest in the unique brand of Polish documentary cinema that was labelled by Polish critics 'creative documentary' (*dokument kreacyjny*).[21] Film-makers such as Grzegorz Królikiewicz in *Bracia* (*Brothers*, 1971) and *Nie płacz* (*Don't Cry*, 1972) and, later, Piotr Szulkin (b. 1950) and Wojciech Wiszniewski (1946–81) started to incorporate techniques of fictional cinema into their documentary works. For example, Wiszniewski's stylised documentary film about the Stalinist period, *Opowieść o człowieku, który wykonał 552% normy* (*The Story of a Man Who Produced 552 Percent of the Norm*, 1973), portrays the life of a coal miner-Stakhanovite, Bernard Bugdoł, 'the Polish People's Republic Citizen Kane'.[22] This and another film by Wiszniewski that examines the Stalinist work competition, *Wanda Gościmińska – włókniarka* (*Wanda Gościmiska, the Textile Worker*, 1975), were banned from distribution and not released until 1981.[23]

The Documentary Film Studio in Warsaw produced the majority of Kieślowski's documentary films. Beginning in the late 1960s, Polish Television was also producing more and more documentary films, sometimes of great importance for Polish cinema, for example Karabasz's *The Year of Franek W.* or Piwowski's *Hair*. Another production studio, *Wytwórnia Filmów Oświatowych* (Educational Film Studio), founded in 1950 in Warsaw, also sponsored some notable films, including two classic Wiszniewski documentaries: *Wanda Gościmińska, the Textile Worker* and *Elementarz* (*The First Textbook*, 1976). As in the post-war period, *Wytwórnia Filmowa 'Czołówka'* ('Czołówka' Film Studio) specialised in historical (often propagandist) films and focused mostly on Polish soldiers. One of Kieślowski's later films, *Byłem żołnierzem* (*I Was a Soldier*, 1970), was made for this studio.

Kieślowski began his career with a series of short films produced when he was still a student at the Łódź Film School. His first short narrative film, *Tramwaj* (*The Tram*, 1966), was made under the artistic supervision of Kazimierz Konrad (1921–88), cinematographer and Professor at Łódź, and Wanda Jakubowska (1907–98), film-maker known chiefly for her film about Auschwitz, *Ostatni etap* (*The Last Stage*, aka *The Last Stop*, 1948). The six-minute, black-and-white *The Tram* tells the story of a young man attracted to a good-looking woman whom he sees on a city tram. In this film without dialogue, Kieślowski focuses on the small gestures and discreet glances of the tram passengers, and pays special attention to the shy protagonist-voyeur who observes as the young woman, the object of his attention, falls asleep. When he gets off the tram, he tries to communicate with her once again (he knocks at the window but she is still asleep). Later he decides to run after the distant tram. Kieślowski's film combines several elements characteristic of his future documentary films – the meticulous attention to detail, the dominance of human faces within a frame, and the portrayal of everyday situations and characters, as well as the elements permeating his later 'art' films – ambiguity, open endings and the role of chance.[24]

Another student short film, the six-minute documentary *Urząd* (*The Office*, 1966), was made by Kieślowski under the supervision of Bossak, Karabasz and Kurt Weber (the Polish School cinematographer). The 'office' of the title, the Łódź branch of the National Insurance Company (*Państwowy Zakład Ubezpieczeń*), deals with human tragedies and intimate problems in an impersonal, unfeeling and routine manner. Kieślowski's film, however, is not only a satire on bureaucracy; like a number of other institutions and places portrayed in Polish cinema, the office clearly stands for the whole communist system.

The last student film, *Koncert życzeń* (*Concert of Requests*, 1967), produced under Konrad and Jakubowska's supervision, is a longer (17-minute) exercise in fictional cinema. Kieślowski contrasts two groups of young people spending their weekend holiday on a forest lake: a couple travelling on their motorcycle and a rowdy group on a bus tour. A sensitive young man observes both groups. The film offers small sociological observations of the behaviour of young people, introduces another sympathetic observer-voyeur, and like other films by Kieślowski relies on small observations of a given reality and captures meaningful gestures and glances. Kieślowski briefly appears in the film's final scene as a man on a bicycle.

In his first professional film, *The Photograph*, made in 1968 for Polish Television, Kieślowski appears once again, this time as a film director with his crew searching for two boys from a photograph that was taken after the liberation of Warsaw. The investigative process and its documentation are as important as the subjects of *The Photograph*. The camera, unusual for Kieślowski, intrudes into the private life of the subjects of the documentary. The director learns that the two boys from the photograph are brothers. When one of them looks at the picture, it brings him not joy but sad memories – although the boys are smiling on the photograph, this was the day when they lost their mother.

From the City of Łódź: Images of an Industrial City

The film made one year later by Kieślowski for the Documentary Film Studio in Warsaw, *From the City of Łódź*, is important for a number of reasons. Along with *The Photograph*, it is Kieślowski's graduation film at the Łódź Film School. It also initiates his long-term work for the Documentary Film Studio as well as his collaboration with cinematographer Stanisław Niedbalski and editor Lidia Zonn, who worked on Karabasz's *Sunday Musicians* and *The Year of Franek W.* The 17-minute documentary about the industrial city of Łódź (the second largest city in Poland) also foretells the style and preoccupations of several films produced by Kieślowski in the 1970s.

Since the Film School is located in Łódź, there is a number of short films and documentaries set in this city and devoted to its description.[25] The image of Łódź as the dynamic, multicultural, photogenic and vulgar capital of nineteenth-century Polish capitalism features prominently in an epic novel, *Ziemia obiecana* (*The Promised Land*), written by the Polish Nobel

Images of old Łódź in *From the City of Łódź* (1969)

Prize-winner for literature, Władysław Stanisław Reymont. The novel was successfully adapted in 1927 by Aleksander Hertz and Zbigniew Gniazdowski and in 1975 by Andrzej Wajda (both films under the same title). Wajda's powerful portrayal of Łódź, chosen as the best film in the history of Polish cinema in a popular 1996 plebiscite in the Polish monthly *Film*,[26] offers an almost Marxist picture of the city-Moloch devouring its children.

Kieślowski, however, is not interested in the past glory of the 'Polish Manchester' and presents a different picture of Łódź that focuses on its 1960s photogenic yet dilapidated beauty. In *I'm So-So* he explains: 'Łódź is a very photogenic town, because it's dirty and shabby ... Peoples' faces look like the walls of Łódź. Tired, sad faces with a dramatic meaninglessness in their eyes. Lives spent standing in the same spot, never getting anywhere.' He is even more explicit in his conversations with Danusia Stok: 'Łódź was cruel and unusual. Singularly picturesque with its dilapidated buildings, dilapidated staircases, dilapidated people.'[27] Viewed more than thirty years later, *From the City of Łódź* contains some poignant and almost nostalgic impressions of Łódź, despite its images of poverty, that aptly depict the late 1960s in Poland. The images of impoverished post-industrial landscapes and people inhabiting such places can, however, be found in several other films made in Europe at that time.

The opening scene of Kieślowski's film shows routine (although from today's perspective almost absurd) exercises organised during the production break in a huge textile factory. The camera portrays a young female instructor and female workers mostly in close-ups and medium close-ups. The director then cuts to similarly framed images of workers during the production process, and an image of the whole factory at night, viewed from outside, and portrayed like a giant beehive. The rest of the film includes greyish images of children playing on the street, tired faces of men and women looking through apartment windows, painstaking observations of everyday street life, small gestures and facial expressions. The film also portrays the workers' passionate defence of one of Łódź's mandolin bands (very popular in the 1960s), conducted by Edward Ciuksza and no longer sponsored by the authorities. One of the older female workers states emphatically: 'If they want to take it away, they should take away our lives. Because this is the closure of our old lives.' The director then cuts to the Ciuksza mandolin band during a rehearsal. Its music, Parisian in spirit, provides an illustration to the old, run-down parts of Łódź. Another scene shows an official yet emotional farewell gathering in a textile factory, organized to honour an elderly female worker on the day of her retirement. Kieślowski cuts between the images of young and older faces of the female workers during the farewell speeches and songs.

The film ends with a series of events in a city park (where Kieślowski appears briefly as a bystander), including a man with a bizarre apparatus testing the ability to endure different levels of electric voltage, and the performance of

Observations of everyday life: female workers in *From the City of Łódź* (1969)

a pretentious Warsaw operetta singer. His song, about yearning for a different, better place to live that is 'somewhere', is juxtaposed with the final panorama of Łódź. Originally a different ending was intended but was vetoed by the censor. As Kieślowski recalls, in the first version the final song was accompanied by images of people returning home after work by city trams going into different directions from the Freedom Square in Łódź. Apart from the pessimistic tone of that scene, the censor evidently objected to its specific setting; the square's central monument of the freedom fighter Tadeusz Kościuszko (1746–1817), the national hero who led the abortive 1794 insurrection against Prussia and Russia, must have suggested some obvious political messages to Polish viewers skilled in Aesopian reading and perpetually hunting for messages written in an invisible ink.[28]

Psychological Portraits

In a documentary film on himself, *I'm So-So*, Kieślowski states that his early films were made in order to get 'a common portrait of our mental condition'. The filmic portrait of working-class Łódź belongs to a group of works that, like the earlier *The Office*, paint the picture of communist Poland. Films such as *Fabryka* (*Factory*, 1970), *Refren* (*Refrain*, 1972), *Robotnicy '71: nic o nas bez nas* (*Workers '71: Nothing About Us Without Us*, 1972) and later, *Szpital* (*Hospital*, 1976) and *Gadające głowy* (*Talking Heads*, 1980), focus on different institutions and see them as reflections of the bigger issue – the communist state. They also introduce the 'collective hero'. For example, the working class in *Workers '71* and medical practitioners in *Hospital*, although dealing with everyday struggle and hardships, reveal the hopes and aspirations of different social strata of Poles.

At the beginning of the 1970s Kieślowski also produced two promotional documentaries, commissioned by the copper mine in the industrial town of Lubin. *Między Wrocławiem a Zieloną Górą* (*Between Wrocław and Zielona Góra*, 1972) advertises Lubin as a place to work and live, and *Podstawy BHP w kopalni miedzi* (*The Principles of Safety and Hygiene in a Copper Mine*, 1972) is a typical training film. He also produced the documentary *Przed rajdem* (*Before the Rally*, 1971) about the preparations for the Monte Carlo car race by Krzysztof Komornicki driving a Polish Fiat. The film focuses on Komornicki's desperation to participate in the race, along with the bureaucracy and the economic limitations of 1970s Poland. The film ends with a sentence stating that the driver was unable to complete the Monte Carlo race. Like in a number of other Kieślowski's films, the protagonist struggles against overwhelming apathy, bureaucracy and absurd regulations.

Like several other Kieślowski's documentaries, *Factory* clearly serves as a metaphor of communist Poland. Made in 1970 – the year of violent workers' strikes in the Baltic ports, the film juxtaposes images of long managerial meetings and assembly-line workers at work at the Ursus tractor plant. Kieślowski crosscuts close-up shots of engineers and party functionaries with primarily long- and medium-shots of factory life. The dynamic factory sequences, portraying workers during their daily routines almost in the manner reminiscent of socialist realism, contrast the endless talk ('talking heads') of the male-only factory administrators who gather in a smoke-filled conference room to discuss co-operations, production plans and supplies. The film ends with an image of new tractors leaving the factory, against all odds. The ending, writes Paul Coates, 'is a deadpan epiphany: the pandemic production problems give the completion of anything a near-miraculous air'.[29]

A similar attempt to reflect the state of mind of the working class in Poland after the strikes of 1970 is presented in *Workers '71: Nothing About Us Without Us*, directed together by Kieślowski, Tomasz Zygadło, Wojciech Wiszniewski, Paweł Kędzierski and Tadeusz Walendowski. The very title of this film explains its political message, more fully realised by the workers themselves during the Solidarity period (1980–81). *Workers '71* suffered from the censor's intervention. Despite the directors' objections, it was re-edited and re-titled as *Gospodarze (Housekeepers)*, and in that mutilated form shown on Polish Television.

The film is divided into several segments titled 'Morning', 'The Division of Labour', 'Tools', 'Mass Gathering', 'Hands', 'Heads' and so forth. It opens with images of an early morning working day in several Polish cities: crowded trains delivering tired people to work, workers reading newspapers and listening to early radio news and communist slogans seen from passing trains. What follows are images of, predominately, miners, steelworkers and female textile workers at work and expressing their concerns about salaries, work organisation, norms and the abuses of the system. The more open spirit of the early Edward Gierek years, who succeeded Władysław Gomułka as the Communist Party leader in 1970, is clearly seen and heard in the picture. Like other films by Kieślowski, *Workers '71* is deprived of voice-over narration and relies on diegetic comments expressed by workers. Their voices display the gap between the official communist newspeak and the true concerns of the working class. The subtitles indicate the content as well as the style of a particular segment. For example, close-ups and extreme close-ups dominate segments titled 'Hands' and 'Heads' while long- and medium-shots feature prominently in parts such as 'Factory Conference'.

Kieślowski's attempt to reflect the state of mind in 1971 Poland certainly influenced some seminal documentary films produced later, during the Solidarity period. For example, the very title of what is probably the most significant documentary made in 1980, *Robotnicy '80* (*Workers '80*), directed by Andrzej Zajączkowski and Andrzej Chodakowski, refers directly to Kieślowski's work. Other film-makers, for example Andrzej Piekutowski in *Chłopi '81* (*Peasants '81*, 1981) and *Górnicy '88* (*Miners '88*, 1988), strive to achieve a similar goal, which is stressed by referring to the same documentary tradition of Polish cinema.

Another documentary work produced by Kieślowski in 1972, *Refrain*, lacks the serious tone of his two previous films and shares similar features with the earlier film, *The Office*. The ten-minute-long *Refrain* deals with a funeral home and targets bureaucracy, corruption and dispassionate attitudes toward sorrowful fellow citizens. The film also reveals some macabre, almost Kafkaesque humour familiar to those who lived under the communist system, for example in the scenes when clients apply for graveyard lots. *Refrain* opens with an image of erasing the name of a recently deceased person. The last scene not only displays Kieślowski's black sense of humour, but also provides a universalising metaphor: to the sound of Vivaldi's music, the camera portrays a number of newborn babies in a hospital, each being assigned its identification number.[30]

In 1976 Kieślowski produced *Hospital*, the 1977 winner of the Festival of Short Films in Kraków. The film deals with Warsaw orthopaedic surgeons who are portrayed working long, 32-hour shifts. The camera follows them in the operating theatre, admittance room and smoky offices. They are portrayed as struggling with faulty equipment and overcoming fatigue. The film focuses on everyday hospital situations without any voice-over comments, with the passage of time carefully indicated every hour. The surgeons are portrayed as skilled workers in this, to use Kieślowski's words, 'film about some brotherhood'.[31]

Kieślowski's later film *Dworzec* (*Station*, 1980) portrays the atmosphere at Central Station in Warsaw after the rush hour. It opens with the main television news at 7:30PM, providing information about the communist party leader, Edward Gierek. The recurrent image, Orwellian in spirit, of security cameras watching people, organises the film. In the last scene the camera moves inside the surveillance room and presents various images of the station on multiple screens. Its political, Orwellian touches aside, *Station* is chiefly admired for its attention to detail, its portrayal of tired, almost inanimate faces, 'people looking for something',[32] the reality that has nothing to do with the optimism of the television news. Scholars often quote the confiscation of *Station* by the

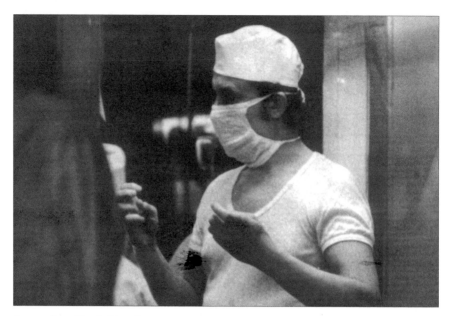

A scene from *Hospital* (1976)

police, searching for a murder suspect at the Central Station and hoping that Kieślowski accidentally filmed her. As Kieślowski explains to Danusia Stok, this event, which could have jeopardised his filmed subjects, contributed to his abandonment of documentary cinema.[33]

Personal Stories

Unlike the majority of Polish film-makers in the 1970s, Kieślowski shows serious interest in everyday, often working-class, protagonists. His stories completely focus on a character or a group of characters linked by the same experience or profession. He allows them to express themselves and abstains from intrusive, didactic off-screen authorial comments. Images, close-ups of faces in particular, tell the whole story.

In his 1970 film, *I Was a Soldier*, Kieślowski offers a simple story that contrasts with the propagandist accounts about heroic soldiers. He interviews seven ordinary men who lost their sight during the war, who now only 'see in their dreams', and have to rely on others to survive. It is a simple film: the characters sit and talk and are portrayed in close-up shots. Every scene ends by fading to white. The whole film, however, ends by fading to black, thus stressing the blindness of the ex-soldiers. Kieślowski depicts the side of war that is not often present in Polish mainstream war films concerned with its heroic or propagandist aspect. His modest film has nothing to do with extremely popular Polish television series such as *Czterej pancerni i pies* (*Four Tankmen and a Dog*, 1966–67, 21 episodes) directed by Konrad Nałęcki, and *Stawka większa niż życie* (*More Than Life at Stake*, 1967–68, 18 episodes) directed by Janusz Morgenstern and Andrzej Konic. *I Was a Soldier* belongs to a small group of Polish documentary films made at the beginning of the 1970s, such as *Don't Cry* by Grzegorz Królikiewicz and *He Left on a Bright, Sunny Day* by Krzysztof Wojciechowski, that deliver personal anti-war messages.

Murarz (*Bricklayer*), made in 1973 but released during the Solidarity period, deals with an exemplary worker of the Stalinist era and Stakhanovite competition. In Kieślowski's film, the middle-aged bricklayer, Józef Malesa, recalls his life while participating in the May Day parade. Bitter yet proud about his achievements, Malesa talks about his communist upbringing and his own fascination with communist ideology. He recalls the way he was courted by the communist system that resulted in his work as a party apparatchik and his gradual disenchantment with this ideology. After the 'Polish October' of 1956, he returned to his original work as a simple bricklayer and felt much happier. Kieślowski does not comment on, ridicule or contradict his protagonist with visual images. Instead, he lets him speak, while the screen is filled with 'socialist realist' songs and images of Warsaw – the city Malesa helped to re-build.

Kieślowski's *Bricklayer* belongs to a group of important Polish documentaries made at the beginning of the 1970s that, despite censorship, wrestled with the Stalinist period. Bohdan Kosiński's *Budowałem miasto* (*I Was Building a Town*, 1972) introduces another worker, Szczepan Brzeziński, who remembers the building of Nowa Huta (steelworks and town) near the old Polish capital, Kraków. Blinded by his achievements, he expresses his love for Nowa Huta and dislike for Kraków that is 'too old' for his taste. The year 1973 marks the production of two films that deal with the exemplary workers of the Stalinist era, Polish Stakhanovites, and the phenomenon of socialist work competition: Wojciech Wiszniewski's *The Story of a Man Who Produced 552 Percent of the Norm* and Ryszard Bugajski's *Słowo o Wincentym Pstrowskim* (*A Word on Wincenty Pstrowski*). Stories from the above-mentioned films return powerfully in Andrzej Wajda's seminal narrative film, *Człowiek z marmuru* (*Man of Marble*, 1977).

In some of Kieślowski's films, for example in *Prześwietlenie* (*X-Ray*, 1974), the viewer may trace autobiographical elements. The film depicts tuberculosis patients in a sanatorium in Sokołowsko near Jelenia Góra (southwestern Poland) where Kieślowski's father was once treated for tuberculosis. *X-Ray* includes close-ups of four men talking to the camera about their illness and uneasy state of mind. They feel as if they are on the margins of society, redundant and forgotten.[34]

First Love: An Atypical Love Story

Gradually, Kieślowski moved away from a traditional pure documentary by incorporating scenes that were carefully staged ('manipulated' or 'provoked' are his terms)[35] for dramatic purposes. The incorporation of such scenes, however, does not alter the existing vision of the director. Instead, such cinematic devices help Kieślowski to uncover the hidden layers of reality.

The much-celebrated, 30-minute film, *Pierwsza miłość* (*First Love*, 1974), serves as a good example here.[36] It deals with the crucial nine months in the life of two young Warsaw inhabitants: the 17-year-old Jadźka (diminutive of Jadwiga) and her boyfriend, the 20-year-old Romek (Roman), both working and completing high school. The camera follows them from the moment Jadźka discovers that she is pregnant, to the birth of their daughter Ewa. Initially Kieślowski intended to make a film about a single mother. When Jadźka introduced her boyfriend, Romek, he decided to incorporate him into the film and follow his life as well. Also, as the cinematographer Jacek Petrycki reveals, 'The idea as such appeared after the Kielowski's child had been born. The pregnancy, the delivery and the first days after it were not as simple and euphoric as they expected. This inspired us to show a girl coping with a much more difficult situation than that of a talented fashion designer and wife of an established film-maker.'[37]

The pre-credit scenes of *First Love* move right into *medias res* by introducing Jadźka who is learning from a physician about her pregnancy, and Romek standing in front of the military recruitment committee declaring that he is going to marry his pregnant girlfriend. Kieślowski often portrays his protagonists separately, as if presenting two parallel stories; for example, Romek talks with his friends and explains the reasons for his unanticipated marriage and Jadźka meets her female friends and an unfriendly group of teachers at her school. Kieślowski documents Romek and Jadźka's preparations to live together (they are renovating a tiny apartment belonging to her grandmother and learning about parenthood), their simple and emotional wedding ceremony and the birth of Ewa. The film ends with a scene of Jadźka and Romek beside their baby girl's crib, pondering her future.

First Love is an atypical love story deprived of romantic clichés, set against the background of the unglamorous Polish reality of the mid-1970s. The young lovers in the film have to overcome a number of obstacles characteristic of the communist era, such as a long waiting list to have a

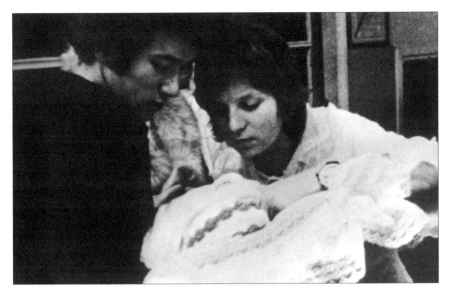

The life of two young Warsaw inhabitants, Jadźka and Romek, in *First Love* (1974)

flat at the housing co-op, problems with residence registration and the state bureaucracy. The extended 12-month period of production of *First Love* forced Kieślowski to incorporate scenes that are reconstructed (such as the opening conversation between Jadźka and the gynaecologist that, in reality, took place before the filming), predetermined (such as the meeting with friends, the wedding and the birth of Ewa) or provoked by the director (such as the visit by a militiaman who checks the residence registration of the young couple). Regarding the latter, Kieślowski comments in his conversations with Danusia Stok,

> I sent in a policeman, who arrived and complained that they weren't registered, that they were living there illegally and could be thrown out. I deliberately found a policeman whom I thought wouldn't cause much harm, although Jadzia was in her eighth month by then and the whole thing could have been quite risky – an unexpected visit like that could have induced labour. Everybody was frightened of the police in Poland at the time, especially if they weren't registered where they were living.[38]

However, as the cinematographer Jacek Petrycki recalls, the conversations were not imposed and several situations and dialogue that look as if they were carefully planned to suit the film's goal were spontaneous. According to him, only the final scene was 'deliberately made as if it was a feature film':

We told them [Jadźka and Romek] to stand and walk, we set the lights and took it. Of course, we did not give them any hints as to what they were supposed to say. Outside it was getting dark and through the window one could see an ice-rink in a distance. When they said something that sounded like a coda and perfectly suited an ending, Krzysztof, who was sitting behind me, tapped me on my shoulder and I focused on what was going on outside, that is, on the ice-hockey players. I must have taken at least five such shots.[39]

Kieślowski's idea of documenting the first twenty years of Ewa, the baby girl in *First Love*, was taken up by his close collaborator, Krzysztof Wierzbicki, in his *Horoskop* (*Horoscope*, 2000), the 47-minute film made for Polish Television's Channel 2. He documents Kieślowski's protagonists, now living in Edmonton, Canada, talking about their life. Wierzbicki employs some footage by Kieślowski, who planned this continuation as a film about Ewa from her childhood to adulthood (working titles: *Ewa*, *Ewunia* and *Horoscope*), but Kieślowski interrupted this project since he was afraid that his film might be used against the protagonists. According to the often-cited comment by Kieślowski, 'documentary films shouldn't be used to influence the subject's life either for the better or for the worse. They shouldn't have any influence at all.'[40]

The Workings of the System

The mechanisms of the communist system, portrayed through its representatives or through people contaminated by the totalitarian ideology, are addressed in Kieślowski's *Życiorys* (*Curriculum Vitae*, 1975) and two films made in 1977: *Z punktu widzenia nocnego portiera* (*From the Point of View of the Night Porter*) and *Nie wiem* (*I Don't Know*).

Ironically, *Curriculum Vitae*, made with the approval and assistance of the Polish Communist Party (PZPR), is certainly an anti-communist film. It portrays the true nature of the communist system, shows its functionaries in action and reveals the mechanisms governing their actions. The Party Board of Control (*Komisja Kontroli Partyjnej*) that examines the life of one of its members in *Curriculum Vitae* is real, but the overall situation is arranged by Kieślowski. He convinced the real party committee to judge the character chosen by him. Kieślowski invented the protagonist's name, Antoni Gralak, as well as his resumé. He also got, in his own words, 'the most enlightened, the most liberal, the most circumspect Party Board of Control in Warsaw … So everything about the Party Board of Control in the film is a true record of its authentic reactions and behaviour. Whereas everything that the main character brings in – that is, the man they're judging at this Party Board of Control – is fictitious: a life history – made up of a combination of life-histories – written by me.'[41]

The cross-examined member of the communist party, Gralak, faces often-ridiculous accusations from the committee that meddles with his private, even romantic life (for example, he is told that his wife is 'alien to him with regard to her class'). As in a number of other Kieślowski's films the faces, sometimes partly hidden in darkness, fill the screen. Mikołaj Jazdon aptly writes that 'The faces of the members of the Party Board of Control are as indistinct as their views, and the hewed, meekly-lit face of Gralak resembles the well-known image of Franz Kafka. Thanks to that, the whole situation in the film inevitably carries associations with *The Trial*.'[42]

Why was Kieślowski able to make this film? Certainly, the party authorities could not expect a pro-communist film from Kieślowski but they counted on his ability to capture generational or social portraits. The finished film was shown at communist party instructional meetings. Today, it remains one of the unique insights into the world of secretive communist politics by portraying the real party activists in action. It is a view from inside the system produced by an understanding and patient observer/film-maker.

Made two years later, *From the Point of View of the Night Porter* is among Kieślowski's best-known works. It won the Grand Prix at the 1979 National Short Film Festival in Kraków and also received the FIPRESCI Award there. The filmic portrait of a night porter, Marian Osuch, a fanatic of law and order, was also popular abroad; for example, it received the Jury Prize at the 1979 International Short and Documentary Film Festival in Lille.

Kieślowski portrays his disciplinarian and semi-fascist protagonist in everyday situations: during his work as a night porter, when he is patrolling the banks of the Vistula river in search of fishermen without fishing permits and when he is checking on young people in a park. Osuch is a simple man who says that 'regulations are more important than people'. He thinks of reality in terms of total control and is a proponent of tough laws and public executions. According to his film-making credo, Kieślowski never comments and never searches for easy effects nor labels the protagonist. He does not mock him but lets him talk freely about his love for order and discipline in a simple, often ungrammatical language. The images of Osuch in action and what he has to say are enough for the viewer to reach conclusions. The final scene, when a teacher asks a group of children who Osuch is, and no answer is provided, invites viewers to contribute their own comments.[43]

Although known to festival audiences and documentary film buffs, the film was shown for the first time to a general public on Polish television after

The night porter Marian Osuch in *From the Point of View of the Night Porter* (1977)

Kieślowski's death. He objected to its general release, being afraid that the film may harm its protagonist: 'I thought that if the film was shown on television then it could cause the porter greater harm. His acquaintances, family, neighbours, daughter, son and wife would see it and it would either make a laughing stock of him or humiliate him.'[44]

Kieślowski voiced similar reservations regarding another film, *I Don't Know* (1977), the straightforward account of a plant manager in Lower Silesia who exposes crimes and corruption involving the local communist party leaders. This is one of the least-known documentaries by Kieślowski. In order to protect his protagonist (who was earlier physically threatened for his actions), Kieślowski not only obscures the names in the manager's testimony by the sound of a typewriter, but also was against the release of the film in order not to harm the central character. Like *Curriculum Vitae*, *I Don't Know* offers an account by the man from within the system, somebody who benefited from it but then tried to turn against it. The simple film, relying on the manager's monologue and close-ups, is presented to the viewer as representative of certain behaviours in the film's preface. The final comment by the protagonist, 'I don't know how to live', not only provides the film's title, but also summarises the questions asked by several protagonists of Polish films of the 1970s.[45]

It is tempting to see the climax of Kieślowski's documentary style in two films made before the Solidarity period: *Siedem kobiet w różnym wieku*

(*Seven Women of Different Ages*, 1978) and *Gadające głowy* (*Talking Heads*, 1980). *Seven Women* received the Grand Prix at the 1979 National Short Film Festival in Kraków (jointly with *From the Point of View of the Night Porter*). The film portrays the world of ballet, but focuses on meticulous observations of everyday backstage routines and rehearsals rather than on public performances. For seven days, the camera captures a different group of female dancers starting with young girls, through mature ballerinas, to an older ballerina working as a ballet teacher. The titles, indicating different days, also mark different chapters of the film that offers seven biographies or, perhaps, one biological cycle. The cycle ends with the old ballerina teaching young aspiring girls who were portrayed at the beginning of the film. The faces, not the elaborate routines and movements, tell the whole story. The expressions of the faces, their beauty as well as signs of fatigue, are more important for Kieślowski than short moments of artificial beauty during a performance in front of the public.

The ironic title of *Talking Heads* is partly an answer to the accusations raised by a prominent Polish film critic, Zygmunt Kałużyński, at the beginning of the 1970s. They concerned the misappropriation of television style, which relies on dialogue (usually medium-shots of characters talking directly to the camera), in documentary films made by Kieślowski and his friends.[46] That style has been characterised by the contemptuous term *gadające głowy*

A scene from *Seven Women of Different Ages* (1978)

('talking heads'). Kieślowski's *Talking Heads* serves as the culmination of his interest in human faces.[47] He interviews (we only hear his voice) forty people, a spectrum of Polish society – workers and university professors alike, young and old. He begins with a toddler, born in 1979, and ends with a 100-year-old woman, asking the same elementary questions: 'When and where were you born?'; 'Who are you?'; 'What matters most to you?'

The film is structured around the years of birth of Kieślowski's inter-locutors who appear on the screen. Their answers to Kieślowski's questions are not spontaneous but are often prepared in advance and range from everyday and unsophisticated to idealistic and political, stressing the importance of democracy, freedom and self-development. Although the film's message is pessimistic, it ends on an optimistic note by introducing the oldest person, an old woman barely hearing Kieślowski's questions, who answers: 'I'd like to live longer.'

Although Kieślowski was making both documentary and narrative films until 1980, his interest gradually was shifting towards the latter. A number of factors contributed to this move: the experiences during the making of *Station*, which was confiscated by the police, the shelving of *Bricklayer*, Kieślowski's reluctance to screen *From the Point of View of the Night Porter* and *I Don't Know* in order to protect his protagonists and the mutilation of *Workers '71*. In *I'm So-So* Kieślowski admits that his and other film-makers' 'descriptive tools had been used for propagandistic purposes'. Lastly, documentary films often collided with his film-making ethics: 'I managed to photograph some real tears several times ... I am frightened of those real tears. In fact, I don't know whether I've got the right to photograph them. At such times I feel like somebody who's found himself in a realm that is, in fact, out of bounds. That's the main reason why I escaped from documentaries.'[48]

Kieślowski's last attempt at documentary cinema appears as late as 1988 with *Siedem dni w tygodniu* (*Seven Days a Week*), his 18-minute contribution to a compilation film produced in Holland. Photographed by Kieślowski's regular documentary cinematographer, Jacek Petrycki, the film depicts daily routines of one three-generational family in Warsaw. Each member of the family is portrayed independently, beginning on Monday. Only when they are seated together on Sunday morning at the breakfast table in their overcrowded apartment does the viewer learn what the connection between all the characters is.

As pointed out by several scholars, Kieślowski organises his films into distinct segments. He precisely punctuates his films with titles (*Workers '71*), hours (*Hospital*), days (*Seven Women of Different Ages, Seven Days a Week*), dates of birth of people interviewed (*Talking Heads*), and recurrent cinematic devices (for example, fades to white in *I was a Soldier* or images of a surveillance camera in *Station*). According to Paul Coates, he does so for two reasons: the first is analytical – 'the material is to be ordered in accordance with an idea'; the second reason has to do with 'the desire for relief and release' since works 'focusing on suffering (*X-Ray*) or bureaucratic routine (*The Office*, *Refrain*) may require interruption by the image of an elsewhere, a place where suffering and oppression disappear'.[49] From today's perspective, the documentary works by Kieślowski constitute an apt reflection of the Polish communist past. Unlike a number of Polish film-makers who either embraced or contested the communist ideology, Kieślowski portrays the 'unnatural rhythm' of the communist system. As Mikołaj Jazdon writes, 'Kieślowski's camera does not look in reality for something that is everlasting but looks for something that destroys a certain everlasting order. Kieślowski shows that the situations described by him are not unique to the world of the Polish People's Republic, but typical. He meticulously describes the rules governing this world, like a physician who scrutinises and notes the symptoms of disease.'[50]

CHAPTER TWO

Film-Essays: Kieślowski and Polish Cinema in the 1970s and During the Solidarity Period

I do not believe in my profession's beauty, social mission, 'beautiful ephemerality', social efficiency, or that a box with celluloid will survive for somebody – I absolutely do not believe in all that. I make films to register. I am attached to reality because everything that exists there is wiser and richer than myself, and for me, to register this existence is perfectly satisfactory.

> – Krzysztof Kieślowski[1]

The late 1970s in Poland signalled a major generational change of guard in Polish cinema: the advent of film-makers born after the war whose first major political initiation was the year 1968 with its brutally crushed student demonstrations (the March Events) and the following anti-Semitic campaign. The campaign was orchestrated by a nationalistic faction of the Communist Party in order to remove some seasoned party and security force members, many of whom were Jewish, from their privileged positions. This new wave of film-makers came to be associated with the term 'The Cinema of Distrust'.[2]

The collection of essays written by two Polish poets, Julian Kornhauser and Adam Zagajewski, *Świat nie przedstawiony* (*The Unrepresented World*, 1974),[3] became the manifesto and the theoretical formula for the generation sometimes known as the 'Young Culture' (*Młoda Kultura*).[4] In an essay on post-war Polish literature Zagajewski writes that the most basic disparity in Polish culture is between 'what is and what should be ... Due to the fact that what exists remains unrecognised, reality itself is incomplete and lame because to exist means to be described in culture'.[5] He attacks the older generation of writers for their artistic compromises, escapist works that avoid questioning the false image of the Polish People's Republic. Zagajewski strives to observe the true, unrepresented world that consists of myriad things: 'conferences and children's camps ... dual faiths, hypocrisy and hope ... party meetings and soccer matches, the Race for Peace and political jokes, hospitals and parade banners, death and new investments, pensioners and personnel, House of Culture and brawls at village weddings, Youth Songs and budding scientists, libraries and beer halls'.[6]

The need to represent the 'non-existent world' resulted in a move away from fiction. Tadeusz Lubelski comments that, 'in the light of the political situation in Poland at that time, getting away from fiction acquired almost an ethical dimension. "Make-believe" was associated with lying, so it was up to a writer's honesty, different from the world of official culture that was full of lies, to give an authentic account of everyday experience.'[7]

The absence of life 'as it is' on Polish screens prompted audiences to practice allegorical Aesopian reading.[8] The audiences often looked for references, frequently non-existing ones, to Polish reality. The need to describe the unrepresented world, the world not present in official arts, had been advocated by a number of film-makers. In publications and interviews they strongly manifested their generational bonds. Agnieszka Holland explains: 'I know that this was the formation created thanks to a certain generational experience – the meeting of people sharing similar sensibility, and a strong need to receive feedback from the audience. This was not the film criticism that invented "moral concern" ... This phenomenon was not artificial; it truly existed on the basis of "social request". It was created by the viewers.'[9]

Attempts to depict the 'unrepresented world' united established masters, such as Krzysztof Zanussi and Andrzej Wajda, and young film-makers, such as Kieślowski, Janusz Kijowski, Feliks Falk, Piotr Andrejew, Agnieszka Holland and Janusz Zaorski. The Cinema of Distrust representative films, Krzysztof Zanussi's *Barwy ochronne* (*Camouflage*, 1977), Feliks Falk's *Wodzirej* (*Top Dog*, 1978), Janusz Kijowski's *Indeks* (*Index*, 1977, released in 1981), Andrzej Wajda's *Bez znieczulenia* (*Rough Treatment*, aka *Without Anesthesia*, 1978),

Agnieszka Holland's *Aktorzy prowincjonalni* (*Provincial Actors*, 1979) and Krzysztof Kieślowski's *Camera Buff* (1979), became emblematic works of the late 1970s in Poland.

This series of contemporary realistic films centred on the conflict between the state and the individual and examined the massive gap between the 'progressive' ideas and their implementation. Due to state censorship, the system had not been attacked directly; the films targeted its institutions and functionaries and focused on corruption and social maladies. The mechanisms of manipulation and indoctrination had been examined on a metaphorical level. For example, the summer camp in *Camouflage* or the world of show business in *Top Dog* served as microcosms of Polish society. These films also portrayed the emergence of the arrogant new communist elites, hypocrisy, conformity and other social and political effects of the communist system. Often set in provincial Poland (perhaps to indicate that these problems are far from centre?), they provided thinly veiled allusions to the political and social present.

In the documentary *I'm So-So*, Kieślowski stresses that 'living in an undescribed world is hard ... It is like having no identity'. In the second part of the 1970s several documentary and narrative films, including films by Kieślowski, attempted to uncover the unrepresented reality and to examine social issues. Interestingly, Polish Television, an institution usually associated with manipulation and indoctrination, produced some of them. For example, Polish Television produced Kieślowski's *First Love*, *The Calm*, *Short Working Day* (with Tor film studio) and in the 1980s, *Decalogue*.

Although frequently discussed by critics as one of the leading directors in the Cinema of Distrust, Kieślowski's vision of political and social reality in Poland is more complex and avoids the easy conclusions present in a number of films made by his contemporaries. In an interview conducted in 1993, Agnieszka Holland comments: 'We were delighted that we could code the message in a film that "evil is linked with communism". It seems that this is the basic weakness of these films.'[10] The clear divisions between the positive and the negative characters frequently produce types rather than real-life characters in the Cinema of Distrust.

Kieślowski's films, however, never suffer from this schematism. They portray a world in which the lines are often blurred between the official sphere, represented by the communist authorities, and the 'silent majority' of Kieślowski's countrymen. His films may be also interpreted as political essays commenting on the undescribed reality. Like the film-makers he admired, for example Miloš Forman, Jiři Menzel, Ermanno Olmi and Ken Loach, Kieślowski focuses on simple, ordinary people and events. He portrays a mosaic of pre-1989 Polish society: a young sensitive theatre tailor, a factory manager, a petty criminal trying to lead a 'normal life', a simple factory worker obsessed with film-making, and a medical student. Unlike Menzel in *Ostře sledované vlaky* (*Closely Observed Trains*, 1966), Forman in *Lásky jedné plavovlásky* (*Loves of a Blonde*, aka *A Blonde in Love*, 1965) or Olmi in *Il posto* (*The Sound of the Trumpets*, aka *The Job*, 1961), Kieślowski never tries to balance between comedy and tragedy, between hilarity and seriousness. Although some of his films contain scenes bordering on tragicomedy, he is a compassionate realist, capturing with his camera the seemingly meaningless gestures and behaviours of his protagonists.

A feeling of authenticity and naturalness permeates Kieślowski's films made in the late 1970s. Despite their apparently simple narrative plots, they reveal complex meanings. Kieślowski keeps his camera on a character, often an insignificant, all-too-human one, and tells the story about the impossibility of achieving a fulfilling life within the colourless and oppressive communist system. His films' *mise-en-scènes*, deprived of glamour and capturing life as it is, stress the importance of the human face. Dialogue, often painfully theatrical in Polish cinema, in Kieślowski's films is down-to-earth, vernacular, matter-of-fact and easily recognisable as belonging to the 1970s. Expressions on the protagonists' faces, their small gestures and acute, detailed observations of their unkind environment tell their own unfeigned stories. In his interest in common, often working-class characters, Kieślowski continues, in a sense, the trend of the 'plebeian cinema' originated in the films by Kazimierz Kutz made during the Polish School period such as *Krzyż Walecznych* (*Cross of Valour*, 1959) and *Ludzie z pociągu* (*People from the Train*, 1961). The questions Kieślowski poses and dilemmas he portrays have a lot of in common with several films made by his friend and mentor, Krzysztof Zanussi, such as *Struktura kryształu* (*The Structure of Crystals*, 1969), *Iluminacja* (*Illumination*, 1973) and *Bilans kwartalny* (*Balance Sheet*, aka *Balance* or *A Woman's Decision*, 1975).

Kieślowski remarked in 1976: 'I started to combine elements of both filmic genres – documentary and fiction – from the documentary taking the truth of behaviour, the appearances of things and people, and from fiction, the depth of experience and action – the driving force of this genre.'[11] The use of documentary techniques by Kieślowski in his early films is not unique in the context of Polish cinema. The documentary background of the majority of Polish film-makers, the influence of Italian Neorealism and, in particular, the Czechoslovak New Wave are evidenced in several Polish films made in the 1970s by their tendency to use non-professional actors, the desire for authenticity and attempts at 'small realism'. For example, the concern for real life and authentic characters is present in Krzysztof Wojciechowski's narrative films. In *Kochajmy się* (*Let Us Love*, 1974) and later in *Róg Brzeskiej i Capri* (*The Corner of Brzeska and Capri*, 1980) he employs a cast of non-professional actors and offers an almost 'ethnographic experience' concerned with, respectively, the developing village and the impoverished working-class Warsaw suburb. The same spirit prevails in a number of television films. For example, at the beginning of the 1970s Janusz Kondratiuk directed *Dziewczyny do wzięcia* (*Marriageable Girls*, 1972) and his brother Andrzej Kondratiuk directed *Wniebowzięci* (*The Ascended*, 1973), two cult films in Poland both made in the spirit of an early Miloš Forman. Kieślowski's friend and the co-director of *Workers '71*, Wojciech Wiszniewski, produced his only fictional film, the medium-length tragicomedy *Historia pewnej miłości* (*The Story of a Certain Love*, 1974). Its dark portrayal of everyday reality postponed the release of this now classic film until 1982. One has also to mention films by Andrzej Trzos-Rastawiecki such as *Zapis zbrodni* (*The Record of Crime*, 1974) and *Skazany* (*Sentenced*, 1976) and Marek Piwowski's *Rejs* (*The Cruise*, 1970). The latter, a fine satire on communism, at first glance looks like an amateurish production without an underlying structure due to its improvised dialogues and quasi-documentary look, along with the presence of non-professional actors/types. But its situational humour and dialogue refer to the current political reality of the time and satirise the schizophrenic absurdities of communist Poland.

The early stages of Kieślowski's artistic career developed similarly to those of a number of film-makers of his generation. Like numerous others, his road to mainstream cinema included documentary and short-film stages, followed by a period of medium-length television productions. Beginning in the late 1960s, television became a training ground for a number of young film-makers as well as a venue for documentary films. Established film-makers as well as recent graduates from the Łódź Film School produced television films. The latter often started their careers by producing medium-length television films. For example, Krzysztof Zanussi attracted international attention with his diploma film, *Śmierć Prowincjała* (*Death of a Provincial*, 1966), which won awards at the Venice and Mannheim film festivals, and in 1968 he directed two television films, *Twarzą w twarz* (*Face to Face*) and *Zaliczenie* (*Pass Mark*). In 1971 Zanussi produced *Za ścianą* (*Next Door*, 1971), perhaps one of the finest Polish television films. Other notable directors such as Agnieszka Holland, Janusz Zaorski and Edward Żebrowski also took that route. Furthermore, a number of established film-makers, including Andrzej Wajda, occasionally made television films, some of them with a theatrical release in mind as was the case of Wajda's television film *Brzezina* (*Birchwood*, 1970), first distributed theatrically.

Kieślowski's career since 1974 is inseparably linked with Tor film studio in Warsaw.[12] Founded in 1967, Film Unit Tor (since 1989 Tor film studio) was originally managed by one of the most respected Polish School directors, Stanisław Różewicz,[13] and drew a number of prominent directors such as Andrzej Wajda (who later headed his own film unit, X), Janusz Majewski and Krzysztof Zanussi – Tor's manager since 1979. *Personel* (*Personnel*, aka *Personel Subsidiaries*) is Kieślowski's first film co-produced by Tor film studio with Polish Television. The majority of his subsequent narrative films would be produced or co-produced by this studio.

Pedestrian Subway: A Short Film About Marriage

Kieślowski narrated simple, semi-documentary stories in some of his early short films. These were unpretentious anecdotes featuring non-professional actors and students, frequently Kieślowski's friends from the Łódź Film School. Kieślowski's first true attempt at combining his documentary experience with a fictional story came in 1973 with a modest medium-length, black-and-white film, *Przejście podziemne* (*Pedestrian Subway*), scripted by Kieślowski and an accomplished poet and playwright, Ireneusz Iredyński (1939–85). Photographed by one of Kieślowski's future regulars, Sławomir Idziak (b. 1945), the film features Teresa Budzisz-Krzyżanowska in the role of Lena, a woman working as a store decorator, and Andrzej Seweryn as Michał, her estranged husband who comes to Warsaw to win her back. After a night of talks and a dispassionate lovemaking scene, the film ends with the husband leaving the store and his wife for his small town.[14]

Kieślowski narrates the story about this failed attempt to revive love and save the marriage in a semi-documentary manner. The film's minuscule action is basically limited to one night and only one setting – the underground shop Lena decorates at night. The newly opened underground passage in the centre of Warsaw, the pride of the Gierek's era, provides an apt 'cold' setting for this chronicle of marital breakdown. The limitation of the action (the outside world is seen only through a small window) and harsh neon lighting enhance the claustrophobic and melancholic mood of *Pedestrian Subway*.

Personnel: Art and Politics

Kieślowski's *Personnel* heralds the tone and thematic preoccupations of several later films of the Cinema of Distrust. It introduces the coming-of-age story of a young trainee theatre dresser working in the wardrobe department of the Wrocław Opera, and focuses on his professional initiation, as well as his introduction to the world of art and politics. Romek Januchta, played by future film director Juliusz Machulski,[15] is an idealistic young man, an observer rather than participant in the internal games and quarrels of the opera house. Despite that, theatre remains a magical place for him. The chief of opera technical staff (Włodzimierz Boruński), who introduces Romek to his supervisor ('you'd better not embarrass your aunt'), comments that 'working here is like a bird flying. Art! Art! We all feel it. This is in the air, inside of us. Do you understand this? Can you feel it?' Romek responds by saying that 'this is such a feeling as if one has risen'.

Later, however, Romek has to take sides in a power struggle at the opera. His friendship with an older theatre worker, the tailor Sowa (Michał Tarkowski), who is critical about the artistic programme of the theatre and who is in conflict with one of the narcissistic and confrontational opera singers, is tested by the opera management and the head of the communist youth organisation (played by Tomasz Zygadło, one of the leading directors of the Cinema of Distrust).[16] Romek supports Sowa, but is pressured by the opera director to write a report denouncing his colleague in order to succeed in his profession. In the final scene Romek has to make his first adult political decision: whether to act against Sowa, to collaborate and profit from it (which is promised quite openly by the communist activist) or to stay loyal to his friend and himself. The open, ambiguous ending of *Personnel* shows Romek sitting in front of a blank page in the opera director's cabinet, with the pen ready in his hand, deciding 'to write or not to write'. The final credits are interrupted by images of Romek making his decision in the impressionistically sunlit office (with light coming from different directions). He seems to know perfectly that, regardless of his comments, his written statement will be used against Sowa.

The story about Romek's initiation into the multifaceted world of art certainly has its political implications. In a tightly controlled political system almost every situation portrayed, no matter how far removed from politics, prompted Polish viewers to practice Aesopian reading. In Polish cinema of the 1970s the world of theatre frequently served as a coded image of the country and as a microcosm of Polish society. For example, in *Zdjęcia próbne* (*Screen Tests*, 1977) directors Agnieszka Holland, Paweł Kędzierski and Jerzy Domaradzki depict the initiation of a group of young and aspiring film actors. In another film, *Provincial Actors*, Agnieszka Holland portrays a group of dissatisfied young actors unable to fulfil their artistic dreams. Kieślowski stresses this theme in the following way: 'Theatre and opera are always a metaphor for life. It's obvious that the film was about how we can't really find a place for ourselves in Poland. That our dreams and ideas about some

Juliusz Machulski as Romek Januchta (left) and Michał Tarkowski as the tailor Sowa (right) in *Personnel* (1975)

ideal reality always clash somewhere along the line with something that's incomparably shallower and more wretched.'[17]

Sowa's words at the meeting of the opera technical staff, when he defends himself against the opera singer's accusations published in the Warsaw daily paper *Życie Warszawy*, clearly have political meaning. He says that 'the artists ignore us. They ignore themselves, they ignore the audiences, and they ignore us. After all, this theatre is rotten. We play trash here; we work ourselves to death to produce old plays. Let's face it: how many people come? Only half of the seats are filled.' When interrupted by his colleagues that he is exaggerating and that artistic affairs are not the business of the technical staff, he continues with a comment that can be easily applied to the political situation in Poland: 'This is our business. The problem is, we sit quietly and say nothing ... This theatre is dead. It's a corpse ... It stopped talking to people.'[18]

Kieślowski's *Personnel* deals with the confrontation between crude reality and the idealistic concept of theatre envisioned by Romek, between dreams about artistry and the prose of life. The ideal image of the temple of arts, maintained by Romek, proves to be in reality a politicised place full of quarrels and down-to-earth ambitions. Interestingly, the opera house in *Personnel* is seen not from the perspective of a regular audience member or an artist, as is often the case in cinema, but from the perspective of one of its foot soldiers – the dresser. Kieślowski's film stresses the immense gap between artists and the technical crew who dislike the artistic production of the opera house. Romek learns about this division during his first day at work when he is unkindly informed by the porter that there are two separate entrances to the opera – one for the artists and another one for the technical staff. In the course of the film, Romek swiftly learns the political nuances governing his workplace. During his conversation with a communist youth apparatchik, who is clearly trying to bribe him to join the communist party, Romek tries on his glasses and discovers that he 'can see better'; from that moment on he is shown wearing glasses that, according to Tadeusz Lubelski, serve as a 'clear metaphor for intellectual illumination'.[19]

The film opens with a close-up shot of a bewildered Romek on his first day in the opera house. He scrutinises himself in several mirrors, while nervously waiting to be admitted by the personnel department, then he is mystified by a pair of ballet dancers rehearsing and a prop of a horse being lowered down outside the opera window. Witold Stok's camera follows Romek's gaze and, in the course of the film, represents mostly his point of view. As in his later documentary film, *Seven Women of Different Ages*, Kieślowski demonstrates interest in meticulous rehearsals, in the pain of practice rather than the glamour of the opening night. For example, when Romek and his aunt attend the premiere of Giuseppe Verdi's *Aida*, Kieślowski only allows the viewer to see the excitement and preparations before the opening act: the audience slowly filling the theatre and musicians taking their seats. To stress the importance of the moment, Kieślowski portrays Romek and his aunt arriving early and taking their seats to the sound of the overture from *Aida*. The beginning of the opera, however, is only recorded on Romek's face. Later he proudly admits to a girl he met while commuting to work that he works for the opera and he tells his impressions of the premiere. As if developing the story from his 1966 short film, *The Tram*, Kieślowski also depicts the developing romance between a young man who is overcoming his shyness and an attractive young woman. The romantic violin music accentuates Romek's glances during the first three silent meetings on the train.

Kieślowski in *Personnel* examines the issue of being loyal to one's convictions in the manner of documentary cinema. Several Polish film critics rightly point out the Formanesque observations in *Personnel*, especially the influence of *Černy Petr* (*Black Peter*, 1963). Both films share a simplicity of narrative (disregard for a well-developed narrative), a documentary-like unobtrusive observation of the portrayed group of people, an improvisation on the set, an episodic plot, a reliance on a number of non-professional actors (real Wrocław Opera tailors, Kieślowski's former teacher – Irena

Lorentowicz, among others), a hand-held camera, the focus on people's faces and everyday behaviour, and finally, a thinly veiled political and social criticism. However, unlike Forman in *Black Peter* and in his other Czech films, Kieślowski is not interested in hilarity and comic banality exposed in everyday situations.

Some similarities, not only related to the narrative aspect, do exist between *Personnel* and Olmi's *The Sound of the Trumpets*. Like Olmi (and Forman for that matter), Kieślowski focuses on seemingly meaningless gestures, daily routine and the vulnerability of his protagonists. Witold Stok's camera stays close to characters and in an almost *cinéma-vérité* fashion records their reactions in close-ups. Professional actors interact with non-professional actors who simply play themselves. Kieślowski comments that he 'rented an opera house in Wrocław with all people who worked there, directors, tailors, etc., and we asked them to continue their daily routine – to work, talk and move. Then we let in our people, film-making students, who tried to behave like them.'[20] The film is built around small, detailed observations and relies on everyday talk (about Polish women, television personalities, soccer) that helps to paint a broad picture of the represented reality rather than to move forward the film's minuscule action.[21]

Personnel belongs among Kieślowski's most autobiographical films. Like the film's protagonist, Kieślowski completed the Warsaw College for Theatre Technicians in 1962, and spent one year working as a dresser at the prestigious *Teatr Współczesny* in Warsaw. As he later recalls in his conversations with Danusia Stok, 'I was constantly dealing with brilliant actors who now appear in my films. We still like each other very much but the relationship is entirely different. The actors include Zbyszek [Zbigniew] Zapasiewicz, Tadeusz Łomnicki, [Aleksander] Bardini, [Edward] Dziewoński – many people who are now in my films. I used to hand them their trousers, wash their socks and so on. I used to attend to them behind the scenes and watch the performances.'[22] Also, like Kieślowski, Romek is not a big-city person, but rather a shy provincial dwarfed by the big-city experience.

Kieślowski's film, despite being a modest television drama, received a number of awards in Poland and abroad. The film was awarded at the Mannheim International Film Festival and also received two prizes at the Festival of Polish Films in Gdańsk – Grand Prix in the category of television film and the journalists' award. Equally important was the Andrzej Munk Prize for the best debut.[23] It is also important to point out that the critical success of *Personnel* came at a time when Polish cinema was dominated by lavish, artistically sophisticated adaptations of the national literary canon, a trend reflected at the 1975 festival in Gdańsk: the Grand Prix (Golden Lions) went to Jerzy Antczak's *Noce i dnie* (*Nights and Days*) and Andrzej Wajda's *Ziemia obiecana* (*The Promised Land*).

The Scar: Managers and Their Dilemmas

In 1976 Kieślowski made two feature films that aptly reflect the reality of communist Poland: *Blizna* (*The Scar*) and *Spokój* (*The Calm*, released in 1980). In several interviews, and in his typical self-deprecating manner, Kieślowski expresses his dislike for *The Scar*. In his conversations with Danusia Stok, for example, he calls it a socialist-realist film *à rebours*.[24] He is even more explicit in an interview conducted in 1995 by Paul Coates; Kieślowski claims that *The Scar* is 'probably badly directed' and also that it is 'muddled, messy, badly made, badly acted, badly edited, overlong and, in general, I don't know if it's any good for anything to anyone.'[25]

Although extremely harsh in his criticism of *The Scar*, Kieślowski succeeds in portraying a multifaceted, well-meaning manager of a huge chemical industrial complex, Stefan Bednarz (Franciszek Pieczka). The film is based on a story by journalist Romuald Karaś who is also listed as the co-author (with Kieślowski) of dialogue. The story deals with the middle-aged manager who, after almost twenty years, returns from Silesia to his small hometown of Olecko where he builds a chemical plant despite the vocal opposition of the local residents. The construction of the plant, which is planned by the over-ambitious and simple-minded town authorities led by the manipulative chairman of the regional council (Mariusz Dmochowski), completely changes the local community. People have to be resettled, houses bulldozed and the forest cleared, despite the presence of a nearby wasteland that is more appropriate for the factory but belongs to another administrative region. Although facing numerous conflicts with the local population and the authorities, Bednarz is able to finish the construction. After four years, in 1970 – the year of violent workers' protests – he decides to end his career. Criticised by the local population for not listening to their voiced concerns, and by the local communist party executive committee for not fully cooperating with them, the embittered Bednarz retires and returns to his family in Silesia. In the final scene he helps his baby grandson learn to walk. The ending may be described as typical of later Kieślowski: it offers a retreat from politics, an escape from the political to the private, a move portrayed in *The Calm*, *Camera Buff* and *Blind Chance*.

The protagonist of *The Scar* is shown as a progressive manager entangled in communist bureaucracy. Like the majority of Kieślowskian characters, he is good by nature and well-meaning. According to the film's logic, it is not

Franciszek Pieczka as Stefan Bednarz, a well-meaning manager of a huge industrial plant in *The Scar* (1976)

Bednarz, but the political and social circumstances that are to be blamed for his failure and the failure of the industrial project. It is the system that is the guilty party here, that very system that tolerates the disparities between lofty verbal declarations and dishonest practice and ignores the widening gap between the communist elites and the masses. In the film, the gap between the authorities and the people finds its equivalent in Bednarz being isolated from the local population and the journalists by his manipulative, career-oriented assistant (Jerzy Stuhr). Although the film is set in the late 1960s, its spirit, its images referring to sped-up yet badly planned industrialisation, and the idea of political leaders being isolated from the masses by the Communist Party apparatchiks, clearly refer to the mid-1970s in Poland.

The realistic, sometimes even paradocumentary, portrayal of the Polish managerial class in *The Scar* and the atmosphere surrounding typical 'communist industrial sites' are well-balanced and devoid of clichés. Sławomir Idziak's camera records the 1970s' pomposity, rituals and communist decorum: official visits by the party authorities and the minister (Stanisław Igar), all driving the emblematic communist cars – the black Volga, the masses organised by the party activists to cheer and show support for their plans, and then silently leaving the place after they are no longer needed, May Day parades, the ritualistic opening of the plant, social functions and professional meetings. The chairman of the regional council explains the nature of the political system to a party activist: 'We are doing it for them [the masses]. And they want it. Yes, and you have to bring them together, so they will say that they want it. This is your job – it's not a laughing matter.' Bednarz defends the factory in a similar manner in his conversation with a television reporter (Michał Tarkowski): 'I think that people will slowly start to consider it as their own.'

The communist system, as portrayed by Kieślowski, reveals a number of surreal qualities. For example, prior to the opening credits, *The Scar* opens with a puzzling long-shot of a group of workers in the forest, pouring water with buckets into the forest. The director then cuts (as he did in his documentary *The Factory*) to a meeting of local party activists who are working on a bid for the factory project. To market their town as an ideal location, they stress the underdeveloped nature of the place – people living in old, dilapidated houses and desperately waiting for a change. The enigmatic opening scene finds its explanation when the chairman of the regional council is informed that the river flooded, as he carefully planned it. Other scenes also border on the surreal: the cavalcade of Volgas on a small dirt road leading into the deep forest and the images of party apparatchiks debating in the forest, all wearing dark suits and appearing incongruous with the pastoral scenery.

By and large, *The Scar* reveals the documentary style that originated in Kieślowski's early films, for example images of Olecko and its inhabitants seen through Bednarz's point of view as he discovers it anew after twenty years, and the intense atmosphere of meetings between the authorities and the local population resemble the spirit of *From the City of Łódź*. The similar portrayal of a party executive committee meeting, which debates Bednarz's managerial style, appears earlier in *Workers '71* and *Curriculum Vitae*. The visual style of Kieślowski's film, however, also displays some poetic qualities present in his later works. They include the frequent panoramas over a desolate landscape that are juxtaposed with images of the plant, images of the forest being removed as portrayed in a series of jump cuts and images shot through and reflected in a window.

Apart from being a political drama, *The Scar* also offers a psychological portrait of the managerial class in Poland. Bednarz lives for his job and, as a consequence, is lonely, has marital problems and has problems with his adult daughter Ewa (Joanna Orzeszkowska). His wife (Halina Winiarska) does not want to join him in Olecko and prefers to reside in Silesia. The circumstances of their departure for Silesia twenty years earlier, probably the result of a conflict, apparently of political nature connected with the most enigmatic character in the film, Stanisław Lech (Jan Skotnicki), are never fully revealed in the film. The protagonist is isolated from his family, from the local population and from the centre in Warsaw. Although his private life is on the margins of Kieślowski's interests, it surfaces in one of the most interesting scenes in the film – Bednarz walking his dog, looking in the darkroom at the photographs he has just taken and resting in his modest flat in an unglamorous apartment building. Franciszek Pieczka (b. 1928), who started his career with an episodic role in Wajda's *Pokolenie* (*A Generation*, 1955) and is known for numerous fine performances in a wide range of films, adds humanity to his character. He underscores Bednarz's good nature and the layer of mellowness behind the tough-man facade, and the gap between his private and professional life. For this role he received the Best Actor award at the 1976 Festival of Polish Films in Gdańsk.

The episodic, occasionally awkwardly narrated film with several underdeveloped characters (such as Bednarz's wife and Lech), *The Scar* features unusual music composed by Stanisław Radwan. The soundtrack relies primarily on the unsettling beats of drums, pulsating rhythms and natural sounds of the construction site. It also emphasises the internal landscape of the protagonist, serves as the expression of his feelings and supplements or even substitutes for dialogue. As always in Kieślowski's early films, dialogue aptly captures the official 1970s language – newspeak.

The Scar is not the only Polish film in the mid-1970s that deals with communist managers and their dilemmas. The realm of the managerial class and communist politics is also examined in several popular television series. They range from the reflective picture of the factory managers presented in the very well-received television series *Dyrektorzy* (*Directors*, six episodes, 1975, Zbigniew Chmielewski) to the popular humorous depiction of life during the Gierek period in *Czterdziestolatek* (*The Forty-Year-Old*, 21 episodes, 1974–76, Jerzy Gruza) and its big screen version, *Motylem jestem, czyli romans czterdziestolatka* (*I Am a Butterfly, or the Love Affair of the Forty-Year-Old*, Jerzy Gruza, 1976). Other television films, for example *Najważniejszy dzień życia* (*The Most Important Day of Life*, 1974, nine episodes, Andrzej Konic, Sylwester Szyszko and Ryszard Ber), *Znaki szczególne* (*Identification Marks*, 1976, six episodes, Roman Załuski) and *Ślad na ziemi* (*The Sign on Earth*, 1978, seven episodes, Zbigniew Chmielewski), also deal with similar issues. Directors of mainstream films in the 1970s, however, abstained from these subjects, never popular among Polish audiences, tainted by the socialist realist dogma and clichés and dangerously close to the domain of schematic propagandist works. Some notable exceptions include, for example, Kazimierz Kutz's ambitious but failed *Linia* (*Line*, 1974), a film about a provincial party secretary, described by several Polish critics as a work about 'the dilemmas of the authorities' (similarly to *The Scar*), and Roman Załuski's *Rdza* (*Rust*), made during the Solidarity period but released in 1982 after the introduction of martial law.

As in *Curriculum Vitae*, in *The Scar* Kieślowski strives to portray the communist system as if from inside by choosing a subject and a character commonly associated with socialist realist works. He finds himself in a situation resembling the one faced by a group of young sociologists in *The Scar*. Although shrewd and ambitious, they are unable to move beyond what is expected from them by the authorities. Being well paid by the factory and dependent on its management compromises their research on the malfunctioning factory. Attempting to deal with some weaknesses of the communist political system, Kieślowski is perfectly aware of the unwritten 'rules of the game'; he never seeks to offer any 'dissident views', and never openly questions or ridicules the system. Instead, he tries to understand its mechanisms, to portray its representatives and to document their actions. The presence of two Cinema of Distrust directors, Kieślowski's friends, Tomasz Zygadło as a young sociologist and Agnieszka Holland[26] as the secretary to Bednarz, emphasises the generational aspect of this film as well.

The disparity between slogans and grey reality, between the rulers and the ruled, that Kieślowski attempts to portray in *The Scar*, is, however, far better represented in Polish documentary cinema, including Kieślowski's own works. A number of such documentary works dealing with everyday hardship, social pathologies and the world of cynicism and incompetence were shelved by the authorities in the late 1970s and not released until the Solidarity period. Some of the finest examples include Marcel Łoziński's *Próba mikrofonu* (*Microphone Test*, 1980), Irena Kamieńska's *Robotnice* (*Female Workers*, 1980) and Piotr Szulkin's *Kobiety pracujące* (*Working Women*, 1978).

The Calm: Life as It Is

Jerzy Stuhr (b. 1947), who plays a supporting role in *The Scar* as an opportunistic assistant to director Bednarz, appears in his first leading role in Kieślowski's modest, yet superb, film – *The Calm*. He stars as Antoni Gralak (also the name of the protagonist of documentary *Curriculum Vitae*), a simple man recently released from prison after three years, who wants to lead an undisturbed life and stay out of trouble. After learning that he cannot return to his previous life (his family as well as his fiancée reject him), he moves to a small Silesian town where he earlier worked as a prisoner. He gets a simple job, rents a room in an apartment owned by an older woman (Izabella Olszewska) with whom he has a brief affair, and begins his new life. Gralak explains his dreams to his new colleagues in the following way: 'A woman, children, a place of one's own.' Soon he marries a young woman (Danuta Ruksza) who showed him some sympathy when he was a prisoner. Drab reality, however, offers him no chance to fulfil his modest dreams. He is caught in the middle of the growing conflict between the director of the small plant (Jerzy Trela), where he was employed despite his prison record, and his fellow workers. The mismanagement and theft of building materials result in the reduction of workers' wages, and this prompts them to go on strike. Both sides reject the protagonist; he is manipulated and blackmailed by the management and, in the final scene of the film, is beaten up by his fellow workers, who feel betrayed by him. Lying on the ground and bleeding, Gralak mutters several times the word 'calm'.

The word 'calm' plays a seminal role in Kieślowski's films and in his artistic biography. It is also repeated in other films and often used by Kieślowski in his interviews. For example, asked by his friend and long-time collaborator, Krzysztof Wierzbicki, in the documentary *I'm So-So*, 'What do you want?' he answers briefly, 'Calm.'

The Calm strikes the viewer with its paradocumentary flavour: down-to earth story and characters, everyday situations and colloquial dialogue. The film was produced by Polish Television, scripted by Kieślowski and based on a short story by Lech Borski 'Krok za bramę' ('The Step Outside the Gate'), which was published in 1973 in a collection entitled *Noc gitarzystów* (*The Night of Guitarists*).[27] Kieślowski and his principal actor, Stuhr, are credited as the authors of the dialogue. The versatile Stuhr, with an ear for real-life dialogue,[28] imprints his mark on this film and the whole Cinema of Distrust. He creates a panorama of characters ranging from uprooted careerists (*The Scar*, *Top Dog*, *Rough Treatment*) and people struggling with the pressure of politics and everyday hardship (*The Calm*) to passionate and sincere ordinary characters (*Camera Buff*). Along with another fine actor, Zbigniew Zapasiewicz, known chiefly for his characterisations of cynical intellectuals in *Camouflage* and *Rough Treatment*, he became one of the emblematic actors of the late 1970s.

Similar to several of his early films, in *The Calm* Kieślowski focuses on the underprivileged, those living on the margins of society, underdogs, those who do not make the front pages and rarely read more than the front page. He deals with small-town life and similar aspirations. Even such humble aspirations, however, prove themselves impossible to fulfil in the world portrayed on the screen. In *The Calm* Kieślowski attempts, in his own words, to 'register on film the story of a man who had a minimum programme for his life, and was not allowed to realise even this small aim because he was entangled in dirty business against his own will'.[29] Stuhr's down-to-earth

Jerzy Stuhr as Antoni Gralak and Danuta Ruksza as his wife in *The Calm* (1976)

Gralak is deprived of any romantic gestures and grand romantic aspirations; he just yearns for basic privacy. In the context of Polish cinema, favouring the portrayal of individuals at the mercy of cruel history (history as a destroyer of happiness and a meddler into private affairs), Kieślowski's character seems apolitical, to the point of being narrow-minded, in his focus on private life, on achieving 'calm'.

Kieślowski's frequent collaborator, cinematographer Jacek Petrycki (*First Love* and *Curriculum Vitae*), captures the images of colourless provincial Poland and the mundane situations, behaviours and gestures that aptly reflect the Gierek decade in Polish history. The film is closer to documentary cinema than fictional film; in Petrycki's words, it is 'the fictional film that is like life'.[30] The narrative of this paradocumentary film, however, contains a metaphysical element, which perhaps foretells the 'art film poetics' of Kieślowski's later films. The symbolic image of galloping horses appears three times on the screen.[31] The first time they appear on a television set and interrupt the television test image. When Gralak is badly beaten by his co-workers, the image is juxtaposed with the picture of the horses. The image of a galloping horse also ends the film, providing an ironic commentary on the fate of the protagonist on his search for unattainable calm. In the documentary *I'm So-So* Kieślowski provides a considerably straightforward explanation; he says that the horses on the screen may represent 'a longing for the quality they possess. They can do as they want. They can run free and have no obligations.' The horses, according to Kieślowski, have nothing to do with politics or social issues but function purely as a metaphysical element.[32]

The painful realism of Kieślowski's film and the inclusion of some images forbidden by the state, such as the workers' strike (though the word strike is not uttered there but rather the simple phrase 'we don't work') and prisoners working outside of a prison, resulted in the belated premiere of *The Calm*. Made during the period of unrest in 1976, the film premiered in 1980, weeks after signing the 'August Agreements' between the striking Solidarity members led by Lech Wałęsa and the representatives of the Communist Party. With his portrayal of the workers solidarity, Kieślowski's film clearly heralds the events of 1980 in several Polish Baltic ports. One Polish film critic justly titles his 1980 review: '*The Calm*, or About Solidarity.'[33]

When the film was released on Polish television, however, it was not compatible with the spirit of the times that was probably better represented by narrative films such as *Człowiek z żelaza* (*Man of Iron*, 1981) by Andrzej Wajda or documentaries such as *Workers '80* by Andrzej Chodakowski and Andrzej Zajączkowski. Unlike Kieślowski, Wajda offers a one-dimensional, melodramatic characterisation typical of socialist realist cinema with clear divisions between the communist and dissident side, a romantically portrayed union between the working class and the intellectuals and students. Kieślowski's disdain for 'revolutionary pathos' and concern for the everyday is probably closer to another emblematic film of that period, Kazimierz Kutz's *Paciorki jednego różańca* (*Beads of One Rosary*, 1980), which also revolves around the struggle for human dignity, for 'calm', and for the right to live the desired life. When screened at the 1981 Festival of Polish Films in Gdańsk, *The Calm* won the Special Prize shared with another 'unshelved' film, Antoni Krauze's *Meta* (*Shelter*, 1971), made for Polish television.

In February 1976 Kieślowski received the award *Drożdże* (*Ferment*) given by the prestigious weekly *Polityka* to those young Poles who 'stir an intellectual ferment'. This comparatively liberal journal (interestingly, led by the future Communist Party General Secretary, Mieczysław Rakowski), gave an award to a film-maker known to the relatively small circle of film viewers familiar with *Personnel* and documentaries such as *First Love* and *Curriculum Vitae*, the film-maker who was still before the theatrical premiere of *The Scar* and *The Calm*. In 1977, despite the fact that the censor shelved *The Calm*, Kieślowski's name appears among the twenty distinguished Poles in a poll undetaken by the daily *Sztandar Młodych* (The Banner of the Youth). As evidenced by these awards, Kieślowski often blurred boundaries between the oppositional and communist sides, between being considered by viewers and critics as a dissident and a pro-party artist. Certainly, he was respected by the authorities (although some of his films were shelved) and this brought accusations of conformity. Such charges would resurface later, after the release of *No End*.

Camera Buff: Meditations on Film-making

Camera Buff, Kieślowski's first internationally acclaimed film, received awards at the Moscow, Chicago and Berlin film festivals. It also won the 1979 Festival of Polish Films in Gdańsk. At the same festival in Gdańsk, Jerzy Stuhr received the Best Actor award for this film and also for his performance in Feliks Falk's *Szansa* (*Chance*). The film was exceptionally well received in Poland, praised for its reflections on the nature of film-making and on the social and moral responsibilities of being an artist.[34]

Kieślowski's film remains one of the most intricate works of the late 1970s in Poland. The deceptively simple story of *Camera Buff* introduces Filip Mosz (Jerzy Stuhr), an ordinary thirty-year-old man working in a small-town factory as a purchasing agent. When his wife Irena (Małgorzata Ząbkowska) becomes pregnant, he buys an 8mm movie camera to record the growth of their child. Raised in an orphanage (the aspect primarily stressed in the published script)[35], Filip has everything the protagonist of *The Calm* truly wanted: a family, a place to live, a job and a group of friends. His friend and supervisor Stanisław Osuch (Jerzy Nowak) comments when he observes the joyous Filip after the birth of his child: 'Now I can see what happiness is all about.' Yet, as Filip later tells his wife, film-making means more for him than his home and family. Irena's nightmare at the very beginning of the film, during her pregnancy, about a hawk attacking a white chicken in a sense foretells the future events.

Filip begins his passionate affair with film by making a home movie that documents the birth and first months of his baby daughter. Later, however, he becomes more and more preoccupied with the world around him. Invited by the factory manager, Halski (Stefan Czyżewski), he becomes involved in making a film about the 25th anniversary jubilee in his factory. He becomes the visual chronicler of official factory functions as well as an observer of simple everyday events in his small town. The camera enables him to see more, to go beyond the facade of things and to grow as a person and as a political being. While making a film about his hometown, he documents his small discoveries: the divergence between the main streets and the back streets, the shabbiness behind a pretty facade. In a memorable and symbolic scene, in a long hand-held take, Filip moves from the front of a well-kept street through the gate leading to a dilapidated rear side. He portrays the two sides of reality in one take: the official truth and the unrepresented reality.

Jerzy Stuhr as amateur film-maker Filip in *Camera Buff* (1979)

The themes of Filip's first films are not necessarily expected by the director of the factory who would like to see a straightforward documentation of the factory life rather than films peppered with small, sometimes critical, social observations. Filip, however, with the help of Anna Włodarczyk (Ewa Pokas) from the federation of amateur film clubs, is nominated and wins the third prize for 'The Jubilee' at an amateur film festival in Warsaw. He also gets an invitation to work for a manipulative television producer (Bogusław Sobczuk, known for similar roles in Wajda's *Man of Marble* and *Man of Iron*). Filip begins to look at the world from a film-maker's perspective; for example, when his wife leaves him, he frames her with his fingers as though she stars in his film. Filip slowly becomes a small-town celebrity and with a circle of friends who gather around him he forms a film club sponsored by the factory. When he stamps his forehead with the official seal of his amateur cine club he is symbolically marking his new identity.

Filip also begins the rapid process of self-education. He is reading more, including film and political journals read by Polish intelligentsia in the 1970s such as *Polityka*, *Kultura* and *Film*, and he is also learning about the masters of cinema such as Ken Loach, much admired by Kieślowski. We watch him reading Jerzy Płażewski's *Film History for Everybody*[36] and paying attention to images from Andrzej Wajda's *Popiół i diament* (*Ashes and Diamonds*, 1958),

István Szabo's *Apa* (*Father*, 1966), Károly Makk's *Szerelem* (*Love*, 1970), Jiři Menzel's *Closely Watched Trains* (1966) and Ken Loach's *Kes* (1969). Gradually, Filip learns the responsibilities of being a film-maker. Although he is still allowed to make films ('You are young, you can make mistakes', the factory manager tells him), one of his films destroys the careers of other people, including his friend Osuch. As a result, the shaken Filip destroys his new film about brickworks, produced for television. He overexposes the film when he suspects that his work, which uncovers the mismanagement of the brickworks, can be used against the people he portrayed there.

Filip's problems as a film-maker are also paralleled by his personal problems; the more he focuses on film-making, the more estranged he becomes from his wife who, being pregnant with their second child, finally leaves him taking their daughter with her. In the frequently cited final scene, the disappointed protagonist takes the factory's newly acquired 16mm Soviet-made camera 'Krasnogorsk' and turns it on himself. He realises that observing external reality has isolated him personally and politically. After exposing the lives of others he is now exposing himself, retreating from socially committed observations to the exploration of his own life and mind.

As observed by several critics, Kieślowski produces a self-reflexive film – a meditation on film-making, its pleasures and dangers, an essay about being faithful to oneself and personal sacrifice, as well as about the responsibilities

Filip (Jerzy Stuhr) and his wife Irena (Małgorzata Ząbkowska) in *Camera Buff* (1979)

A scene from *Camera Buff* (1979): Jerzy Stuhr as Filip (right) listens to comments about his film. Stefan Czyżewski as the factory manager Halski (centre), Jerzy Nowak as Stanisław Osuch (left), and Tadeusz Bradecki as Witek (far left)

of being an artist. In the last scene, when the protagonist puts the camera in front of himself and re-tells his experiences from the beginning of the film (the birth of his child), Kieślowski explains that he 'simply realises that, as an amateur film-maker, he's found himself in a trap and that, making films with good intentions, he might prove useful to people who'll use the films with bad intentions'.[37] In Krzysztof Wierzbicki's documentary, *I'm So-So*, Kieślowski is more explicit: 'He realises that one can only portray the world through oneself.' According to Jerzy Stuhr, Kieślowski originally intended a different ending with the character destroying the negative and thus symbolically finishing his career as a film-maker. After several weeks, Kieślowski added the actual ending, claiming that it is 'more truthful' (he identified himself with the protagonist).[38]

Filip's realisation of the futility of all the efforts he put into filming culminates in his 'suicide' as a political film-maker (he 'shoots' himself with his camera). This meaning of the ending of *Camera Buff* had been scrupulously analysed by Polish critics who, by and large, did not share Kieślowski's own interpretation, but treated the ending as a sign of capitulation. For example, according to Jan F. Lewandowski, Filip has to look for 'substitute themes due to the pressure of politics and the inability to deal with political and social issues'.[39] The last scene of *Camera Buff* and Kieślowski's statements on the arduous task of describing the unrepresented world herald, perhaps, his future films preoccupied with metaphysical issues and more and more removed from the Polish political and social context.

Saturated with subtle humour, *Camera Buff* examines the impact of film on a life, the process of self-discovery through the arts and the pressure of political censorship. When the factory manager reminds Filip that 'film is the most important of all arts', and Filip briskly adds that these are Lenin's words, they stress only what is convenient for them. Polish film-makers and critics, desiring to defend the high status of film among other arts and wanting to defend their own projects, frequently used Lenin's words. The political context as well as the true meaning of this often (mis)quoted term is, however, missing: as originally formulated, film is the most important art for propaganda purposes and therefore should be used properly by the film-makers, who were aptly nicknamed by Stalin 'engineers of human souls'.

Camera Buff can be also discussed as an essay on censorship and self-censorship; on making compromises and learning that the world is grey rather than black and white. Filip, the passionate neophyte who gets a camera, a tripod and an editing table, intends to 'make simple films about people and their feelings', as he explains to his colleagues. Soon, however, he learns that the plant director demands the editing out of some scenes, simple observations of reality that do not comply with the official truth. Later Filip makes another film called 'Pracownik' (Worker) about his co-worker Wawrzyniec, who is a dwarf. Wawrzyniec is a simple model worker who has worked for 25 years at the factory, and his equally simple life has revolved around work and small 'communist luxuries', such as going on Sunday to a coffee shop for dessert with his wife. Although Filip produces a moving film about Wawrzyniec's fight for dignity through exemplary work ('it is more difficult for him to be good'), his bosses are not pleased: the film does not conform to the expected portrayal of socialist work and workers. The understanding and paternalistic factory manager Halski explains to Filip the meandering nature of communist politics during their walk in the wooded area that is overlooking the town. He defends the actions taken by the authorities because 'it just so happens that public life cannot always be open. One has to be very careful how one says something, in order not to ruin something. One has to know a lot.' When Filip protests, 'everybody should know', Halski's response is that 'not everybody is mature'. Pointing out a picturesque valley, he also suggests that 'it doesn't seem like much, but the world is so beautiful. People live, people love, and it's worth seeing sometimes. And everything in you is so grey and sad.' Filip concludes ironically that, indeed, 'only nature can be public'.

The problems that the film-maker/amateur encounters in his small town certainly parallel the problems of the Polish professional film-making community. Paul Coates comments that *Camera Buff* 'hovers between the Fellinian mode of autobiography and straight narrative'.[40] Krzysztof Teodor Toeplitz writes in a similar manner that, thematically, *Camera Buff* can be approached as the *8½* of contemporary Polish cinema. The unique character of Kieślowski's film, writes Toeplitz, has to do with its protagonist and his moral dilemmas. He is neither a film-maker, as was the protagonist in Federico Fellini's film or in Wajda's *Wszystko na sprzedaż* (*Everything For Sale*, 1969), nor a refined intellectual as in Zanussi's films, but a simple character with sophisticated dilemmas. The film tells us that 'problems concerning the creativity and morality of art – often ascribed to the neurosis or hypersensitiveness of overly-sensitive artistic people – are in fact universal problems, accessible to anybody who, even by a small degree, crosses the border of everyday "peaceful calm"'.[41] Here, Kieślowski works against the pervasive stereotype (prevalent not only in Polish cinema) that certain topics are reserved for specific social groups. For example, when Filip discovers the camera's ability to immortalise, thanks to casual footage of his friend's mother taken shortly before her death, he expresses some ontological questions about the nature of cinema asked by several film-makers and film theorists.

As if to stress Krzysztof Zanussi's importance to the Polish film-making community, and to Kieślowski himself (he made *Camera Buff* for Zanussi's Tor film studio), Zanussi himself participates in a meeting after a screening of his film *Camouflage*, and he comments on film-makers' moral obligations. Later Zanussi visits Filip's film club in Wielice, where the poster of his film, *Balance Sheet*, is proudly displayed on the wall, and offers some practical advice. The scene obviously pays tribute to Zanussi as the key figure of the Cinema of Distrust, and earlier, as one of the key figures in Polish amateur film-making movement and cine clubs. The same scene, however, as pointed out by Jadwiga Anna Łużyńska, provides an almost ironic comment on Zanussi's celebrity-like status and the ritualistic nature of Polish cultural life. Kieślowski achieves this effect by cutting from the scene in *Camouflage*, when the cynical *Docent* (Professor) instructs the Teaching Assistant that those who avidly greet their bosses will profit from it, to the scene portraying the warm welcoming of Zanussi by the members of Filip's cine club.[42]

Apart from Zanussi, *Camera Buff* also features other members of the Polish film-making community, including Andrzej Jurga, a film-maker and a professor at the Katowice Film School, as himself (Jurga also produced television programmes about amateur film), and Tadeusz Sobolewski, one of the leading Polish film critics. In episodic roles Kieślowski casts a group of non-professional film-makers from Silesia, and Marian Osuch, the night porter in *From the Point of View of the Night Porter*, who appears briefly as the man in charge of a gas-mask drill in the factory and as a factory porter.[43]

It is tempting to see *Camera Buff* as a film about Kieślowski, his disenchantments with the realistic portrayal of 'unrepresented reality', his previous bitter experiences with documentaries (such as *I Don't Know*) that, instead of helping, could have been used against their protagonists. The film also may refer to Kieślowski's own struggles with censorship, for example as was the case of *Workers '71*, re-edited without his permission, and *Bricklayer* and *The Calm*, shelved by the authorities after their production and released during the Solidarity period. An observant viewer will find in *Camera Buff* scenes similar to those included in the earlier documentary *First Love* – stopping the cars on the street to get to a hospital with a pregnant wife, or watching the window of the hospital in the hope of seeing the newborn baby. Commenting on *First Love*, Kieślowski admitted that the whole situation was inspired by the birth of his daughter Marta ('I had the feeling of déjà vu')[44]. Kieślowski also utilises his earlier unfinished documentary projects, for example about a worker-dwarf, that are produced in *Camera Buff* by Filip.[45] Furthermore, Filip's documentary method of filming 'what is there', as his colleague puts it, is Kieślowskian in spirit and very close to his numerous statements. It can also be argued that, like the protagonist of *Camera Buff*, in his future films Kieślowski gives up the attempt to uncover external political reality in order to focus on inner feelings and experiences. Unlike Filip, however, Kieślowski neither made amateur films, nor was he involved in the cine club movement: 'I wasn't ever fascinated with a camera like that', he reveals to Danusia Stok.[46]

Camera Buff remains Kieślowski's breakthrough film, a pinnacle of the early stage of his career as a director of fiction. In his first narrative films Kieślowski deals with well-intentioned male characters struggling for calm and dignity in a political system that favours conformism, servility and dishonesty. The rites of passage of a young tailor and an aspiring amateur-film-maker are depicted against the background of meticulously portrayed Polish political reality. That reality forces the protagonists to make important political choices – the subject more explicitly represented in Kieślowski's later *Blind Chance*. His protagonists, be they simple-minded workers in *The Calm* or the managers in *The Scar*, suffer disappointments. It is worth noting that Kieślowski's early protagonists are surrounded by women who do not 'stand behind their man', do not understand them and care only about personal life. According to Alicja Helman, due to their 'particular conservatism and narrowness … [they] do not want to see any changes, and fear anything that might divert their husbands' attention from them and the "nest" they have built'.[47] 'Don't win', shouts Irena in *Camera Buff* when Filip goes by train to attend the film festival in Warsaw, and she observes, with barely masked disapproval, Filip's new passion that takes him away from what she expected from him. This treatment of women (seen also in *The Scar*), reproached by Polish film critics, was replaced in Kieślowski's later films by some strong, differently portrayed female characters.

Short Working Day: Mechanisms of Power

Short Working Day, based on Hanna Krall's novella *Widok z okna na pierwszym piętrze* (*The View from the First-Floor Window*), was made in 1981 for Polish television but with a possible theatrical release in mind. Unlike Kieślowski's other films, *Short Working Day* deals with a significant moment in Polish post-1945 history. The film retells the violent workers' riots in the city of Radom in June 1976 that started after a sudden television announcement of major food price rises and soon changed into social and political protests. The protesters besieged and torched the regional communist party headquarters and clashed with riot militia (ZOMO). The protests, which quickly spread to other Polish cities and were violently suppressed by the authorities, consolidated the political opposition in Poland. For example, following the events, the Committee for the Defence of Workers (KOR) was formed, which played an important role in the future political struggle for freedom. Due to its subject matter, *Short Working Day* was immediately shelved by the authorities and was never released theatrically. Kieślowski often stressed the weaknesses of this film and, in the course of time, was against its release.[48] The film premiered on Polish television after Kieślowski's death, twenty years after the Radom events, to little critical response.

The film begins with a pre-credit sequence introducing the protagonist in the year 1968, a turbulent period in Polish history marked by student demonstrations and an anti-Semitic campaign orchestrated by the communist party. The protagonist denounces the 'firebrands' manipulating the students and, most probably, this opportunistic action secures him the position of the district party secretary in the industrial city of Radom in 1975. In a television appearance five years later (during the Solidarity period) he defends his actions of 25 June 1976.

Like *The Scar* and a number of Kieślowski's documentary films, *Short Working Day* deals with the mechanisms of power portrayed from within the system. The film offers the point of view of the local Communist Party secretary, played by Wacław Ulewicz, whose office building is besieged by striking workers. The viewer learns what prompts the workers to take such

A scene from *Short Working Day* (1981): reconstruction of the workers' riots in 1976

desperate measures via the inclusion of the documentary footage showing Piotr Jaroszewicz, the then Polish Prime Minister, announcing in a televised speech an average 69 per cent increase in food prices (of meat, in particular). The Radom party secretary does not know how to deal with the workers' protest: 'We'll have to promise them something. It doesn't matter what', he explains in his interior monologue; 'The party activist cannot take offence at the working class, even if the working class is mistaken', he continues his newspeak observations. Despite the secretary's voice-over narration, his apparently endangered life and his position as a loner facing the hostile and unpredictable crowd, it is difficult, if not impossible, to sympathise with him. The party secretary is portrayed as incompetent and indecisive, a typical party activist who tries to calm the situation by winning the militant workers and pleasing his bosses in Warsaw. Narrating the film through the eyes of the communist apparatchik certainly alienated Polish viewers and the majority of Polish critics uncertain of Kieślowski's intentions. 'I had set myself a trap', recalls Kieślowski, 'because in Poland at that time – and even more so now – there was absolutely no question of the public wanting to understand a Party Secretary.'[49]

Stylistically, Krzysztof Pakulski's photography emulates the roughness of documentary films. The incorporation of documentary segments (Polish newsreels and television programs with political figures such as Lech Wałęsa and Piotr Jaroszewicz) enhances this experience. The film is filled with shots of the brownish interiors of the Communist Party headquarters, long shots of the restless crowd seen from the first-floor window where the cabinet of the party secretary is located and close-ups of the faces. Sometimes Kieślowski focuses on a single character, freezes the image and allows for a brief flashforward that introduces the character's future fate, before returning to the main action. Thanks to this device, Kieślowski links the Radom events with the birth of Solidarity. For example, the viewer follows a worker being beaten with batons by militia after his arrest, brought to court and sentenced for hooliganism. Other flashforwards introduce, among others, a young KOR activist helping a persecuted female worker and a group of future Solidarity activists.

As always, Kieślowski avoids sharp divisions, satire or caricature in portraying the picture of Polish society in 1976. *Short Working Day* is a docudrama capturing the spirit of the Radom events. The 'short day' of the title refers to the party secretary's day at work. Usually, as he admits, he works long hours but on 25 June when factories in Radom go on strike, he ends his working day abruptly, around two in the afternoon, being evacuated with the help of secret police before the party headquarters is set on fire. The no-star cast of the film helps to enhance its almost documentary flavour.[50] The lead actor Ulewicz, who is always at the centre of the film, is undoubtedly typecast

Wacław Ulewicz in *Short Working Day* (1981): Communist Party secretary in action

by Kieślowski due to his roles of communist party apparatchiks in some of the films produced in the infamous (because of its nationalist and communist bias) film studio Profil, headed by Bohdan Poręba. Ulewicz appears, for example, in *Gdzie woda czysta i trawa zielona* (*Where the Water is Clear and Grass Green*, Bohdan Poręba, 1977), *Hotel klasy Lux* (*Five Star Hotel*, Ryszard Ber, 1979) and *Wysokie loty* (*High Flights*, Ryszard Filipski, 1980). Kieślowski's original idea of casting Filipski,[51] a fine actor yet a controversial political figure, certainly would have moved this uneven film to another level.

Writing in 1981, Kieślowski notes that, 'at that moment the artist's inner self, his heart-searching and angst, were of less importance ... Today telling the truth about the world, though still essential, is no longer enough. We must look for more dramatic situations, for morals reaching beyond the everyday, for more universal and sagacious diagnoses.'[52] These comments as well as the poetics of Kieślowski's *Blind Chance* foretell his future cinematic style.

CHAPTER THREE

Choices, Chances and Politics

My films are always observations of a man in a situation which forces
him to make a choice to define his standpoint.

– Krzysztof Kieślowski[1]

Leaving its political implications aside, the imposition of martial law by
General Wojciech Jaruzelski on 13 December 1981 seriously affected
the cinema in Poland.[2] The film landscape in Poland was changed by the
communist ban on 'unwanted' Polish films, by the emigration of young
film-makers such as Ryszard Bugajski and Agnieszka Holland and by the
silence ('internal exile') of others, such as Wojciech Marczewski. Accused of
seditious activities, Andrzej Wajda was removed as the head of the film studio
X in April 1983, together with his close collaborators, the producer Barbara
Pec-Ślesicka and the literary director Bolesław Michałek. Wajda also resigned
as the head of the Polish Film-makers Association, which was suspended, like
the majority of other Polish associations, after December 1981.

The political situation after 1981 deepened the divisions between the
film-makers who supported the introduction of martial law and those who

did not. Comments such as 'Poland's quality cinema is now either silent or working in exile'[3] certainly oversimplify the problem, yet aptly reflected the heated atmosphere with its intensified divisions between 'us' and 'them'. Once again, a film's political aspects became more important than the film itself. The unofficial boycott of certain pro-communist film-makers and the attempt to boycott film-making in general, and film-making for state television in particular, were unsuccessful. The boycott did not affect established film-makers (some of whom, like Andrzej Wajda or Krzysztof Zanussi, were working abroad) but negatively affected the careers of young, emerging film-makers and actors. The latter were either unable to produce films or had to comply with the dominant aesthetics in order to be considered legitimate artists. Film director Waldemar Krzystek commented sarcastically: 'Immediately after martial law, it was not the best time to break with the artistic preferences of "moral concern". The country was again in need, the nation suffered, and mothers shed tears.'[4]

A number of films that had been made and released during the brief Solidarity period (1980–81) were immediately banned by the authorities, among them Kieślowski's *Przypadek* (*Blind Chance*), Wajda's *Człowiek z żelaza* (*Man of Iron*) and Wojciech Marczewski's *Dreszcze* (*Shivers*), the latter of which premiered on 12 December 1981 – one day before the declaration of martial law. The same thing happened to a group of politically uncompromising films finished at the beginning of 1982, including Janusz Zaorski's *Matka Królów* (*The Mother of Kings*) and Ryszard Bugajski's *Przesłuchanie* (*The Interrogation*). Due to the absence of Polish films that expressed dissenting views, distorted pro-communist interpretations of recent events were propagated in films such as Roman Wionczek's 1984 *Godność* (*Dignity*).

The banning of several Polish films, the reduction of Western films in Poland (only nine such films in distribution in 1982),[5] and the impact of the (mostly pirated) video market which heavily promoted commercial cinema, alienated a number of sophisticated Polish viewers. The elimination of politically minded cinema from distribution and the growing importance of locally-made popular genre films prompted several Polish critics, who supported the thematic preoccupations of the political cinema in the late 1970s, to speak of the danger of imminent commercialisation. The critics singled out films by Juliusz Machulski, the former principal actor of Kieślowski's *Personnel*, such as *Vabank* (*Va Banque*, 1982), its sequel *Vabank II, czyli riposta* (*Va Banque II*, 1985) and *Seksmisja* (*Sex Mission*, 1984), that referred to Western cinema rather than a Polish national context, to cinema conventions rather than life 'as it is'.

Polish critics favoured and wanted to protect politically committed cinema against the encroachment of commercially minded films. Some critics saw the appearance of popular cinema as a cynical move on the part of state authorities to divert the attention of Polish viewers from matters of primary importance. They did not object to Machulski's films or to Radosław Piwowarski's unpretentious *Yesterday* (1985), a sentimental and comic coming-of-age story about Beatlemania in Poland. Their primary target remained films such as the erotic *Thais* (Ryszard Ber, 1984) and the 'erotic horror' *Widziadło* (*The Phantom*, Marek Nowicki, 1984). The problem, however, was not the genuinely popular films but rather the mass of mediocre products, neither popular nor artistically or politically-minded, swiftly rejected by new audiences that had been educated by pirated videos of American popular cinema.

Kieślowski acted as the Vice-President of the Polish Film-makers Association (*Stowarzyszenie Filmowców Polskich*) in turbulent times from 1978 to his resignation in 1981: 'I realised it wasn't my world', Kieślowski later recalled; 'I wasn't cut out for such revolutionary times'.[6] Between 1979 and 1982 Kieślowski also taught at the Katowice Film School, originally established in 1978 for the television industry exclusively.[7] He worked there with, among others, Kazimierz Kutz, Andrzej Wajda and Krzysztof Zanussi – film-makers and teachers who were unwelcome at the Łódź Film School for political reasons. Critics in Poland often juxtaposed the documentary-oriented style of Katowice, labelled 'kieślowszczyzna' (Kieślowskism) after Kieślowski, with the formal concerns of Łódź, known as 'łodzizm' (Łodzism).[8]

Blind Chance: Variations on Fate

> I still think that, together with Munk's *Bad Luck* and Zanussi's *Illumination*, *Blind Chance* belongs to our most important achievements of intellectual cinema.
>   – Tadeusz Sobolewski[9]

The script of *Przypadek* (*Blind Chance*) was written before the Solidarity period and was later published in 1981 in a prestigious journal on drama, *Dialog*.[10] Produced in 1981, the film was immediately shelved by the authorities after 13 December of that year. A still from *Blind Chance* appeared on the front cover of the last issue of the monthly *Kino*, published before the introduction of martial law in Poland. Six years later, in 1987, *Blind Chance* was quietly released with a group or other distinguished banned films including Janusz Zaorski's *The Mother of Kings* and Jerzy Domaradzki's *Wielki bieg* (*The Big*

Run, 1981). In 1988, Agnieszka Holland's *Kobieta samotna* (*A Woman Alone*, 1981) was 'unshelved' as was the preeminent Polish film of the early 1980s, Ryszard Bugajski's *The Interrogation*, one year later. At the 1987 Festival of Polish Films in Gdańsk, Kieślowski was awarded the Best Screenplay Award for *Blind Chance* and its star Bogusław Linda received the Best Actor Award (the award also recognised his performance in Filip Bajon's *Magnat* [*The Magnate*]).

While early narratives by Kieślowski demonstrate his fascination with capturing life 'as it is', they go beyond narrowly understood realism. Kieślowski admits in his conversations with Danusia Stok that describing the undescribed world had its limitations and, therefore, *Blind Chance* offers 'no longer a description of the outside world but rather of the inner world. It is a description of the powers which meddle with our fate, which push us one way or another.'[11] In a characteristically self-critical manner, Kieślowski blames the film's flaws on the imperfections of his script. (Interestingly, Polish critics mostly praised the script of *Blind Chance*, which was also awarded in Gdańsk.) The move to the 'inner world' and metaphysics, heralded earlier by Kieślowski in the ending of *Camera Buff*, finds its epitome in *Blind Chance*.[12]

Kieślowski's *Blind Chance*, which at the beginning of the 1980s quickly attained dissident cult status, portrays an undergraduate medical student Witek (diminutive form of Witold) Długosz, played by Bogusław Linda, whose future is determined by whether he is able to jump onto a moving train. This is the beginning of Witek's three different life paths: he is a young party apparatchik manipulated by old party functionaries, a dissident activist involved in underground publishing and a person isolated from others by his desire for privacy. In each 'what-if' scenario an accidental element determines the protagonist's life – a fact stressed by the film's title. The Polish title *Przypadek* is usually translated as *Blind Chance*, but it could as easily be translated as 'the coincidence' or 'the case' (that is, the case of Witek).

The pre-credit scene of *Blind Chance* opens with a puzzling close-up shot of a young man's face who is screaming in horror 'No!' The camera pulls toward his open mouth and the credits follow. Then the viewer sees several perplexing, short scenes that make sense only during the course of the film. They provide the summary of Witek's life prior to his run after the train (perhaps Witek is looking back at his life at the moment of his death). These scenes include the death of Witek's mother during his birth at the time of bloody strikes in Poznań in 1956 (a heavily bleeding man is dragged across the hospital corridor), images of his father and Witek's farewell to Daniel, his Jewish friend who leaves Poland for Denmark during the anti-Semitic campaign of 1968. In other glimpses of the protagonist's past we see Witek kissing his first love Czuszka, Witek making love to a fellow medical student Olga, the death of Witek's father and Witek's outburst of sadness at the train station.

Only those viewers who are familiar with Polish history can understand the importance of several scenes and dates in *Blind Chance*. The protagonist is born on 27 June 1956 in Poznań. The opening scene in a hospital, filled with the dying and wounded, blood on the floor, refers to the violent workers' protest in Poznań in June 1956. (The opening image is repeated later in the film.) During the strike, which concerned working conditions, reduction of work loads and salary increases, riots broke out and the army and security forces intervened and opened fire on the protesters.[13] Witek's mother dies, along with his twin brother, while she is giving birth; the medical personnel are too busy with the wounded. As Witek later remarks, he survived because he was the first one to be born. (The death of Witek's twin brother at birth perhaps anticipates the future story about Weronika and Véronique in *The Double Life of Véronique*.) The film makes other important historical references when Witek reveals to his girlfriend Werka that both his great grandparents participated in the 1863 uprising (the so-called January Uprising) against the tsarist regime, that his grandfather took part in the 'Miracle on the Vistula' – the decisive battle on the outskirts of Warsaw during the 1920 Polish-Soviet war, and that his father participated in the September 1939 campaign against the advancing German troops and in 1956 took part in the Poznań strikes. Witek's family history and his symbolic date of birth make him a generational protagonist. This is not, however, the generation to which Kieślowski belonged. Witek, like the author of this book, belongs to the generation born after the Stalinist period, too young to remember the year 1968 in Poland, whose formative years were the late 1970s, during the Gierek's era of 'small prosperity'.

The opening segment of *Blind Chance* also contains an important telephone conversation between Witek and his dying father. The father's last words – 'I'd like to tell you something because it might be too late: you don't have to do anything' – are taken literally by Witek. He takes a leave of absence from the medical academy (where he presumably was studying to please his father) and tries to find his own way. The rest of the film is built around three different stories, three films within a film. They offer three hypothetical generational biographies or three variants of the same biography, three alternative life paths, three outcomes of Witek's chase after the moving train.

The three separate stories originate with a simple incident at the Łódź train station. Three times Witek runs through the station and bumps into an older woman who drops some coins and curses him. The camera then follows one rolling coin that is picked up by a middle-aged alcoholic man who uses it to

Bogusław Linda as Witek running after the moving train in *Blind Chance* (1981)

pay for a glass of beer. In the meantime, Witek buys a discounted student train ticket and, running to the platform, either barely misses or bumps into the man with the beer, which either enables him to catch or causes him to miss the train to Warsaw (perhaps the train of destiny). Witek's three attempts to board the train are emphasised by the same memorable musical score by Wojciech Kilar, one of the most accomplished Polish composers.

In the first story, which is the longest, lasting 49 minutes, Witek runs and catches the Warsaw train. On the train he meets an old-time communist party activist Werner (Tadeusz Łomnicki) who introduces him to the world of official politics. Once in Warsaw, he invites Witek to his apartment and explains events from his political and private past. Also, thanks to his high-level contacts, the now semi-retired Werner helps Witek advance his career by introducing him to his friend, a prominent party apparatchik Adam (Zbigniew Zapasiewicz). The ambitious and eager Witek is sent by another party official (Jerzy Stuhr) to quell a rebellion, caused by alleged harsh treatment, at a rehabilitation camp for drug users supervised by the Union of Socialist Youth (*Związek Młodzieży Socjalistycznej*, ZMS). Although threatened by the patients, Witek succeeds in releasing their hostages, all of whom are doctors, and returns to Warsaw. Also in the first story, thanks to another chance, Witek meets his first love Czuszka (Bogusława Pawelec), now involved in dissident activities, and mixes with her circle. Due to his political naïvety, however, Witek betrays Czuszka and her friends by revealing their political actions (distributing underground books) to Adam. After her arrest, the outraged Witek strikes Adam, thus ending his flirtation with the communist ideology. The story ends bitterly. Witek's much anticipated trip to France is stopped at the last moment (at the airport) by the authorities because of strikes in several Polish Baltic ports – obviously referring to the advent of Solidarity in August of 1980.

Kieślowski paints a picture of the end of Gierek's era in Poland with a small number of representative characters, some of them almost bordering on clichés. Three different characters represent the communist side in *Blind Chance*: Werner, Adam and the apparatchik played by Jerzy Stuhr. Werner belongs to the embittered yet still loyal generation of communists. Arrested in 1948 and released from prison after Stalin's death in 1954, Werner tells the story of his life to his earnest apprentice Witek and ends it thus: 'If we haven't done things right, maybe your generation will. You, for instance.' The participation of Tadeusz Łomnicki (1927–92) as Werner adds another dimension to this character. This great actor, known chiefly for his theatrical performances, whose filmic career began in 1955 with Andrzej Wajda's *A Generation*, was also known for his involvement in official politics as a member of the Central Committee of the Polish Communist Party. Another activist, Adam, represents the conformist mainstream of the party and is played by Zbigniew Zapasiewicz, an actor known chiefly for his role as a cynical and embittered professor in Zanussi's *Camouflage*. Interestingly, he also plays a similar, Adam-like character in another shelved film, Janusz Zaorski's *The Mother of Kings*. Jerzy Stuhr, as the young party apparatchik, portrays a typical 1970s scoundrel. The 'oppositional side', represented by Czuszka, also seems to have been taken from the prop-room of the Cinema of Distrust. The young rebels at the hospital may strike contemporary viewers as equally clichéd, with their 'angry and non-conformist' look and 'freedom songs' such as 'we are different, that's why you don't want to know us, we are different, but capable of many things'.

In the 35-minute second story the protagonist runs after the train, but is stopped by a railway militiaman (*sokista*), struggles with him, and is arrested. As a punishment, Witek is sentenced to community service. While working in a park on a gigantic flowerbed in the shape of an eagle (the Polish emblem), he meets an underground activist Marek (Jacek Borkowski) and, through him, other dissidents. After meeting wheelchair-bound priest Stefan (played by one of the leading actors of politically-minded cinema of the late 1970s, Adam Ferency) who is helping the dissidents, Witek converts to Catholicism and is baptised. The combination of the Roman Catholic faith and an anti-communist stance marks Witek as the emblematic Polish hero of the Solidarity period.

Like other underground activists, Witek helps with the printing of dissident literature and is preoccupied with the underground 'flying university' and with organising a free workers' union. He also helps those who are harassed by the authorities. For example, he is sent by his organisation to an older woman, an underground activist, most probably a KOR (Committee for the Defence of Workers) member who was providing legal and financial aid to arrested workers. Her apartment has just been ransacked by security service (SB) men posing as grateful workers. Her calm ('Life is a gift,' she tells Witek) contrasts sharply with the dangerous situation she has just faced.

In the second story Witek also meets his childhood Jewish friend, Daniel (Jacek Sas-Uhrynowski), who comes from abroad to attend the funeral of his mother, and Daniel's sister Werka (Marzena Trybała), the married woman with whom Witek later has an affair. Witek's involvement with the political opposition is abruptly terminated after the search and arrest of his friends' cell active in underground publishing, when he is unjustly accused of betraying them. Ready for a trip to France to attend a meeting of the Catholic Youth, Witek refuses to cooperate with the security service which makes it impossible for him to get a passport. Returning home, he learns about the 1980 strikes in several Polish cities from his aunt (Irena Byrska), an old-time idealist communist, now listening to Radio Free Europe.

The third story, which is only 20 minutes long, begins again with the image of the running Witek who misses the train and meets his university friend and lover Olga (Monika Goździk) on the platform. They subsequently marry; Witek resumes his medical studies, interrupted in the first two variants, and leads a calm and politically uninvolved life. During his work at the medical academy, under the supervision of his former dean (Zygmunt Hübner), he refuses to take sides: 'I don't want any part of one or the other', he explains, and does not sign a petition to release a group of political prisoners, including the dean's son. When the dean asks Witek to replace him and deliver a series of lectures in Libya, he agrees and decides to travel, via Paris, three days later, on 11 July 1980, after his wife's birthday celebrations. Before boarding a train he learns that they are expecting a baby girl. The story and the film end with the image of the plane exploding shortly after take-off from the Warsaw airport.

In *Blind Chance*, Kieślowski questions the 'us' and 'them' division that defined the Polish political as well as cultural life under communist rule. He expresses disillusionment with life in Poland and favours uninvolvement – the model of life revolving around the personal rather than the public.[14] According to the film's logic, one can be honest, regardless of one's political stand, even being on the side of the Communist Party. *Blind Chance* offers no proper solution for Witek. The fatal plane to Paris waits for him in every

Witek (Bogusław Linda) and Werka (Marzena Trybała) in *Blind Chance* (1981)

variant of his life; even being uninvolved cannot save him from his fate. In the first two variants, however, when Witek is politically active on either side of the political barricade in Poland, he is saved. As Kieślowski explains, being focused on one's personal life cannot change the world because 'the world has to be changed'.[15] Being politically involved, however, Witek gets another chance. In part two, the likeable protagonist's aunt tells him: 'I'm glad you didn't go away, not at a time like this.'

In all three parts of *Blind Chance*, regardless of his political stance, Witek is basically the same: sincere, honest, decent, passionate, eager to act and trying to do his best in given circumstances. In every story Witek also finds for himself a different surrogate father (Werner, Stefan, Dean), and falls in love with a different (with regard to her appearance, psychology and aspirations) woman. Although fate meddles in Witek's affairs and alters (or ends) his life, he remains good by nature. Perhaps Kieślowski argues that decency can be found on both sides on the political division in Poland – certainly an unpopular view in the bitter atmosphere of the early 1980s in Poland. 'Blind chance may shape one's life but does not shape the human being', writes Polish critic Maciej Pawlicki.[16] Perhaps, as Tadeusz Sobolewski convincingly argues, Kieślowski stresses that political and ideological divisions in Poland are a fiction and do not reflect true differences.[17]

Blind Chance might be considered a pessimistic philosophical parable on human destiny shaped by occurrences beyond individual control. On the one hand, Kieślowski's treatment of the matter stems in large part from his documentary beginnings; in this light, the film could be considered a political essay. On the other hand, by introducing the element of chance (perhaps destiny) into his protagonist's actions, the director is able to deal with questions present in his later, internationally acclaimed films, starting with *Decalogue*. Kieślowski comments that his films 'are always observations of a person who must choose in order to define one's place. This is always an attempt to consider what proper, objective reality is, or to understand the motives of a person who acts against this reality.'[18]

Kieślowski's film about human destiny also bears some similarity to the *Three Colours* trilogy. *Blind Chance* offers three films within a film and the characters, by reappearing in other stories, sometimes add an ironic twist to the action. In the second part, for example, Witek, standing in front of the Warsaw Central Station building, asks Werner for directions. In the final part of the film, before Witek's doomed flight to France, he is at the airport where a group of young pilgrims, headed by Stefan, wait for their plane to Paris. In the same scene, a flight attendant from the first part runs with passports belonging to the young party apparatchiks. Coins also link *Blind Chance* with the *Three Colours* trilogy, specifically the rolling coin in *Blind Chance* and Karol's French two-franc coin in *Three Colours: White*.

Kieślowski deals with a personal experience but universalises Witek's experience in a parable on destiny and choices. By providing his protagonist with an almost stereotypically patriotic biography, he generalises his experiences and his dilemmas. Given his patriotic-nationalist family up-bringing, however, Witek is certainly portrayed as too naïve when it comes to communist ideology in the first story of the film.

The star of *Blind Chance*, Bogusław Linda (b. 1952), at that time also appeared in a series of acclaimed political films, including Agnieszka Holland's *Gorączka* (*Fever*, 1981) and *A Woman Alone*, Andrzej Wajda's *Man of Iron* and *Danton* (1983) and Janusz Zaorski's *The Mother of Kings*. He became one of the idols of the Solidarity generation, although the censor shelved most of the films he appeared in. Later, at the beginning of the 1990s, Władysław Pasikowski's *Psy* (*The Pigs*, 1992) and its sequel released in 1994, *Psy 2: Ostatnia krew* (*The Pigs 2: Last Blood*), established him as a new charismatic Polish star. In the 1990s, Linda became an icon for another generation, the post-Solidarity generation, and represents its nihilism and disillusionment with the new reality. The tough guy aura and cynical attitude of the protagonists he portrays in Pasikowski's films reflect the reality of the first period of unfettered Polish capitalism. Linda often stresses that the evolution of his image, from romantic, frequently anti-totalitarian heroes to the fallen angel of the old system in the 1990s (as in *The Pigs*), is intentional, an integral part of his artistic development: 'The time came when I felt that I had had enough of roles as an intellectual. I felt that such a person, without any major life experiences, torn by idealistic differences, was not a hero for the present.'[19] Nevertheless, this shift has prompted some Polish critics to accuse the actor of betraying his initial image. Tadeusz Lubelski, for instance, declares that contemporary Linda 'remains merely a caricature of himself'.[20]

Kieślowski's film, firmly set during the decline of Gierek's regime, was released in a different political climate and reached another generation of film viewers for whom the experience of martial law (after 13 December 1981), rather than the Solidarity period (1980–81), had become the most important generational experience. *Blind Chance* was received by the majority of Polish critics as an apt reflection of the state of minds of the pre-Solidarity era. Due to its shelving, however, instead of introducing an intellectual ferment to Polish cinema, it became, as Tadeusz Sobolewski puts it, 'a souvenir of the past'.[21] Another critic called it a postscript to the Cinema of Distrust but intellectually more refined.[22] The almost clinical study of the three life variants, presented by Kieślowski, certainly has more in common with Krzysztof Zanussi's philosophical parables such as *The Structure of Crystals* and *Illumination* than with the Cinema of Distrust from the late 1970s.

Due to its cold narrative and unclear political sympathies, Kieślowski's film became an easy target for politically-minded film critics. His project had already been attacked at the script stage by functionaries of the Ministry of Internal Affairs as an 'anti-state and anti-socialist demagogy', apologetic towards the opposition and falsifying reality.[23] Certainly, some pro-communist party critics considered its fatalistic message, the view that life is governed by chance rather than the class background or our conscious actions, as anti-Marxist.

On the other side of the political spectrum, Solidarity critics, for example Krzysztof Kłopotowski, labelled Kieślowski 'a socialist film-maker' – a derogatory term in mid-1980s Poland.[24] *Blind Chance*, according to another Polish critic, writing under the pseudonym Marcin Sułkowski, offers 'an ironic summary of the aspirations of the [Polish] generation formed by the 1970s'.[25] The same critic claims that Witek is like a top-of-the-class student who wants to be the best without questioning, who naïvely follows the crowd and does not search for the true meaning of life. In all three stories Witek behaves like an eager beaver and his life is ruled by blind chance. Witek, writes Sułkowski, 'resembles a mirror, a smooth surface that reflects encountered persons', and takes on alien shapes.[26] That is probably why, in a conversation with Witek, his ailing father says, 'your good grades annoyed me. You noticed, didn't you? Know what pleased me? When you hit the teacher in the seventh grade and then got nothing but Cs. I don't like eager beavers. I never did. My dislike rubbed off on your school.'

The unique narrative strategy of *Blind Chance* influenced, to a certain degree, two films released in 1998: *Sliding Doors*, a British film directed by Peter Howitt, and *Lola Rennt* (*Run, Lola, Run*), a German film directed by Tom Tykwer. *Sliding Doors* offers not three but two versions, depending on whether Helen (Gwyneth Paltrow) catches a London train. The protagonist also does not face Witek's dramatic ideological choices. *Run, Lola, Run* relies on its MTV-like brisk editing and deals with a young punk in Berlin (Franka Potente) desperately trying to save her gangster boyfriend by getting him 100,000 German Marks. As Slavoj Žižek fittingly comments on *Run, Lola, Run*: 'The first words of the film ("the game lasts ninety minutes, everything else is just theory") provide the proper co-ordinates of a video game: as in the usual survival video game, Lola is given three lives. "Real life" itself is thus rendered as a fictional video-game existence.'[27] Tykwer's film offers a postmodern sensibility and, although it does not have the depth of Kieślowski's film, it is saved by its venomous kinetic energy.

No End: Requiem for Solidarity

This is a film about people with bowed heads.
          – Krzysztof Kieślowski[28]

The first film that Kieślowski made after the imposition of martial law in December 1981, *No End*, avoids easy generic classification. It contains elements of psychological drama, ghost story, romance and courtroom drama, as well as political and metaphysical film. Along with Agnieszka Holland's *A Woman Alone*, *No End* is among the bleakest films ever made in Poland.

Kieślowski's film was made in difficult times for ambitious uncompromising political cinema. Although for a number of Western critics and viewers political films formed a 'genre' virtually synonymous with Polish cinema, intimate psychological dramas, safe literary adaptations and commercial films formed the canon of Polish cinema in the mid-1980s. The oppressive, highly politicised atmosphere of these years better suited films like the winner of the 1985 Festival of Polish Films in Gdynia, *Kobieta w kapeluszu* (*A Woman with a Hat*, 1985), scripted and directed by Stanisław Różewicz, a subtle morality play devoid of direct references to Polish politics. Nevertheless, finished in 1984, but released on 17 June 1985, *No End* joined a small group of distinguished films that, due to political restrictions, received only limited release in 1985. Such films include *Nadzór (Custody)* by Wiesław Saniewski, a prison film set in a women's penitentiary, and 1984 Venice Film Festival winner, *Rok spokojnego słońca (Year of the Quiet Sun)*, by Krzysztof Zanussi, a tale of unfulfilled love set against the gloomy background of Polish post-1945 reality.

No End is an unusual film set during the period following the events of 13 December 1981 which ended the brief period of the Solidarity movement. The first film that touched upon the political and psychological situation of that dark period in Polish history was Leszek Wosiewicz's medium-length *Wigilia '81 (The Vigil of 1981*, 1982) which premiered as late as 1988. Wosiewicz's film was made during martial law for the new experimental production collective, Karol Irzykowski Film Studio in Łódź, later known for a series of significant films made by the younger generation of film-makers. The simple action of *The Vigil of 1981* is limited to an old apartment and its inhabitants, three women waiting in vain at Christmas Eve Supper for the interned Witek – their grandson, son and husband.

To reflect the reality of martial law in Poland, Kieślowski initially attempted to make a documentary film about political trials that were held after December 1981. Although this project never materialised, with the help of his new friend and scriptwriter, Krzysztof Piesiewicz, Kieślowski was able to record several court cases held before the public and military courts. Being a respected defence lawyer, known for his involvement in several high profile political cases since 1982, Piesiewicz offered first-hand knowledge about the mechanisms and abuses of law in post-1981 Poland. The appearance of Kieślowski's crew with a camera in court usually resulted in milder sentences for political prisoners. As Kieślowski recalls in his conversations with Danusia Stok,

> The judges didn't want to be recorded at the moment of passing unjust sentences, because they knew that if I turned on the camera, then some time in the future, after three, ten or twenty years, somebody would find this film. And they'd see themselves … Just as at the beginning nobody wanted to let us in on any trials – the lawyers, in particular, defended against this, and the defendants – so later they were all begging us to film their cases. It got to the point where I had to hire a second camera in order to make it from one trial to another on time. When a camera was in the courtroom, the judges didn't pass prison sentences. So I didn't even load the second camera with film because there wasn't any need. They were simply dummy cameras which were only there so that through plain human fear, the judges wouldn't pass sentences.[29]

Convinced of the impossibility of documentary means to aptly reflect the depressing state of affairs after the implementation of martial law, Kieślowski turned to narrative film. Co-scripted with Piesiewicz, *No End* reflects the disheartening reality of martial law – 18 months of curfew and militarised administration in Poland. It does so, however, without portraying all the elements that form the external reality of that period in Polish history: riot militia (ZOMO) in full gear, violent street protests, people lining up for food, mass arrests, curfew, television news delivered by television personnel in military uniforms, General Jaruzelski in dark glasses announcing the imposition of martial law, and harsh living conditions, among others. Furthermore, the word 'Solidarity' is absent from the screen due to the censorship practices of the day.

Instead of an overtly political film, Kieślowski tells the story of the death of a renowned lawyer, Antoni (the diminutive form Antek is used throughout the film) Zyro, who defended political prisoners immediately after the introduction of martial law. The lawyer dies prematurely in 1982, apparently of a heart attack. He leaves behind his beautiful, confused and grieving wife of eleven years, Urszula (the diminutive form Ula is used in the film), played by Grażyna Szapołowska, and their young son Jacek. Antoni Zyro is played by Jerzy Radziwiłłowicz (b. 1950), the symbol of 'Solidarity cinema', known chiefly for his lead roles in Andrzej Wajda's seminal political films: *Man of Marble* and *Man of Iron*. In *No End* Kieślowski consciously typecasts Radziwiłłowicz in the role of a person who is 'extremely clean, extremely pure, extremely clear'.[30]

Although politics plays an important role in *No End*, psychology is much more meaningful; it is not politics but a personal loss that really matters to Urszula. This is not to say, however, that *No End* is deprived of political and social observations. Kieślowski captures some aspects of the psychological reality of the post-martial law situation: illegal groupings, private calls monitored by the authorities (even a call to find out the time), candles burning in the apartment windows to commemorate the introduction of martial law, the specific language of the street associated with the time, certain physical types of young, angry, bearded underground activists (like the one nicknamed Rumcajs played by Adam Ferency), Przemysław Gintrowski's emblematic political songs, Andrzej Czeczot's and Andrzej Mleczko's political cartoons and the sharp political divisions within society and within families.

The metaphysical element, present earlier in *The Calm* (the intriguing, symbolic horses appearing on the television screen) and, more importantly, in *Blind Chance* (the discourse on chance and destiny), governs the story of *No End* from its pre-credit scene. The opening scene offers a bird's-eye view of a cemetery with flickering burning candles during the All Souls' Day on 1 November – a genuinely meaningful day in Poland. Zbigniew Preisner's intense, repetitive and sombre musical score supports this image. The scene sets the dreary and melancholy tone of the film and introduces its major themes of death, memory and love.

After the credits, a man wearing a black suit appears on the screen. As the viewer learns later, this is the ghost of Antoni Zyro, wandering through his young son's room and looking at his own reflection in the window and the glass of a bookcase. Then, in the family bedroom with his wife asleep behind him in the bed, he faces the camera and begins his dispassionate monologue. The lawyer introduces himself by saying, 'I died. Four days ago', and continues with details concerning the circumstances of his death. The simplicity of this introduction, which accounts for its great effectiveness, bears strong resemblance to the final scene of *Camera Buff* when Stuhr's character addresses the camera in the same immediate manner, this time talking about the birth of his child. After the short explanatory comments addressed directly to the camera (and the viewer), the ghost of the lawyer remains silent for the rest of the film. He quietly observes how his wife is coping with loneliness and tries to protect her. He also witnesses the development of 'his' court case involving a young worker, Solidarity member Dariusz (Darek) Stach (played by Artur Barciś), accused by the communist authorities of organising a factory strike after the introduction of martial law.

The film portrays Urszula's sadness and her gradual alienation from people and the outside world. She feels the ghost's presence. The more she learns about her deceased husband, the more she loves him. She discovers things from the past, for example her husband's humility and that he knew about nude pictures she had taken when she was young and desperate for money. Urszula also feels guilty about certain aspects of their relationship and she is jealous about his past friendships. At one point she makes love to a stranger, an English-speaking tourist met in a coffee shop who mistakes her for a prostitute and whose hands resemble those of her dead husband. After a graphic lovemaking scene, Urszula explains her union with Antek in Polish (although she is a translator of George Orwell), so the stranger cannot understand her feelings, and then hurriedly leaves his hotel room.

To liberate herself from the past, Urszula attempts to erase Antek from her memory. She visits a young hypnotist (Tadeusz Bradecki) and undertakes therapy without telling him that her husband is dead. During the session, however, she sees Antek, exchanges secret signs with him, and watches as he makes an eerie sound by moving his finger on an empty glass. Almost two months after the lawyer's death (we see the date of his death, 7 September, on his tombstone), Urszula and Jacek are portrayed among many fellow Poles during All Souls' Day at the Powązki cemetery in Warsaw. In a scene referring to the pre-credit images, Kieślowski captures the ocean of candles at the cemetery and people's faces. Shown in a close-up at Antek's grave, Urszula whispers, 'I love you.'

After several unsuccessful attempts to overcome her sadness and longing for Antek, Urszula leaves her son at his grandmother's and methodically

Grażyna Szapołowska as the grieving widow Urszula and her son Jacek (Krzysztof Krzemiński) in *No End* (1985)

prepares her suicide. It can be read as her will to be reunited with Antek. She dresses in black, brushes her teeth, tapes her mouth, symbolically cuts the link with the outside world (the phone cord), shuts all the vents and turns on the gas in the oven. She sits in front of the stove waiting for death, the camera behind her, as if representing her dead husband's point of view. The screen darkens as the camera pulls into the stove and then pulls back. The director then cuts to a close-up of Antek who greets and hugs Urszula. In an emotionally charged, yet bleak, final scene the couple walks away from the camera in a park-like setting.[31] Preisner's music once again fills the screen with familiar sombre tones and the film's credits roll over a freeze frame of the reunited couple. Kieślowski comments on the nature of Urszula's suicide: 'Only the very young commit suicide because of love. To be sure, my female protagonist of *No End* dies such a death, but this happens because of a total defeat, because of the inability to navigate herself in the world. Perhaps love directs her emotions, but what is she supposed to do when her only link with the world was her husband, who, from the beginning of the film, is dead.'[32]

Although Kieślowski's film invites an interpretation as a drama of mourning (with later *Three Colours: Blue* as its art-film continuation), it is also a courtroom drama set in the highly political climate of the early 1980s in Poland. That part of the film introduces Labrador, played by Aleksander Bardini, a defence attorney who is about to retire. He had defended his countrymen in political trials during the Stalinist period in Poland; later, eschewing politics, he deals exclusively with criminal cases. When Labrador learns from another lawyer about his mandatory retirement at the age of 70, he changes his mind and decides to defend Darek. He attempts to convince Darek to be more pragmatic, in other words to say what the judges want him to say. He tells the accused that 'when one has decided to live, one has to be able to endure a lot'. However, the honest and idealistic Darek (who represents the 'naïvety' of many of his contemporaries opting for similar desperate measures at that time) prefers a hunger strike, and he persists.

Labrador finally wins the case with the help of his assistant (Michał Bajor) by securing a letter of recommendation for Darek written by the pro-government new unions established in Darek's factory during his imprisonment. As a result, Darek gets only an 18-month sentence which is suspended for two years. When the sentence is passed, however, nobody shows any signs of joy. The verdict is greeted with silence indicating a feeling of resignation on the part of the accused, his family and the public gathered in the courtroom. The silence continues when Darek, his family and Labrador linger in the empty courtroom, the ghost of Antoni Zyro among them. 'The small victory seems insignificant when compared with the enormous quenched hopes ignited by

Jerzy Radziwiłłowicz as the ghost of lawyer Zyro in *No End* (1985)

Solidarity', writes Paul Coates.[33] Is this really a small victory? As portrayed in the film, the scene rather signifies a defeat, especially for those who, wanting to see Darek as a Solidarity martyr, hastily leave the courtroom. Commenting on the whole situation in a meaningful gesture, Labrador puts a finger to his head as if he wants to shoot himself. Interestingly, Philip Strick compares this gesture with that of 'the amateur movie-maker of Kieślowski's *Camera Buff*, once the naïve documentarist, now a self-censoring manipulator of information [who] finally "shoots" himself with his own camera'.[34] Labrador also provides an additional reflection when, after the trial, he reads to Urszula a poem by Ernest Bryll (unacknowledged on the screen): 'I don't even know how it happened, that I changed from a young wolf to an old dog ... maybe nobody had to put this dog-collar on me, nobody came after me, and I, myself, went serving humbly like a dog. Lord ... assure me that I'm living free although I weep.'[35] Aleksander Bardini (1913–95), known for his roles as professors, lawyers and doctors in films by Andrzej Wajda, Krzysztof Zanussi and Janusz Majewski, brings to this role the same screen persona that will later appear in films by Kieślowski, including *Decalogue 2* (doctor), *The Double Life of Véronique* (orchestra conductor) and *Three Colours: White* (lawyer).

The ghost of the lawyer appears seven times throughout the film, either silently observing Urszula or intervening in her daily matters. Although only a mysterious black dog that appears three times in the first part of the film seems to recognise his presence, a number of puzzling events in the film call attention to the presence of the supernatural: Labrador's watch, a gift from his student Zyro, falls and stops during his conversation with Darek's wife Joanna (Maria Pakulnis), while a man in black (perhaps Zyro) passes by; the mysterious red question mark appears on the directory of attorneys next to Labrador's name; Urszula's Volkswagen car stops on the street for no visible reason, saving her, in all likelihood, from a deadly accident; a newspaper disappears which is important in the context of the worker's trial. In another scene, when Darek awakens in his prison cell during the hunger strike, the ghost is there and quietly looks at him. As a result of this visit, Darek changes his mind and ends this suicidal action.

What is the role performed by the ghost in *No End*? Perhaps, unlike several 'active ghosts' in mainstream cinema (and one can list myriad examples, among romantic melodramas especially), the ghost in *No End* serves clearly as the symbol of the suppressed (as if dead) Solidarity movement, the symbol of pacified resistance, physically absent from political life, yet whose spirit is still present and felt by the majority of Poles. At the film's opening, Zyro's ghost tells the viewer about his sudden death (resembling the abrupt termination of the Solidarity movement on 13 December 1981) and, although he is no longer able to defend the young worker, he helps to assign his mentor Labrador to

Political trial in *No End* (1985): Aleksander Bardini as attorney Labrador (centre), Michał Bajor as his assistant (left) and Artur Barciś (far right) as the accused Solidarity activist, Dariusz Stach

the case. The ghost functions as the spirit that cannot be erased from memory, as evidenced by the widow's failed hypnotic session. The ghost of Solidarity is 'alive' and impossible to forget even by those who openly do not share his convictions (like Labrador). Furthermore, Labrador's unusual name (at least in the Polish context) reinforces the issue of fidelity to the cause ('faithful as a dog'). Urszula's fidelity to her husband also extends beyond the grave.

Another question is equally puzzling. To what is the title of the film referring? No end to what? There are several possible answers. On a personal level, the title of Kieślowski's film refers to the relationship between Urszula and Antoni. On the political level, the 'no end' refers to the issue of fidelity to the spirit of Solidarity. It may be, however, also a reference to the political and economic misery and other problems experienced by Poles at the beginning of the 1980s (not portrayed on the screen).

Tadeusz Sobolewski writes that the film is a 'sometimes risky attempt to look at social drama exclusively from an individual perspective'.[36] Indeed, Kieślowski does little to go beyond one individual case to portray, for example, a national or generational experience. Co-scriptwriter Piesiewicz, however, defends this approach: 'In the years 1982–83 we lived in Poland in a somewhat unreal atmosphere. Seeking a refuge in religion or in spiritualism, as in this film, became a kind of escape from reality.'[37]

When No End, released in a limited number of prints several months after its production, finally reached divided and highly politicised Polish society, critics, regardless of their political stance, attacked the film and as a consequence it received no prize at the 1985 Festival of Polish Films.[38] This can be attributed to the film's complex poetics, its mood of despair and defeat, its prominent metaphysical component, and its retreat from the para-documentary realism that had been much praised by Polish critics in Kieślowski's earlier productions. Kieślowski remarked that his film 'was terribly received in Poland. Terribly. I've never had such unpleasantness over any other film as I had over this one. It was received terribly by the authorities; it was received terribly by the opposition and it was received terribly by the Church. Meaning, by the three powers that be in Poland.'[39] The harsh criticism of No End, and the sense of being ostracised, would certainly later contribute to Kieślowski's reluctant and bitter attitude toward Polish critics, his aversion to politics and his move to international co-productions.

A penetrating observer of the new Polish cinema, critic Tadeusz Sobolewski, comments: 'The experiences of martial law developed ritual reactions within Polish culture: poetry was composed to commemorate particular occasions, along with paintings depicting the martyrdom of victims of the regime, Romantic Messianism came back to life, or rather the parody of it.'[40] It is not difficult in this context to understand why the film was so disliked by the three powers in Poland. The Polish Roman Catholic Church despised this film's aura of hopelessness, the graphic portrayal of casual sex, the protagonist's suicide and the depiction of love for a dead husband being stronger than maternal love. *No End*, obviously, did not meet the expectations of the communist authorities either, and was criticised by the pro-Communist Party critics because it portrayed martial law as the defeat of the communist regime.

Solidarity activists and critics associated with this political formation also found it impossible to embrace *No End*. The film has nothing to do with previous 'oppositional' films made in Poland because it portrays no clear conflicts between political factions. Instead, an atmosphere of death and despair permeates *No End*. Solidarity activists expected a film more in the spirit of Wajda's propagandist *Man of Iron* that encourages the suppressed union members to maintain their struggle. Instead of characters taken from a Solidarity poster and a simplified representation of the political life in Poland they were offered images of powerlessness, protagonists unable to overcome the mood of defeat, living with a sense of loss. In the opposition journals published underground, Kieślowski was accused of painting a stereotypical picture of the post-1981 situation, psychological improbabilities and, what was probably extremely painful for the director, of collaborating with the communist regime. Equally harsh comments were expressed in prestigious official journals such as *Kultura* and *Odra*.[41] According to a number of Polish critics, Kieślowski, like the ghost in the film, only observes his fellow countrymen's misery and suffering without attempting to change it. Kieślowski's almost entomological, 'un-Polish' treatment of explosive political issues, his rejection of traditional romantic and revolutionary heroes and his metaphysical bias prompted such a response. It must be stressed, however, that supernatural phenomena are present in some canonical examples of Polish national drama, for example Adam Mickiewicz's Romantic *Dziady* (*Forefather's Eve*) and Stanisław Wyspiański's fin-de-siècle *Wesele* (*The Wedding*), both adapted for the screen. Equally political in nature, *No End* deals with the impossibility of overcoming the burden of the past. The dead lawyer, one of many phantoms from the nation's intricate history, serves as a reminder of the past. His very presence brings some hope for the future.

I saw the film when it was released first in Poland. It left me indifferent due to its inability to depict my own experience of martial law and what I perceived then as its psychological incongruities. In the course of time, and with repeating viewings, the film has become for me synonymous with one aspect of that experience, the atmosphere of despair, and accurate in its representation of the spirit of martial law. Two other aspects that I associate with that period however, pathos and 'laughter through tears', are captured in the films made by Kazimierz Kutz in 1994: *Zawrócony* (*The Turned Back*) and *Śmierć jak kromka chleba* (*Death as a Slice of Bread*). The tragedy and pathos of the sit-in strike at the Wujek coal mine in *Death as a Slice of Bread* contrasts with the almost farcical and grotesque representation of events in *The Turned Back*. Interestingly, with the exception of the critically acclaimed and generally popular *The Turned Back*, *No End* and *Death as a Slice of Bread* worked against the trend and alienated Polish viewers with their refusal to introduce easily identifiable characters and typical 'revolutionary' Wajda-like (pro-Solidarity) narratives. Also both films, the first made during the suppression of the Solidarity movement and the latter during the period characterised by the depreciation of its myth, may serve as powerful farewells to the epoch of Solidarity.

Despite its important subject and the presence of popular Polish actors,[42] *No End* has never achieved the popularity it deserves. It is, however, an important work in Kieślowski's *oeuvre* and in the context of Polish cinema. With *No End* Kieślowski begins his collaboration with composer Zbigniew Preisner (b. 1955) and scriptwriter Krzysztof Piesiewicz (b. 1945) who will both help to define the style of 'mature Kieślowski'.[43] Their impact on Kieślowski's cinema will be discernible in a ten-part television series, *Decalogue*, and, in particular, their most acclaimed collaboration – the *Three Colours* trilogy.

CHAPTER FOUR

Entomological Observations and Metaphysics in Decalogue

Decalogue is an attempt to narrate ten stories about ten or twenty individuals who – caught in a struggle precisely because of these and not other circumstances which are fictitious but which could occur in every life – suddenly realise that they're going round and round in circles, that they are not achieving what they want.

— Krzysztof Kieślowski[1]

We wanted to go beyond Polish iconography to get rid of that unbearable polonocentrism: the constant weeping, the paraded pain and the conviction that we are the centre of the universe.

— Krzysztof Piesiewicz[2]

Decalogue, a ten-part series of loosely connected television films, offers a pessimistic picture of a harsh world in which moral choices must be made against the pressure of politics and economics. In spite of its apparent religious connotations, Decalogue is not only an exploration of religious or metaphysical issues but also an acute analysis of the mental condition of Polish society before 1989. The bulk of the action takes place in the same drab Warsaw apartment building complex, the Ursynów housing estate, built in the late 1970s. The ugliness and greyness of the dehumanised urban setting dominate the filmic landscape, together with close-ups of the people who endure these harsh conditions. Kieślowski's 'entomological observations' of desperate and unhappy characters inhabiting the unfriendly space give *Decalogue* the feeling of a documentary film.

Prior to the *Decalogue* series, Warsaw tenement blocks by and large did not provide the scenery for existential television dramas. These places were, after all, symbols of development in an underdeveloped country, symbols of the communal way of life. Given that representatives of all strata of society lived there, and that numerous people wanted to move there (and could not because of the shortage of apartments), it comes as no surprise that this was the setting for success stories about social advancement: films about migration from villages and small towns to the capital city. From the popular 1965 television series, *Wojna domowa* (*Civil War*, fifteen episodes), to the mid-1970s production, *The Forty-Year-Old*, both directed by Jerzy Gruza, this was also the setting for light comedies that often, in a thinly veiled manner, poked fun at the absurdities of the Polish People's Republic. Beginning in the 1980s, living in standardised apartments like Ursynów was no longer associated with success but necessity. For example, Stanisław Bareja's television series, *Alternatywy 4* (*Alternative Street, No. 4*, 1983, premiere in 1986/87, nine episodes), is a satirical portrait of the inhabitants of one apartment block also situated, interestingly enough, at the Ursynów housing estate.

The idea for a series of films based on the Ten Commandments originated around 1982 and 1983. Christopher Garbowski writes that scriptwriter Krzysztof Piesiewicz

was in part inspired by a Gothic altarpiece in the National Museum in Warsaw displaying the Ten Commandments in ten different scenes. In the altarpiece, the scenes are placed symmetrically. One might detect a similar symmetry in the *Decalogue* series when you consider the fact that after the first five episodes the style and tempo are somewhat different; there is also a framework of violence in the first and fifth episode which mark that part of the series apart.[3]

As Kieślowski mentioned on several occasions, he initially wanted to finish the script with Piesiewicz, give it to younger film directors and supervise the whole project through his Tor film studio. Eventually, he became emotionally involved with the project and decided to direct it for Polish television. The carefully planned shooting took eleven months in 1987 and 1988. Limitations – a small budget, relatively short episodes (approximately 56 minutes) and production time constraints – mark the *Decalogue* series. To lower the costs, Kieślowski frequently worked on more than one film simultaneously, enabling various cinematographers to use the same locations during one day. To recover costs, he also decided to produce extended versions of two parts of *Decalogue* to be shown in cinema theatres. Kieślowski himself selected part 5 of *Decalogue*, leaving the second choice for the Polish Ministry of Culture. The ministry selected part 6 and funded both productions. The theatrical version of *Decalogue 5*: *A Short Film About Killing*, premiered in Polish cinemas in March of 1988; the theatrical version of *Decalogue 6*: *A Short Film About Love*, appeared later in the same year, in October. The *Decalogue* series was shown on Polish Television in the winter of 1988 and 1989.

Despite their earlier harsh treatment of *No End*, the majority of Polish film critics praised Kieślowski's new work; successful screenings abroad of the two *Short Films* certainly helped the reception of Kieślowski's films at home. For example, *A Short Film About Killing* received the FIPRESCI Award and the Jury Prize at the 1988 Cannes Film Festival, and also earned the Best European Film Award ('Felix') in 1988. *A Short Film About Love* was honoured with the Special Jury Award, the FIPRESCI award and the Catholic Jury Prize at the 1988 Film Festival in San Sebastian. The television series *Decalogue* was also shown on the big screen abroad and received yet another FIPRESCI award and the 'Youth and Cinema' Prize at the 1989 Venice Film Festival and Catholic Jury Prize at the 1989 Film Festival in San Sebastian, among others.

International recognition aside, the Polish premiere of *A Short Film About Killing* coincided with a heated debate in Poland about capital punishment. At the annual 1988 Festival of Polish Films in Gdańsk, the two *Short Films* received the Grand Prix ('Golden Lions of Gdańsk'). *A Short Film About Love*, in particular, received critical acclaim and numerous awards in Gdańsk: Best Script Award for Kieślowski and Piesiewicz, Best Actress Award for Grażyna Szapołowska, Best Supporting Actress for Stefania Iwińska and Best Cinematography for Witold Adamek. In the following year, the two leading actors of *A Short Film About Love*, Grażyna Szapołowska and Olaf Lubaszenko, were voted the best Polish actors in a popular plebiscite of the cinema weekly *Film*.[4]

When Kieślowski and Piesiewicz started their work on *Decalogue*, Polish cinema was dominated by safe literary adaptations such as *Nad Niemnem* (*On the Niemen River*, 1987), directed by Zbigniew Kuźmiński, and intimate psychological dramas such as *A Woman with a Hat*, directed by Stanisław Różewicz. The mid-1980s were also characterised by the growing role of popular cinema, both locally-produced films and imported action cinema watched mostly on video format. The success of *Decalogue* and its two big screen versions also came during a period marked by the release of several films produced during and immediately after the Solidarity period and promptly shelved by the communist authorities. Films such as Janusz Zaorski's *The Mother of Kings*, Jerzy Domaradzki's *Wielki Bieg* (*The Big Run*, 1981) and Kieślowski's own *Blind Chance* were released in 1987; television films such as Robert Gliński's *Niedzielne igraszki* (*Sunday Pranks*, 1983), Leszek Wosiewicz's *The Vigil of 1981*, and Wiesław Saniewski's *Wolny strzelec* (*The Freelancer*, 1981) had their premieres in 1988. Also in 1988, the authorities released Agnieszka Holland's powerful *A Woman Alone*. With the addition of the paramount film of the early 1980s, Ryszard Bugajski's *The Interrogation*, released one year later, these temporarily dislodged films formed the most visible group around 1988.

The release of Kieślowski's ten television films referring to the Biblical Ten Commandments in a communist-bloc country by a director who considered himself agnostic may be seen as an anomaly. Despite the strength of the Polish Catholic Church, Krzysztof Zanussi became virtually the only Polish film-maker in the 1980s producing films that could be labelled 'Christian' or 'religious'. His filmic biography of the 'Polish Pope', *From a Far Country: Pope John Paul II* (1981) and a hagiography of the saint Maksymilian Kolbe, *Życie za życie* (*Life for Life*, 1990), may serve as the best examples. Katarzyna Jabłońska is perhaps right in saying that '*Decalogue* is an exceptional challenge to Polish Catholicism. To be sure, it is a polemic with false, superficial religiosity. It is also a provocation directed against a certain religious infantilism, against treating religion as an escape from responsibility for one's own life and for the life of others.'[5] Scriptwriter Piesiewicz admits that 'in 1985 the very idea of dealing with the Decalogue was already a certain provocation, almost a manifesto because it was clear that we wanted to focus on a real human being in real circumstances, situations and conflicts. We wanted to completely detach ourselves from that very general way of describing the world, from the relationship between "the political world and the human being", or "the political person and the world".'[6]

The political climate in Poland during the last years of communist rule contributes to the final shape of *Decalogue*, but the long-lasting economic, political and moral crisis, gloomy prospects for the future and the resulting mass emigration of Poles are deliberately subdued in Kieślowski's series. He intentionally ignores certain everyday aspects of life that dominated the reality in Poland in the late 1980s: politics, social rituals and images of day-by-day hardship (for example food rationing, queues). Disenchanted with politics,

Kieślowski attempts to depict 'individuals in difficult situations'[7] instead of explicitly political issues and situations familiar from numerous television productions. In the introduction to the English edition of *Decalogue* Kieślowski writes: 'The films should be influenced by the individual Commandments to the same degree that the Commandments influence our daily lives. We are aware that no philosophy or ideology had ever challenged the fundamental tenets of the Commandments during their several thousand years of existence, yet they are nevertheless transgressed on a routine basis.'[8] In Kieślowski's series, the biblical Commandments are not illustrated but are, rather, referred to in ten anecdotes, each with two or three leading characters. Also the setting is by and large limited to the same Ursynów housing estate. Although each part of the series usually refers to one single commandment, sometimes a film may refer to more than one commandment; occasionally, its reference is not clear at all (such as *Decalogue 6*).

The *Decalogue* series introduces undistinguished characters, mostly intelligent professionals dwarfed by an oppressive political system. The viewer watches them in situations that require immediate and vital decisions and is introduced to their moral dilemmas. The serious, dark, almost depressing tone of the majority of the *Decalogue* films prompted some critics to discuss it in terms of some mysterious East-Central European malady. For example, Tim Pulleine writes that Kieślowski's perception of the world is saturated with 'East European sinisterness'.[9] Even if one agrees with this comment – suggesting that the characters in *Decalogue* are themselves the products of specific East-Central European historical, political and cultural circumstances – one also has to notice that they face universal, truly Bergmanesque dilemmas. Kieślowski himself admired some of Bergman's films, *The Silence* (1963) in particular.[10] (Interestingly, in his 1995 interview, trumpeted as 'the last one', Bergman listed *Decalogue* as one of the five contemporary films that he 'most benefited from'.) The open structure of *Decalogue* invites the viewer to interpret the actions of Kieślowski's protagonists, to follow their struggles with destiny in an abundance of chance encounters, symbols, allusions, ambiguity, deliberate slow pace, laconic dialogue and a number of recurring motifs (such as the bottle of milk: sipped, frozen, spilled and delivered).

Decalogue was produced with the involvement of Kieślowski's regular composer since *No End*, Zbigniew Presiner, and nine leading Polish cinematographers (Piotr Sobociński worked on two parts, 2 and 9). Kieślowski assembled a diverse group of cinematographers known for their different aesthetic and working styles. The group included the very experienced Wiesław Zdort (b. 1931), who started his career during the Polish School period and worked as a camera operator in 1958 on such Polish classic films as Andrzej Munk's *Eroica* and Andrzej Wajda's *Popiół i diament* (*Ashes and Diamonds*). His later career is associated with directors such as Kazimierz Kutz and Barbara Sass (his wife). However, the majority of cinematographers working on *Decalogue* belong to Kieślowski's generation: Krzysztof Pakulski (b. 1948), Sławomir Idziak (b. 1945), Witold Adamek (b. 1945), Edward Kłosiński (b. 1943) and Andrzej Jaroszewicz (b. 1938). But Kieślowski also worked with newly emerging cinematographers such as Dariusz Kuc (b. 1951), Piotr Sobociński (1958–2001) and Jacek Bławut (b. 1950), the latter also a director of acclaimed documentary films. On the set of *Decalogue*, the director granted them a lot of freedom to experiment. He tells Danusia Stok: 'I've never given lighting cameramen as much freedom as I did in *Decalogue* … I counted on the competence, on the energy which results from freedom.'[11] Kieślowski's approach toward shooting resulted in slightly different visual styles in the various parts of *Decalogue*. These range from hand-held camera and the extensive use of filters (especially in *Decalogue 5* and *A Short Film About Killing*, photographed by Sławomir Idziak) to 'plain', functional photography (for example by Dariusz Kuc in *Decalogue 7* and by Jacek Bławut in *Decalogue 10*). Kieślowski's authorial signature aside, *Decalogue* also owes its stylistic coherence to Ewa Smal – the young editor who was recommended to Kieślowski by his long-time collaborator, editor Lidia Zonn.[12]

The production of such an ambitious project also had to involve a number of known Polish actors. Several of them appeared in earlier films by Kieślowski: Bogusław Linda, Aleksander Bardini, Jerzy Stuhr, Grażyna Szapołowska and Tadeusz Łomnicki, among others. Kieślowski also cast a group of actors whose names and best-remembered performances are associated with leading Polish directors, including Krystyna Janda and Daniel Olbrychski (Andrzej Wajda), Maja Komorowska (Krzysztof Zanussi), Olgierd Łukaszewicz (Wajda and Kazimierz Kutz). Often he relies on young emerging actors – the stars of the new Polish cinema such as Mirosław Baka, Zbigniew Zamachowski and Olaf Lubaszenko, or theatrical actors, rarely seen in Polish films, such as Anna Polony.

Among Kieślowskian actors there is also Artur Barciś, previously seen in *No End* in the role of the imprisoned striking worker Dariusz Stach. He appears in episodic yet extremely important roles in almost all parts of the *Decalogue* series, with the exception of parts 7 and 10. Like the ghost of lawyer Zyro in *No End*, the character played by Barciś is the silent witness to events in other people's lives. Kieślowski comments on his role: 'I introduced the character whom some called "the angel" and whom the taxi-drivers when they brought him in to the set called "the devil". But in screenplays he was always described as a "young man".'[13] Wiesław Zdort, the cinematographer of *Decalogue 1*, reveals that during his first conversations with Kieślowski, they labeled the mysterious character 'the Angel of Fate'. Furthermore, he reveals that it was he who suggested that the Angel of Fate should reappear in other parts of *Decalogue*.[14] Actor Barciś admits in an interview with Tadeusz Sobolewski that he did not receive any specific acting instructions from Kieślowski regarding the character.[15]

The enigmatic angel-like character appears in some decisive scenes of *Decalogue*, during moments in which the fates of the protagonists are determined. The Angel of Fate glues the series together and adds an almost metaphysical dimension. He is portrayed as a person sitting at the campfire near the fatal pond in *Decalogue 1*, as a hospital worker in *Decalogue 2*, as a driver of a tram that nearly crashes into the protagonist's car in *Decalogue 3*, as a sportsman kayaking on the Vistula river and then carrying the kayak on his back when the female protagonist is about to decide her fate in *Decalogue 4*, as an inspector surveying the road and a painter in the prison in *Decalogue 5*, as an elegant man in a white suit in *Decalogue 6*, as a student listening to the protagonist's lecture in *Decalogue 8* and as a cyclist who observes the protagonist's attempted suicide in *Decalogue 9*. The editing often suggests that the Angel of Fate is aware of the complexity of a character's action. He silently warns about the consequences of a character's deed without directly interfering; sometimes he disapproves certain actions and feels sorry for what is happening.

Decalogue 1: I am the Lord; Thou shalt not have other gods before me

The first part of the *Decalogue* series sets the tone for the following films. It opens with a shot of a frozen pond; the camera glides over a thin layer of ice towards a mysterious man dressed in a heavy sheepskin coat sitting near the pond behind a campfire. The camera pauses for a moment in front of him and he looks straight into it. The director then cuts to an image of an older woman whom the viewer later learns is Irena (Maja Komorowska) standing on the street and watching a group of young boys, among them her nephew Paweł, running in slow motion on a television screen that is on display in a store's window. When the screen freezes with a close up image of Paweł, the viewer realises that Irena is crying. Her tears are mirrored by those of the strange man near the pond whose image follows that of Irena. This ambiguous opening suggests that perhaps the events presented later in the film are an extended flashback.

The story of *Decalogue 1* revolves around the relationship between a caring and understanding father – university professor Krzysztof (played by theatre director Henryk Baranowski) – and his gifted ten-year-old son Paweł (Wojciech

Klata)[16]. Krzysztof is a strong believer in science and logic; unlike his religious sister Irena, who helps him take care of Paweł during the (unexplained) absence of the mother, he is an agnostic, convinced that everything can be counted and measured. With his son, who is equally passionate about science and computers, Krzysztof calculates the thickness of the ice on the nearby pond before Paweł can make use of his Christmas gift – a pair of skates. Despite his careful calculations, the ice inexplicably breaks and Paweł drowns.[17]

Ominous signs of things to come and strange premonitions build the atmosphere of the film from its opening scene: the mysterious man sitting at the fateful pond as if waiting for the inevitable; a dead dog, probably frozen to death, found by Paweł; a frozen bottle of milk, and milk that turns sour; and a computer that switches itself on inexplicably. The most important menacing sign parallels the tragedy on ice: when Krzysztof is working at home, a bottle of ink breaks and blue ink gushes over his scientific papers placed on the table. The ink bottle cracks and this inexplicable, irrational incident stuns Krzysztof. When he later washes his hands in the bathroom and stares into the mirror, he senses something dire and beyond his comprehension. At that very moment he can hear sirens and, later, from his window he watches fire trucks heading towards the pond.

Despite its story about 'crime and punishment', Kieślowski's film is not a straightforward illustration of the thesis that the God of the Old Testament punishes those who put knowledge over faith or who worship false 'gods' (science/computer in the film). *Decalogue 1* does not offer a simple clash of 'rational science' versus 'irrational religion'. The father, as if not trusting his own calculations, checks the ice the night before the fatal accident to make sure that it is safe, and in doing so, he is confronted with the warning look of the Angel of Fate during his vigil near the pond. In another scene, when the computer inexplicably turns itself on, it flashes the sign 'I am ready' in English, and behaves as if it has a life on its own. In her analysis of *Decalogue 1*, Lisa Di Bartolomeo argues that 'the film is at one level a battle over Paweł's soul; he is enthralled by the power of technology, the lure of epistemology rather than mystification ... Paweł must lose his life rather than lose his soul'.[18] The 'battle for Paweł's soul' between his father and aunt Irena plays a prominent role in the film. 'It's a form of words of farewell. There is no soul', claims Krzysztof, the advocate of science and computers, who expresses his belief in technological advances best during his lecture on 'the intelligent computers' having their own 'personality'. (His son observes the lecture.) Irena, on the other hand, explains to Paweł that for his father 'measurement could be applied to everything ... Your father's way of life may seem more reasonable, but it doesn't rule out God.'

Decalogue 1 is the only film in the series that contains several direct references to religion, religious education, the 'Polish Pope' and discussions about the nature of God. For example, to explain the existence of God, Irena hugs her nephew and asks: 'What do you feel now?' 'I love you', replies Paweł. 'He is in that', concludes his aunt. Compared to other films in the series, the religious, metaphysical nature of *Decalogue 1* is also stressed by the more significant role of the angel-like character, 'the keeper of the ice' as cinematographer Wiesław Zdort also names him,[19] who appears six times in the film. The final sequence enhances the religious meaning of the film. After the loss of his son, Krzysztof goes to a nearby church, still under construction, and in frustration purposely destroys the makeshift altar with the icon of the Black Madonna of Częstochowa (*Matka Boska Częstochowska*) in the centre. The falling candles leave hot wax on the icon; the dripping wax forms a few 'tears' on the Madonna's face and she looks as if she is crying. Krzysztof tries to calm down by pressing a piece of the frozen holy water, in the shape of the Host, onto his forehead.[20]

The film ends with the image of Paweł, previously seen in the opening sequence, running towards the camera in extreme slow motion. The screen almost freezes, thus almost immortalising the boy, transferring him to another realm, the realm of human memory. The final scene is related to an earlier conversation between Paweł and his father, when the boy raises the issue of death after finding the dead dog. 'So what is left?' he asks, to which his father responds: 'What a person has achieved, the memory of that person. The memory is important. The memory that someone moved in a certain way, or that they were kind. You remember their face, their smile, that a tooth was missing.' Like Filip in *Camera Buff*, capturing a glimpse of his friend's mother soon before her death, the accidental footage taken by a television crew during the visit to Paweł's school extends our failing memory. It preserves the smile on Paweł's face and his moment of happiness.

Cinematographer Wiesław Zdort's elaborate use of the colours blue and green, discussed by Lisa Di Bartolomeo,[21] makes this film one of the most stylistically significant in the series. The combination of blue and green, perhaps symbolically a juxtaposition of the spiritual and the material, also organises the film on the visual level. Blue, the dominant colour in *Decalogue 1*, is associated with television images of Paweł running in slow motion towards the camera, interiors of the nearby church and Paweł's flat, the bluish light given by the reflector operated by the firemen searching the pond, and the whole night scenery near the pond. The colour green features particularly in the scenes with the computer; the green light of its screen is reflected on the boy's face, possibly signalling an attempt to conquer the boy's soul. Perhaps without exaggeration, Slavoj Žižek argues that 'the computer here is mystified into an almost Stephen-Kingesque status of the Green Evil Object'.[22]

Decalogue 2: Thou shalt not take the name of the Lord thy God in vain

Part 2 of the *Decalogue* series, which takes place in a setting familiar from many melodramas – a hospital – tells a story of love, infidelity, mortality and miracles. Kieślowski narrates the story of Dorota (Krystyna Janda), a violinist in a symphony orchestra, whose dilemma is whether to terminate her early pregnancy. While her husband Andrzej (Olgierd Łukaszewicz) is dying of cancer in the hospital, she is pregnant by another man, her lover-musician who never appears on-screen but who leaves her recorded messages (the voice of Piotr Fronczewski). In order to decide, Dorota requests the opinion of the chief surgeon (Aleksander Bardini) taking care of her husband, who also lives in the same apartment building. Her decision concerning the abortion hinges on her husband's chances of survival: she does not want to keep the baby if her husband remains alive.

The tone of the first meeting between the doctor and Dorota foretells future discussions. 'Do you remember me?' asks Dorota. 'Yes, you ran over my dog two years ago', responds the old surgeon. Later, disappointed with the doctor's attitude, she tells him, 'It's a pity that I didn't run over you.' Constantly pressured by Dorota, the doctor refuses to help her, saying he 'is reluctant to give verdicts'. From years of experience he has learned that 'some live who should have died; some die without known causes.' He also advises the impatient Dorota, waiting for her scheduled abortion, that 'all you can do is wait'. Later, however, when she announces that the abortion will be performed in an hour, he tells her that her husband is going to die and, as a result, she keeps the baby. Despite the dark prognosis, her husband Andrzej inexplicably recovers. In the last scene, with happiness emanating from his tired face, he thanks the doctor for his miraculous recovery and proudly announces that he is going to have a child. 'Do you know what it is to have a child?' he asks the doctor. 'I do', answers the surgeon.

The main characters in part 2, the old surgeon and the female violinist, are hardly sympathetic. The embittered surgeon is lonely and removed from other people. His only close contact seems to be with the cleaning lady who once a week takes care of his modest apartment. He tells her in instalments about the plight of his family who perished in a Warsaw building bombed during World War Two. His grief is immense, but private. Expecting a guest, he turns the black-and-white family picture displayed in his living room toward the wall.

Aleksander Bardini as the chief surgeon in *Decalogue 2* (1988)

The tragic death of the doctor's family results not only in his withdrawal from social life but also in his decision to save another child's life, since he knows 'what it is to have a child'. The surgeon's loneliness is visually paralleled by the 'loneliness of cactuses' which he carefully grows in his provisional greenhouse built on the balcony.

Dorota, played by Janda, has a number of psychological characteristics associated with Janda's earlier performance in Wajda's *Man of Marble*: she is independent, aggressive, adamant, a tense chain-smoker. Her dilemmas are externalised: before taking a decisive step, she meticulously destroys the only green plant in her flat; in another scene she deliberately smashes a cup of tea (portrayed in slow motion). Dorota's comparatively privileged material status is established by her metallic Volkswagen Beetle, the expensive stereo equipment in her apartment and the passport that indicates her frequent travels abroad and, therefore, access to hard currency and consumer goods. Although her husband's profession is not stated in the film, according to Polish folk wisdom, he 'ought to be' a scientist, maybe a physicist, since his pastime is mountain climbing.

The doctor and Dorota interfere with God's domain, both try to 'play God' and attempt to decide somebody else's fate: Dorota the fate of her unborn child, and the doctor the fate of Dorota's husband and the baby. Asked by Dorota whether he believes in God, the surgeon answers: 'I have a God; there's only enough of him for me.' 'A private God?' – wonders Dorota – 'Then ask him for absolution.' The Angel of Fate appears twice in the film, as a medical orderly in the hospital. He is present when a medical test shows that Andrzej's disease is spreading beyond control and also when Dorota tells her unconscious (perhaps only sleeping) husband that she loves him.

Edward Kłosiński's camera captures elusive images of early spring coming to the Warsaw suburb. The focus however is on the mental landscape of the film's protagonists. For example, when Andrzej's health deteriorates, he looks resignedly at his hospital room and notices water slowly dripping from a pipe and paint peeling from the ceiling. His decaying physical condition parallels the decay of his surroundings. Later, when he is on the road to recovery, he observes (in extreme close-up) a wasp trying to get out of a glass with strawberry compote given to him by Dorota.

Decalogue 3: Remember the Sabbath day, to keep it holy

The next part of *Decalogue* describes a failed attempt to revive an old, adulterous love affair that ended three years earlier. Ewa (Maria Pakulnis, who previously appeared in *No End* as Darek's wife) interrupts the Christmas Eve of her former lover, Janusz (Daniel Olbrychski), on the pretext of searching for her missing husband Edward. Janusz lies to his wife (Joanna Szczepkowska) telling her that his taxi has been stolen and he disappears with Ewa into the night. They drive together through the almost surreal, deserted city to a hospital, a morgue, an alcoholics' centre and a train station in search of Edward. In the morning Ewa reveals to her reluctant driver and helper that he unknowingly saved her life. Afraid to be alone on Christmas Eve ('It is difficult to be alone on a night like this'), she would have killed herself without his help. After a night full of bitter talk, lies and crude attempts at rekindling the lost love, Janusz returns to his wife on the morning of Christmas Day and promises her not to see Ewa again.

The third part of *Decalogue* refers to the commandment about keeping the Sabbath day holy. The film's action is set on Christmas Eve, a special day in predominantly Roman Catholic Poland, and depicts a number of traditional rituals. The opening scene introduces Janusz dressed as Santa Claus (Polish *Święty Mikołaj*), leaving his taxi in front of the apartment building, and during the most important family gathering in Poland – Christmas Eve Supper –

delivering gifts to his children. The viewer then observes Janusz and his family during the Midnight Mass (*Pasterka*) in a Church where he exchanges discreet glances with Ewa. The presence of decorated Christmas trees and the singing of traditional Polish Christmas carols emphasise the spirit of that holy period.[23] Despite the setting and a story revolving around the religious event, *Decalogue 3* nonetheless has little to do with a typical Christmas tale. Ironically, the first carolling, which is heard over the credits with the panoramic view of Warsaw after dark, is done by a drunk carrying a Christmas tree who reappears twice in the film. He aimlessly wanders the streets, visibly lost, and laments, 'Where is my home?' Later, he ends up in a sobering-up station where a sadistic male nurse waters him with a hosepipe in the presence of Ewa and Janusz. Like the drunk trying to get home, the main characters also seem to be 'lost' – their religiosity is superficial and their unhappiness (despite the 'joy of Christmas') is engraved on their faces. Commenting on the references to Polish reality, Annette Insdorf writes: 'On this holy night in Poland, compassion seems to be in short supply.'[24]

The desperate, suicidal woman, doubly estranged on Christmas Eve (which is also her nameday), finds a compliant but increasingly irritated man with whom she tries to survive the night. Ewa (Eve) performs the role of the classic temptress. Accusing Janusz of revealing their affair to her husband in order to end it, she manipulates him and expresses her profound frustration and anger: 'I wish it was him, or you,' she says in the morgue after looking at the mutilated body of an accident victim. 'How often I've pictured your faces crushed by truck wheels.' The game she plays with Janusz results in a life-threatening situation when their car barely avoids a collision with an oncoming city tram driven by the Angel of Fate.

Paul Coates observes that *Decalogue 3* places its viewer as a detective 'furnishing clues (often objects in close-up, weighed in the palm that stands for the pondering mind), but also precluding identification with the people for whom they are significant, and knowledge of quite what they might signify for them'.[25] Piotr Sobociński's expressive camera also voyeuristically intrudes on characters. For example, Janusz's family, living on the main floor, is observed during the Santa Claus visit by the camera placed outside the window to represent the look of Krzysztof, the grief-stricken father from *Decalogue 1* who lives in the same building. He peeks through the window at Janusz's family like another grieving character, Ewa, who in a later scene glances from outside before interrupting Janusz's family having champagne after the Midnight Mass. The colour red – mostly red-light reflections on the protagonists' faces – and blue – the colour of the night – dominate the film. The night setting of the action explains the prevalence of dark images, mostly images of characters emerging from darkness, with their faces partly hidden in shadows.

The film shares some similarities with Kieślowski's earliest television narrative work, *Pedestrian Subway*: the story about the impossibility of recovering an old love, the night setting and the parting in early morning. Another scene, which takes place at the desolate Warsaw Central Railway Station, may remind the viewer of Kieślowski's 1980 documentary *Station*. Apart (obviously) from the setting, *Decalogue 3* features a scene that structures *Station* – an image of a security camera monitoring the station, from which the director cuts to an image of an empty surveillance room. In charge of the station's surveillance is a young woman played by Dorota Stalińska, an actress known for her portrayal of dynamic, sturdy women in the films of Barbara Sass, such as *Bez miłości* (*Without Love*, 1980) and *Krzyk* (*The Shout*, 1983). Also, as in some of Kieślowski's other films, making bets plays a decisive role in the characters' life. For example, Ewa reveals to Janusz: 'Do you know the game, if a man comes around the corner, it means luck, but a woman means bad luck … I played it today. I thought that if I could get through the night with you until seven in the morning … then everything will be fine.' Later she adds: 'When I was driving to the church, I saw a boy. He escaped from the hospital in his pyjamas. They caught him.'

Among several leading Polish actors appearing in *Decalogue* is Daniel Olbrychski (b. 1945), the emblem of Polish cinema of the late 1960s and early 1970s, an actor associated with several masterpieces directed by Andrzej Wajda in particular. After the introduction of martial law in 1981, he rarely appeared on Polish screens acting instead in foreign films directed by Claude Lelouch, Vojtech Jasny and Margarethe von Trotta, among others.

Decalogue 4: Honour thy father and thy mother

Decalogue 4 examines a father-daughter relationship that turns into an incestuous game. Kieślowski narrates a story about a twenty-year-old acting student Anka (Adrianna Biedrzyńska) who, during her father Michał's (Janusz Gajos) absence from home, discovers an envelope with the inscription 'to be opened after my death'. Intrigued, she opens the envelope only to find inside another one marked 'for my daughter Anka', and left by her mother who died five days after giving birth. Without opening the original letter, Anka invents its content and recites it to her father after his return from a business trip. Anka's version of the letter states that Michał is not her biological father, thus opening for Anka the possibility of playing a game of sexual advances with him. In the new situation, she suspends the family ties and attempts to define the relationship with Michał anew. Instead of following the commandment and 'honouring her father', she shows (though perhaps she is only acting since, after all, she is an aspiring actress) desire for her father and tries to seduce him. Although Michał categorically rejects her incestuous actions, he also gradually begins to question his own fatherhood: 'I never knew for sure, but I always suspected' – he admits to his daughter. In the end, fearing that Michał may leave her, Anka confesses to her deed of forging the letter and they decide to burn it, preferring not to learn its true content. The ending of the film restores the status quo. Annette Insdorf, however, rightly observes that 'the added irony is that her ultimate way of truly honouring the father is to disobey the mother – by destroying her precious letter'.[26]

According to Francis J. Rigney, the film offers 'a story for Freudians: an acted-out (literally) naked Oedipus – more precisely, Electra – complex'.[27] In one of the seminal scenes, Anka reveals to Michał: 'When I first went to a bed with a man, I somehow felt unfaithful. It was you. I am constantly searching for someone. Yet when I'm touched, I think of your hands. Close to a man, I'm not with him at all. How should I address you now?' 'I don't know', responds Michał. In another scene, Anka is unable to stay focused during the drama class and perform a love scene from *Romeo and Juliet* with her fellow student and boyfriend, Jarek. When an older drama instructor (played by the well-known theatrical actor and director Adam Hanuszkiewicz) suddenly takes over the Romeo part, she performs it exquisitely.

Several small realistically observed details contribute to the film's tense atmosphere and its delicate discussion of the incest taboo. For example, the story begins on Easter Monday, during the so-called *śmigus dyngus* – a traditional Polish custom of dousing women. Some innocent morning play abruptly stops when Michał looks at his wet daughter and retreats in confusion. In a later scene, when Anka checks her eyesight, the sarcastic female eye-doctor gives her the letters forming the word in English 'FATHER' ('I check intelligence at the same time', she says, suspecting that Anka guesses rather than reads the letters). The performances of Janusz Gajos, one the most acclaimed actors in Poland, and Adrianna Biedrzyńska, a talented young actress, both highly praised by Polish critics, made this film a believable experience.

Some characters from other parts of the series appear in this episode as well. The old doctor from part 2 and the taxi driver from part 5 appear briefly during the elevator scene. The Angel of Fate makes two appearances during the film's decisive moments. Madly kayaking on the Vistula River toward the bank where Anka considers opening her mother's letter, he looks shrewdly at her when she is about to open the letter. When he passes by her, carrying the kayak on his back, she changes her mind and decides to leave the letter unopened. Artur Barciś's character also reappears toward the end of the film, once again with the kayak which he carries toward an apartment building, when Anka admits to her father that she lied about the content of the letter.

Decalogue 5 and A Short Film About Killing: Thou shalt not kill

Paradoxically, the semi-documentary aspect of *Decalogue* is evident above all in the most stylised part of the series, *Decalogue 5*, and its extended theatrical version, *A Short Film About Killing*. The film tells the story of a young drifter, Jacek Lazar (Mirosław Baka), who commits a callous and brutal murder of a taxi driver, Waldemar Rekowski (Jan Tesarz), and despite the spirited defence by a young lawyer, Piotr Balicki (Krzysztof Globisz), he is sentenced to death for his crime and hanged. Kieślowski once tersely described the film as 'a story about a young boy who kills a taxi driver and then the law kills the boy'.[28]

Although *Decalogue 5* and *A Short Film About Killing* depict the same story, their emphasis and rhythm differ somewhat. Instead of simply cutting the big screen version to 57 minutes of the television episode, Kieślowski adds new scenes and rearranges others in the process of montage, thus slightly changing the film's perspective. As Charles Eidsvik perceptively writes: '*Decalogue 5* is essentially an argument about the senseless cruelty of both a crime and capital punishment as a form of retribution, whereas *A Short Film About Killing* is not only a critique of capital punishment, but also a spectacle of human rubbish, cruelty and despair, an outcry against ugliness in both its moral and its aesthetic dimensions.'[29]

The television version introduces the main three characters in the manner characteristic of several of Kieślowski's films – through their reflections in mirrors or glass. The film opens with a mirror image in medium close-up of lawyer Balicki as he prepares for his final bar examination. In voice-over he comments on the fact that the Biblical law, 'an eye for an eye', does not prevent the proliferation of crime: 'The law should not imitate nature, the law should improve nature. People invented the law to govern their relationships. The law determined who we are and how we live. We either observe it, or break it. People are free; their freedom is limited only by the freedom of others. Punishment means revenge, in particular when it aims to harm, but it does not prevent crime. For whom does the law avenge? The innocent? Do the innocent make the rules?' These comments may also serve as the motto for the entire film.

Decalogue 5 and *A Short Film About Killing* present three distinct viewpoints. Kieślowski crosscuts between the sociopathic murderer, the taxi driver who later becomes his victim and the idealistic lawyer whose first case is defending the killer. *A Short Film About Killing*, which is almost 25 minutes longer, begins however with a brief description of repulsive urban decay. The images of a dead rat in a puddle and a black cat hanged on a clotheshorse set the tone for the entire film. Kieślowski moves rather quickly from one horrifying death sequence to another, both portrayed in a semi-documentary manner. He leaves out two parts that customarily play the most crucial role in the majority of mainstream films: the search for the killer and the courtroom drama. The viewer only learns that Piotr Balicki delivered a great speech against capital punishment ('the best against capital punishment I've heard in years', the Judge tells him privately), but to no avail.

Customarily for him, Kieślowski brings into focus small gritty realistic details. He stresses the graphic, dreadful aspect of both the murder of the taxi driver and the 'killing' authorised by the state. The long sequence during which the taxi driver is killed leaves nothing to the imagination. It is a premeditated murder; Jacek asks for directions to the taxi stand, cuts a cord he has brought with him in a café and puts it around his hand in preparation for the murder. He strangles his victim, beats him with an iron bar and finally smashes his head with a large stone. Despite the taxi driver's frantic attempts to attract somebody's attention with a car horn, nobody ever notices the crime, let alone comes to help. Kieślowski intercuts shots of the vicious murder with the images of a painfully slow cyclist, an equally unhurriedly passing cargo train and the image of a horse that turns his head towards the crime scene. In so doing, as Tadeusz Sobolewski fittingly writes, Kieślowski is able to capture 'fate in action'.[30] Another critic, Christopher Garbowski, in his important study on *Decalogue*, discusses the religious relevance of the murder scene: 'In the face of the cabdriver victim, who has been stranded and clubbed on the head with an iron bar, we seem to see the face of the crucified Jesus with blood streaming down his face as if from a crown of thorns. The victim appears to look at the murderer as if to forgive him. After the deed, the slayer eats the victim's food, just as the soldiers cast lots for Christ's clothes.'[31] Furthermore, argues Garbowski, Jacek is later placed on death row, which is located in the underground, in 'a man-made hell', where the lawyer Balicki 'reaches out to a human being'.[32]

By depicting the execution of Jacek also with all the terrifying details, Kieślowski almost equates the two killings. His chilling depiction of the meticulous preparations for the execution, particularly the scene with the chief executioner dispassionately taking care of business, only foretells future events. The five-minute execution sequence is a frightening spectacle, magnified by the confusion and clumsiness of the whole process: the inept militiamen surrounding Jacek and trying to hold him, the piercing shouting of the assistant to the executioner, Jacek's desperate last-minute resistance and the disturbing shot of the hanged Jacek from underneath the trapdoor, among others. Both 'killing sequences' are longer in the theatrical version, which also contains some graphic material, perhaps unsuitable for television viewers. This includes Jacek repeatedly hitting the lying taxi driver with a stone and the image of the hanged Jacek with his bodily fluids dripping into a plastic container that is placed below him.

Like the gloomy events portrayed in the film, the capital city of Warsaw, where the film is set, is depicted as a repellent, depressing place: grey, brutal and peopled by alienated characters. Almost every scene involving the taxi driver and, in particular, the psychotic drifter Jacek, is set in inhospitable, bitter surroundings. Jacek wanders around this town that is marked by violence on the streets, brutal relationships between people and an atmosphere of impending doom. According to Paul Coates, Jacek 'stalks Warsaw like an edgy, existential angel of doom'.[33] The greenish filters used by cinematographer Sławomir Idziak not only dehumanise and distort the images of Warsaw but also leave some diffused colours in the centre of the frame. Interestingly, parts of the film are set in the most picturesque parts of Warsaw such as the Old Town's Main Square, the King's Castle and the Castle Square. Idziak's known

Mirosław Baka (in the middle) as Jacek in Warsaw's Old Town Square in *A Short Film About Killing* (1988)

The killing of the taxi driver: Mirosław Baka (left) and Jan Tesarz in *A Short Film About Killing* (1988)

predilection for hand-held camera also enables him to achieve an excruciating tension as he follows the daily routines of the film's protagonists.

In this fatalistic film the characters are portrayed very nearly as the victims of their environment. Without any specific reason Jacek throws a stone from a bridge onto a highway, causing an accident. Also, without being provoked, he attacks a man in a public toilet and shoves him to the floor; he splashes coffee dregs at the café's window; he spits into his cup of coffee before returning it; and he chases away pigeons and is cursed by the old woman who feeds them. The final melodramatic scene before the execution reveals, however, a slightly different, more humane side of the supposedly heartless killer, as he talks with his lawyer. Referring to a mysterious black-and-white first communion photograph that he wanted earlier to enlarge, Jacek tells the story about his 12-year-old sister Marysia, killed five years ago by a drunken tractor driver with whom Jacek was drinking before the accident. He also expresses his wish to be buried next to his father and his little sister. If things were different, he concludes to the lawyer, 'perhaps I wouldn't be here today'. Kieślowski depicts the taxi driver in a similar manner. On the one hand, the driver displays several unsympathetic features. He has no respect for the passengers who are patiently waiting for him to finish washing his car, plays nasty tricks and clumsily tries to pick up Beata, a young assistant in the vegetable kiosk. On the other, however, he calls to his handicapped wife during the killing scene and earlier gives half of his sandwich to a homeless dog. Jacek, another rough-living 'dog' that roams the hellish streets of Warsaw, will devour the other half after the murder.

Mostly due to its length, *A Short Film About Killing* contains a number of scenes that are not present in the television version which fill out the characters' psychology. For example, *Decalogue 5* focuses only on the professional life of the lawyer, eliminating affectionate scenes with his fiancée, and thus making him a more one-dimensional character. Destiny and chance meetings between the three characters organise the first part of the theatrical version in particular. The three narratives and three simultaneous actions are set during a single day. The killer is in search of a victim, the future victim unknowingly moves closer to his destiny by turning down several fares before deciding to take his future killer and the sensitive lawyer gears up for his first real case. Their paths cross. For example, the lawyer and his girlfriend celebrate the passing of his final examination, sitting in the same café where Jacek meticulously plans his murder. In another scene, from the taxi driver's point of view, the camera portrays the lawyer driving a motor scooter, stopping in front of him at the intersection, and proudly shouting to another driver that he has just passed his lawyer's exams. When the camera cuts to a close-up shot of the taxi driver, it shows his disapproval of the whole situation. The theatrical version also reveals the link between Jacek and his girlfriend Beata, the shop assistant who, with a mounting horror, recognises the stolen car that belonged to the taxi driver.

The semi-documentary nature of Kieślowski's film is also magnified by the use of actors not widely known in Poland prior to this film. For Mirosław Baka (b. 1963), the role of Jacek was his third screen appearance and his first major role (he graduated from acting school in 1989). Another actor, Krzysztof Globisz (b. 1957), although he appeared earlier in Andrzej Wajda's *Danton*, had been primarily an accomplished theatrical actor, since 1981 associated with *Teatr Stary* in Kraków. The experienced Jan Tesarz (b. 1935) in the role of the taxi driver started his filmic career in 1966 and has been credited with a number of supporting roles and episodes in television and mainstream films, among them the role of the father-in-law of the accused Solidarity activist in *No End*.

As in other parts of the *Decalogue* series, familiar characters reappear in this part as well. Dorota and her husband Andrzej from *Decalogue 2* try to get a cab near their apartment complex but are treated badly by the taxi driver. Also the mysterious character that unifies the whole series, the Angel of Fate, makes two appearances. First he appears as a land surveyor who stands on the road and stops the taxi with Jacek during the fateful ride. As in parts *1*

The death sentence: *A Short Film About Killing* (1988)

and 4 of the series, the film's editing suggests that the Angel of Fate warns the protagonist by looking at him disapprovingly. Later in the film the mysterious young man appears once again, this time as a worker carrying a ladder in the prison where Jacek is held before the execution.

Decalogue 6 and A Short Film About Love: Thou shalt not commit adultery

Decalogue 6 and *A Short Film About Love* introduce a story of peeping Tomek, voyeurism, stalking, lust and sexual humiliation. They examine the unhealthy obsession of a 19-year-old postal clerk, Tomek (Olaf Lubaszenko), with an attractive older woman, artist-weaver Magda (Grażyna Szapołowska), who lives in the apartment building opposite his. The disturbed youth, an orphan staying with the mother of his friend serving in the Polish contingent of the UN forces in Syria, is consumed by his love for Magda. He steals a telescope from a school, sets his alarm clock for 8:30 – the time when she usually returns home and spies on her every evening from his bedroom. Gradually, he begins to meddle in her life. He makes phone calls, tampers with her mail, sends her phoney notifications about money orders, gets a job delivering milk to be closer to her and calls a gas emergency number to report a fake gas leak in her apartment in order to interrupt her sexual encounter with another man. Tomek clearly idealises and objectifies his fantasy woman living on the other side of the square. His infatuation with Magda leads him to admit his activities, to reveal his love for her. Perhaps out of curiosity, Magda agrees to an innocent 'ice cream date' with Tomek in a café where he confesses to his other deeds. She takes him home, plays sexual games with him and makes him ejaculate prematurely. Humiliated, Tomek escapes and tries to commit suicide by slashing his wrists. Consumed by guilt, Magda desperately tries to contact him and watches his apartment with a pair of opera glasses. The film reverses the watcher/watched roles. Now this is Magda trying to contact Tomek who, unknown to her, is recovering in the hospital and will later be protected by his landlady who has witnessed their 'love-making' scene through the telescope. The television version ends with Tomek's laconic 'I'm not peeping at you anymore' to Magda, when she visits him later at the post office.

A Short Film About Love slightly changes the rhythm of *Decalogue 6* by introducing scenes that develop the characters' psychology, for example, that depict Tomek's relationship with his caring, mother-like landlady (Stefania Iwińska) and by adding the framing story that places the bulk of the film in a flashback. This narrative frame, inspired by the lead actress Szapołowska's comment concerning the audiences' need for a conventional story,[34] opens and ends with an image of Magda in Tomek's room. While he is asleep after

Stefania Iwińska (Tomek's landlady) and Olaf Lubaszenko (right) as Tomek in *A Short Film About Love* (1988)

his return from the hospital, she looks through his telescope at her apartment, imagines herself and Tomek talking to each other and reflects on their relationship. Unlike the closed ending of the television film, the expanded theatrical version offers a typical Kieślowskian 'happy ending' that suggests the possibility of a future relationship between Tomek and Magda. As Charles Eidsvik aptly writes, this framing story 'effectively makes the film a story of transgression, pain and a kind of spiritual reconciliation, whereas the *Decalogue 6* story, like most of the other episodes, is a story of transgression and its consequences'.[35]

The action of *Decalogue 6* is essentially confined to two apartments, the square that separates them and the nearby housing-estate post office. Kieślowski comments on the extensive use of subjective shots in the following way: 'We watch from the point of view of the person who is loving and not the person who is loved. The loved one is merely in shreds, an object.'[36] Thus, the events in two-thirds of the film are represented through Tomek's eyes: the voyeuristic shots of Magda in her apartment, the fragmented images of her apartment and the sporadic action on the staircase and the tenement square. The landlady, the only 'objective observer' (although she treats Tomek as a surrogate son), briefly watches him and Magda through the telescope she has just discovered in his room. The last segment of the film belongs to Magda – the previous object of voyeuristic actions. She tries to contact Tomek, spies on him, watches his window through binoculars and visits the post office where he works.

Relying on a long lens (300mm and 500mm lenses), Witold Adamek's camera carefully replicates the perspective of a person watching. Both the theme of voyeurism as well as the dependence on point-of-view long-shots from the perspective of a peeping Tom bring to mind several classic films such as Alfred Hitchcock's *Rear Window* (1954) and Patrice Leconte's *Monsieur Hire* (1988), to name only two. The extensive use of the colour red anticipates to a certain degree the *Three Colours* trilogy: the red cover of Tomek's telescope, Magda's bed cover and telephone, the colour that surrounds them in the corridor when Tomek invites her out to a café for an ice cream. The colour blue serves as the colour of the night as well as the colour that dominates the interior of Tomek's room. Accomplished producer, cinematographer, scriptwriter and director Adamek contributes greatly to the final look of the film. Known chiefly for his contribution as cinematographer to some seminal Polish films of the 1980s, including *The Mother of Kings* and *Custody*, Adamek moved in the late 1990s into directing films, with productions such as *Poniedziałek* (*Monday*, 1998) and *Wtorek* (*Tuesday*, 2001), depicting the darker aspects of the Polish capitalist reality in both a realistic and humorous way.

Critics usually read *Decalogue 6* as a love story, as a narrative about an obsessive, unrequited and destructive love, and Preisner's romantic music clearly emphasises this aspect of the film. Kieślowski modifies the clichéd story about a mature woman who performs the role of sexual educator for a much younger man. Instead of playing with paired opposites such as experience versus innocence and cynicism versus naïvety, he portrays the encounter of two lost souls, two isolated, miserable characters. For Tomek, Magda exists solely as a fantasy object that he fills with his dreams and yearnings. He does not know that Magda is incapable of returning the kind of love he is longing for. 'Why are you peeping at me?' she asks. 'Because I love you. I love you. It's true.' 'And what do you want?' 'Nothing' Tomek replies. For the worldly and promiscuous Magda there is no such thing as love in the abstract, it is expressed physically. 'That's all love comes down to', she tells him after his involuntary climax. Tomek, however, is convinced that, as his landlady put it, 'girls only pretend to be casual, but in fact they need tenderness'.

Despite the persuasiveness of the aforementioned line of argument, I tend, however, to agree with Slavoj Žižek who proposes that Kieślowski's film is not 'a film about love', but 'A Short Film About Self-Killing'. According to Žižek, this film should be viewed 'against the background of "slasher" films, in which a Peeping Tom male character stalks and harasses a woman who traumatises him, finally attacking her with a knife: *Decalogue 6* is a kind of introverted "slasher" in which the man, instead of striking at the woman, turns his murderous rage against himself'.[37] Another psychoanalytically-oriented scholar, Francis J. Rigney, likewise notes that Tomek's attempted suicide can be explained as '"sadism" towards one's self – really a desire to kill her'.[38]

Artur Barciś' character, the Angel of Fate, is seen on the tenement square as an elegant young man wearing light-coloured clothes and carrying luggage. He appears for the first time when Tomek blissfully runs home hauling his milk handcart and almost bumps into him, overjoyed after Magda agreed for an 'ice cream date'. Later, the Angel of Fate watches Tomek running home, humiliated after his sexual experience with Magda. Also, a character from part 9, Roman, makes his brief appearance as the man with a bike who lives in Magda's building. (An observant viewer may also notice Kieślowski's brief cameo appearance: when Magda enters the post office in the hope of seeing Tomek, she sees a man wearing a black leather jacket – Kieślowski with his back to the camera – standing in front of Tomek's closed station.)

Kieślowski once again (after *No End*) relies on the performance of one of Poland's most popular actresses in the 1980s, Grażyna Szapołowska. Readers of the popular Polish weekly *Film* voted Szapołowska and her screen partner, Olaf Lubaszenko (b. 1968), the best Polish actors in 1988. Lubaszenko, who also worked as Kieślowski's assistant on *Decalogue 1, 2, 3,* and *10,* started his career as a child actor in a television series *Życie Kamila Kuranta* (*The Life of Kamil Kurant,* 1982). He appeared in several mainstream films in 1987 and 1988 and furthered his popularity at the beginning of the 1990s acting in films directed by Władysław Pasikowski such as *Kroll* or *The Pigs.* In the late 1990s he also began a career as a film director with *Sztos* (*The Sting,* 1997) and several painfully popular, teenage-oriented films such *Chłopaki nie płaczą* (*Boys Don't Cry,* 2000) and *Poranek kojota* (*The Morning of Coyote,* 2001).

Decalogue 7: Thou shalt not steal

The Seventh Commandment is referred to in the story of a young student, Majka (Maja Barełkowska), who kidnaps her own daughter Ania. 'Can you steal something that is yours?' asks Majka, providing a literal, perhaps too literal, indication of the film's main concern. The six-year-old Ania, who is brought up by her grandmother, Ewa (Anna Polony), is convinced that Ewa is her real mother and Majka her older sister. Unbeknownst to Ewa, Majka snatches Ania during a performance for children and travels with her to a nearby village to see the child's father, Wojtek (Bogusław Linda), whom Majka has not seen for six years. When she was sixteen and a high school student, Wojtek – her Polish teacher – got her pregnant. In order to avoid the scandal, Majka gave birth in a different town and her mother, the school's principal Ewa, later legally claimed the child as her own. Desperate Majka now tries to reclaim her child, to free herself from her controlling mother and migrate with her daughter to Canada. However, she needs Ewa's official permission. Despite Majka's frantic efforts, she is betrayed by her ex-lover and tracked down by Ewa. In the final scene, afraid that she is losing Ania for the second time, Majka hurriedly boards a local train. Torn between the two struggling women, Ania watches her mother – Majka – disappear, possibly forever.

The young Ania, the true victim, becomes an object during the struggle between a mature possessive woman and her neurotic daughter who wants to hurt her mother as much as she wants the child. Ewa, who showed little love and patience to her young daughter Majka, and later was unable to have more children due to some complications at Majka's birth, now does not want to share Ania even with her biological mother. Like several preceding parts of *Decalogue,* part 7 also tells the story of strong women who manipulate and control their men. Alicja Helman writes that,

> even where femininity appears more authentic and complete, finding fulfilment in its material calling, Kieślowski discerns nothing more than

the unrelenting clash of two egoisms, as Majka and her mother battle like tigresses. What prevails here is less high emotions than unadorned, naked animal instinct. The director seems to suggest that woman's every face is terrifying after a fashion. Woman in love, woman as mother, disappointed mother, woman alone: each is a dangerous entity, following an incomprehensible 'female' logic, governed by an unfettered element that overwhelms and flabbergasts the men.[39]

Male characters in *Decalogue 7* are portrayed as passive and weak, at the mercy of the unruly women. Władysław Kowalski, who appears as Ewa's compliant husband Stefan, will almost repeat his role as a caring father in Kieślowski's next film, *The Double Life of Véronique*. Surprisingly, the emblematic actor of Polish cinema in the 1990s, Bogusław Linda, known chiefly for action films 'with an American accent', offers an unremarkable performance in the role of Wojtek. Interestingly, in a 1995 film *Tato* (*Daddy*), directed by Maciej Ślesicki and much-discussed in Poland, Linda is cast as a father in yet another struggle for a child during a bitter divorce case. *Daddy*, however, goes further with its characterisation and portrays an almost misogynist landscape with female characters bordering on caricatures.

To some extent, the visual style of *Decalogue 7* is different, with only the opening scene stylistically close to other parts of *Decalogue*. The camera portrays a familiar apartment building from a low angle and its images are accompanied by a piercing cry of a child. Kieślowski then cuts to the images of Majka terminating her studies and getting her passport with the intention of going to Canada. After the 'kidnapping' of Ania, Dariusz Kuc's camera moves beyond the Warsaw housing estate to a nearby village where Wojtek makes his living sewing teddy bears. (In the late 1980s this was certainly a more profitable job than teaching Polish in a secondary school.) The bulk of the film's action is thus removed from the typical *Decalogue* setting, resulting in the film's brighter tone.

I am in agreement with several critics who point out that *Decalogue 7* is one of the weaker parts of the series, too close to numerous television soap operas. Perhaps Paul Coates is right when saying that the abundance of characters is partly to blame for this film's problems.[40] Perhaps this has also to do with the sharp, 'soapish' polarities between the characters: disciplinarian mother, passive father, obedient ex-lover and depressed daughter. To make matters worse, the film also implies a one-time romantic relationship between Ewa and Wojtek. She tells him 'You haven't much luck with us' and addresses him using his diminutive name 'Wojteczek'. Wojtek also addresses Ewa with her first name (which is unusual in the Polish context, and suggests at least friendship), and is afraid that Ewa could have told Majka 'everything'. The unconvincing story of *Decalogue 7* also does not incorporate an appearance by the Angel of Fate, although he appears in the published script and Artur Barciś is credited at the end of the film. Like the spirit of the best parts of *Decalogue*, the footage with the Angel of Fate never makes it to the final version of the film.

Decalogue 8: Thou shalt not bear false witness against thy neighbour

The eighth entry in *Decalogue* contributes to a discussion on Polish-Jewish relations. Unlike the other parts of *Decalogue*, this morality tale returns to the past and deals with a sense of guilt and the complexities of history.

The story introduces an older professor of ethics at the University of Warsaw, Zofia (Maria Kościałkowska), who is visited by Holocaust survivor Elżbieta (Teresa Marczewska), a New York-based translator of her works. Although they met earlier abroad, only now does Elżbieta reveal the story of her survival. During World War Two, Zofia and her husband refused to shelter her, then a six-year-old Jewish girl who escaped from the Warsaw ghetto to search for sanctuary on the safer side of the wall. 'The false witness they were about to commit consciously was incompatible with their principles', Elżbieta says bitterly. Luckily for her, she was able to stay with other Poles with whom she moved to America after the war. Knowing that the child survived helps Zofia rid herself of the burden of the past. She comments that 'there is nothing more important than the life of a child'.

Zofia is also offered a chance to explain the complexities of the wartime situation and the real reasons for not taking care of Elżbieta. As she explains, her family was active in the Polish underground army, AK (Home Army), and her husband was an officer in one of the most important sections of that army, *Kedyw* (*Kierownictwo Dywersji* – The Command of Diversion) that targeted collaborators and high-profile Gestapo and SS officers, and successfully freed several prisoners. The Gestapo tried to infiltrate the organisation. Information that the man who brought the child to Zofia was a suspected collaborator, and the fear that it might gravely endanger the Polish resistance, prevented Zofia from offering a hideout to Elżbieta. The person unjustly suspected of collaborating with the Nazis and almost executed for a crime he never committed, the tailor (Tadeusz Łomnicki) whom Elżbieta later visits, prefers not to talk about this painful past. In the last scene of the film, from his shop he watches Zofia and Elżbieta on the street, talking to each other, but he cannot share their sense of closeness. The window bars physically and symbolically separate him from the two women.

Tadeusz Łomnicki (as the tailor) in *Decalogue 8* (1988)

In Polish films about the Holocaust and Polish-Jewish relations, Jewish characters are portrayed almost exclusively as figures emerging from the past.[41] These films usually offer either nostalgic pictures that stress the multinational character of pre-1945 Poland or a wartime nightmare everybody wants to forget. For example, in the mid-1980s the following films had been released: Jerzy Kawalerowicz's *Austeria* (1983), Waldemar Dziki's *Kartka z podróży* (*Postcard from the Journey*, 1984), Stefan Szlachtycz's *Tragarz puchu* (*A Down Carrier*, 1984), Jerzy Hoffman's *Wedle wyroków twoich* (*According to the Decrees of Providence*, 1984), Juliusz Janicki's *Nie było słońca tej wiosny* (*There Was No Sun That Spring*, 1984) and Wojciech Żółtowski's *W cieniu nienawiści* (*In the Shadow of Hatred*, 1986). Kieślowski's contribution to the 'cinema of the Holocaust' was produced after the television screening of Claude Lanzmann's *Shoah* (1985), which stirred a heated debate in Poland due to its partial emphasis on anti-Semitic traits in Polish society. Kieślowski's film was also released after the publication of Jan Błoński's influential essay, 'The Poor Poles Look at the Ghetto', which appeared in January of 1987 in the Catholic weekly *Tygodnik Powszechny*.[42]

Błoński's text, which deals with repressed national memories and discusses whether Poles can be blamed for their indifference during the war, is very close to the spirit of Kieślowski's film. Unlike other Polish films about the

Holocaust and Polish-Jewish relations, *Decalogue 8* is set in the present and focuses on the confrontation with the dark and intricate past. Elżbieta visits Poland for the first time since the war ('People don't like witnesses of their humiliation', she reveals to Zofia), bringing back not only memories but also a possibility for reconciliation. The opening scene, shown over the credits, signals this preoccupation with national and personal memory. It introduces a young girl and a man walking together through a labyrinth of old houses. Andrzej Jaroszewicz's camera captures the close-up shots of their hands. Preisner's music, which later reappears throughout the film, adds to the murky and melancholy tone of this opening and refers to the situation in occupied Warsaw. This sharply contrasts with the bright scenery of the subsequent scene which is set in a blossoming park where Zofia is jogging.

Zofia is portrayed as a successful Polish academic, revered by students and translated into English. Her past complements this picture – during the war she was a member of the Home Army and rescued several Jews. Nevertheless, like the painting on the wall of her room that never hangs straight, the spotless picture of Zofia's life reveals one major stain that cannot be easily fixed. The person, who during the war gave false witness against the tailor, changed her life and others' lives.

Despite its examination of Polish morality and the discourse on memory and forgiveness, *Decalogue 8* belongs to the weaker parts of the series. It seems too didactic and does not go beyond conventional wisdom with its emphasis on the 'complexities of the past'. Kieślowski does make use of the Angel of Fate, who is seen at Zofia's lecture sitting among other students. During Elżbieta's story of survival, his close-up is crosscut with that of Zofia, thus suggesting the link between the two, and his knowledge that the story, which other students do not relate to their professor of ethics, really concerns her. Kieślowski also links this film with *Decalogue 10* by introducing Zofia's neighbour (Bronisław Pawlik), a passionate stamp collector who, according to Zofia, shows her postal stamps 'the way people show photographs of their grandchildren or children'. His death will bring his two sons together and, ironically, also will bring his sons closer to him and his stamp-collecting passion. In another reference, *Decalogue 8* also introduces a story within a story that alludes to *Decalogue 2* – one of Zofia's students summarises Dorota's dilemma.

Decalogue 9: Thou shalt not covet thy neighbour's wife

Sometimes called 'A short film about jealousy', *Decalogue 9* focuses on the marital crisis of two Warsaw professionals in their mid-1930s. In the first sequence, the once-promiscuous cardiologist Roman (Piotr Machalica) learns from his medical colleague about his untreatable impotence. His wife Hanka (Ewa Błaszczyk), who works as a ticketing agent at the airport, tries to console him. Roman, however, encourages his wife to take a lover, unaware that she is already having an affair with physics student Mariusz (Jan Jankowski), which she wants to end. When Roman's suspicion is awakened, he not only begins to listen in on his wife's telephone conversations but also makes spare keys to her mother's flat where the lovers meet, and spies on them from a closet. When Hanka discovers him there after parting with her lover, it surprisingly brings the couple closer together despite her initial anger and their mutual humiliation. Later, however, when Hanka goes skiing in Zakopane, the student secretly follows her. Realising that her husband is probably aware of Mariusz's travel to Zakopane and afraid that this may jeopardise their reunion, she takes the first bus home without even changing out of her skiing gear.

Like a number of Kieślowski's films, *Decalogue 9* ends 'happily'. Roman recovers in the hospital in a body cast after attempting suicide by jumping over a ramp on a bike. Terrified after reading Roman's suicide note, Hanka awaits the worst but, instead, she receives Roman's phone call from the hospital. Ironically, Hanka's infidelity cements the union, a union of souls rather than bodies ('Love is in one's heart, not between one's legs', she had told him earlier). Francis J. Rigney asks why Roman is permanently impotent and answers thus: 'Perhaps because the film is set in Poland; in the USA, such an outcome is medically less likely. Anyhow, accepting this base as more than a "movie-type" illness; on it was built a structure of lust, lies and suspicion.'[43]

The film's editing and photography by Piotr Sobociński suggest an almost metaphysical connection between the two main characters. The crosscutting between the faces of Hanka and Roman links them almost telepathically, reminding us of such classics as F. W. Murnau's *Nosferatu* (1922). For example, during the first scene Hanka wakes up from a bad dream, says 'Romek,' and her image reflected in a bedroom mirror is crosscut with that of Roman sitting in his friend Mikołaj's (Jerzy Trela) medical office. The subsequent cutting from one character to another reinforces this connection. Sobociński's camera also captures signs of the marital breakdown by showing the couple together yet psychologically distant, such as during the elevator ride to their apartment when either Roman's or Hanka's face is lighted. As in other parts of the *Decalogue* series, mirror images and reflections fill the screen and small objects play an important role. For example, Roman's car's glove compartment opens without any reason revealing a physics notebook that belongs to Hanka's lover. As usual in Kieślowski's cinema, telephones seem to take on a life on their own – often they determine the protagonists' fate. The accumulation

Ewa Błaszczyk as Hanka in *Decalogue 9* (1988)

of such detailed observations, 'charged with dramatic significance', prompts Annette Insdorf to proclaim *Decalogue 9* 'the most Hitchcockian' part of the series.[44]

The discourse on voyeurism, spying, impotence, jealousy and eavesdropping which permeates *Decalogue 9* heralds Kieślowski's *Three Colours* trilogy. Likewise, the side-story about Roman's patient, a young female singer in love with Van den Budenmayer's music, who has to undergo an operation on her heart to be able to sing, announces the thematic preoccupation of *The Double Life of Véronique*. Like the majority of other parts of the *Decalogue* series, episode *9* also centres on two characters, well played by Ewa Błaszczyk and Piotr Machalica. Kieślowski casts Błaszczyk against her type. She earned critical praise for her roles as tough women in Wiesław Saniewski's *Custody*, István Szabo's *Hanussen* (1988) and Leszek Wosiewicz's *Kornblumenblau* (1989). Interestingly, in 1989 her screen partner Machalica appeared in Jacek Bromski's erotic comedy, *Sztuka kochania* (*The Art of Love*), in the role of a known and well-published sex therapist who experiences sexual problems.

The Angel of Fate appears twice in the film. He is seen for the first time when Roman drives home after the appointment with Mikołaj and, in desperation, Roman almost causes an accident. The angel-like character passes by on a bike and carefully looks at him behind the wheel. Barciś' character reappears toward the end of the film when Roman tries to commit suicide. Still on his bike, he observes Roman pedaling towards the end of a highway overpass, which is under construction, and plunging into the ground. Then he looks at the unconscious man and leaves the scene, as if to get help.

Decalogue 10: Thou shalt not covet thy neighbour's goods

The *Decalogue* series ends on a different note, with a black comedy, a satire on human obsession, greed and egoism. Part *10* tells the story of two brothers, Jerzy (Jerzy Stuhr) and Artur (Zbigniew Zamachowski) who, after two years of not seeing each other, meet at the funeral of their father, who was introduced in part *8* as Zofia's stamp-collecting neighbour who proudly showed her a series of three German stamps from 1931. (The pseudonym 'Root' that appears on his coffin along with his name suggests that, like Zofia, he belonged to the Home Army during World War Two.) While searching his modest apartment, the brothers learn more about their father's stamp-collecting passion ('our misery, mother's wasted life, poor food, lack of money', comments Jerzy), find out that they have inherited a priceless stamp collection and later gradually develop the same venomous obsession with stamps as their father. Repeating their father's path, they sacrifice their careers, family life (in Jerzy's case) and even Jerzy's kidney to get a precious Austrian Rose Mercury stamp from 1851 which is missing from their collection.

During Jerzy's operation, however, when Artur is busy entertaining a willing nurse who recognised him as a celebrity, the stamp collection is stolen. In a display of parallel editing, Kieślowski crosscuts the images of the operating room, Artur and the nurse and the stamp collection being stolen from their father's apartment. The brothers suspect each other, but in the last scene their future priorities are clear. Each of them buys independently an identical new series of stamps at the post office (sold by Tomek from part 6), and they discuss their purchase in the tiny flat that belonged to their father.

The obsession with things that the majority of people may consider trivial takes over the protagonists' lives. Looking at the collection left by his father, Artur wonders, 'Where does it come from, this urge to have something'. In the course of time the viewer learns that the words spoken at the father's funeral by the chairman of the philatelic society perhaps also apply to Jerzy and Artur, 'His family, his professional life and perhaps his emotions he sacrificed for a noble passion.' The two brothers continue the work of the father they hardly knew; as the same chairman tells them later, 'it would be a crime to dissipate somebody's life'. They turn the modest flat into a small fortress by adding to already existing steel-plated doors and nailed-up windows, bars, a sound alarm and a Great Dane.

Kieślowski depicts the origins of the 'urge to have something' in an uncharacteristic manner. Unlike *Decalogue 10*, his earlier films almost never venture into the realm of satire or black comedy, although the communist reality portrayed in his films often, as if by accident, reveals the system's grotesque and preposterous dimension carefully hidden behind the sombre façade. The pair of actors, Stuhr and Zamachowski, whose vibrant performances enhance this part of *Decalogue*, appear later, also as brothers, in another black comedy, *Three Colours: White*. Visually, perhaps, *Decalogue 10* is not as refined as other parts of the *Decalogue* series. Jacek Bławut's functional photography is at the service of the story; the colour symbolism, unusual framing and distorting camera lenses are not essential in this satire filled with black humour.

CHAPTER FIVE

The Double Life of Kieślowski: European Art Film and the Polish Context

The story has to be told in such a way that a viewer, who is used to the poetics of video clips, can get the condensed ideological message we intended.

– Krzysztof Piesiewicz[1]

The year 1989 in Poland marks the peaceful transition from the communist system to democracy. The political and economic changes occurring after the 1989 'freedom shock' also decisively affected Polish cinema. The nationalised film industry, entirely dependent on government funding, was transformed into a free market economy that is now only partly subsidised by the state. A number of organisational reforms were introduced at the beginning of the 1990s to create a new system in which state patronage coexists with private initiatives.[2]

The transition to a market economy in Poland has not been an easy process. At the beginning of the 1990s there were symptoms of a deep economic crisis in the film industry. Figures show that the number of cinema theatres decreased rapidly; another alarming figure was the extremely low average number of cinema visits per inhabitant – one hundred thousand viewers per year in cinema theatres was considered high by Polish standards. Nevertheless, given the difficulties of the transitional period, it is worth noting that the Polish film industry was able to produce more than 20 feature films annually (25 in 1991, 23 in 1992, 21 in 1993 and 20 in 1994). In accordance with expectations, American films clearly dominated the market at the beginning of the 1990s – more than 60 per cent of the Polish repertoire consisted of American films (as much as 73 per cent in 1992). The end of a fully subsidised and centralised Polish film industry controlled through state censorship and the emergence of a new audience, for whom not only communism but Solidarity were history, brought some inevitable changes to film production and distribution, as well as to film thematics and stylistics. Co-productions, multinational enterprises, competition with Hollywood and a plurality of styles and genres changed the film landscape in Poland at the beginning of the 1990s.

Given that cinema has generally been regarded in Poland as more than just entertainment, the situation during the transitional period prompted discussions among film-makers and critics about the future of the Polish film industry. These debates vacillated between voices emphasising the importance of the national character of Polish films and those advocating the universal, cosmopolitan nature of art. Some directors, for example Krzysztof Zanussi, stressed the limits of narrowly understood 'national themes' or the 'Polish perspective' and postulated what can be called 'a European consciousness'.[3] The popular slogan in Poland at the beginning of the 1990s, 'catching up with Europe', expressed a desire to create new post-totalitarian art that, while addressing some universal issues, would reflect national uniqueness. In a move toward European markets, Poland joined the Eurimages Foundation in 1992 (established in 1989), which sponsors European films. Krzysztof Kieślowski's last films were made with its help.

The transition to democracy at the beginning of the 1990s ended film-making as a national and social mission; it has once again became a strictly professional endeavour which exists somewhere on the margin of mainstream Polish life. Film-makers and other artists have been relieved from their traditional duties to the nation, liberated from political pressures and commitments. The political role commonly reserved for artists returned to politicians, political commentators and historians. In the 1990s, however, state-run political censorship was replaced by the economic censorship of the producer which, in many aspects, appeared even harsher. Kieślowski noticed the difficulties of the transitional period and remarked that the communist censorship created conditions in which film-makers 'were in a luxurious and unique situation. We were truly important … precisely because of censorship.

We're allowed to say everything now but people have stopped caring what we're allowed to say.'[4]

Kieślowski's pragmatic move to international co-productions ('it offers me better conditions')[5] was certainly driven by the political changes in Poland. The transformation of the Polish film industry, based on film units, the core of the local film business since 1955, into independent studios subsidised by the state, gave considerable freedom to the companies mainly in the sphere of co-productions and distribution in the West. Despite limited government subsidies via the Cinema Committee of the Ministry of Culture and Arts, this independence forced the companies, such as Kieślowski's Tor film studio, to concentrate on the commercial aspect of their productions. According to some Polish experts, international co-productions almost guaranteed survival for the local film industry.[6] Despite the strong criticism of by some prominent film-makers and critics, who pictured a dark image of Poland being flooded with anonymous international co-productions and at the mercy of the spectre of commercialism,[7] multinational productions began to dominate Polish cinema at the beginning of the 1990s. For example, in 1993, out of 31 films released, 15 were co-productions.

Although there were sporadic attempts at international co-productions during the communist period, such ventures never played a significant role in the centralised Polish film industry. Occasionally, film-makers such as Andrzej Wajda and, in particular, Krzysztof Zanussi, the head of Kieślowski's Tor film studio, either made films abroad or with the participation of foreign capital. For example, Zanussi's extensive list of films includes works produced in Germany such as *Wege in der Nacht* (*Roads in the Night*, 1979), *Versuchung* (*Temptation*, 1981) and *Unerreichbare* (*The Unattainable*, 1982), as well as multinational productions such as *Z dalekiego kraju* (*From a Far Country: Pope John Paul II* (UK/Italy/Poland, 1981), *Imperative* (Germany/France, 1982, in English), *Year of the Quiet Sun* (Poland/Germany/USA) and *Paradigm* (1985, France/Germany/Italy). Andrzej Wajda's *Danton* (1983), a Polish-French co-production starring French and Polish actors (such as Gérard Dépardieu and Wojciech Pszoniak), remains arguably his best film of the 1980s.

The tough economic situation of several Polish film studios after the return of democracy forced them, as well as other film-makers, to look for financing for their projects abroad. Although previously German producers had participated in the production of several notable films, such as Wajda's *Korczak* (1990) and Zanussi's *Life for Life*, the beginning of the 1990s is marked by prominent French involvement. Polish-French films made after 1989 include Waldemar Krzystek's *Zwolnieni z cycia* (*Dismissed from Life*, 1992), Marcin P. Ziębiński's *Kiedy rozum śpi* (*When Reason Sleeps*, 1993) and Jacek Gąsiorowski's *Tak-tak* (*Yes-Yes*, 1993), among others. The French producers also participated in several multinational co-productions involving Polish directors and film studios. For example, they were involved in the production of Andrzej Wajda's *Pierścionek z orłem w koronie* (*The Ring with a Crowned Eagle*, 1993, Poland/Germany/UK/France), Filip Bajon's *Lepiej być piękną i bogatą* (*It's Better to Be Beautiful and Rich*, 1993, Poland/ Germany/France/Ukraine) and Juliusz Machulski's *Szwadron* (*Squadron*, 1993, Poland/France/Belgium/Ukraine). One of Kieślowski's regulars, the renowned cinematographer Sławomir Idziak, directed the multinational film *Enak* (1992, Poland/France/Germany) with the participation of actress Irène Jacob. After the enormous success of Kieślowski's *Decalogue*, particularly in France, he had no problems attracting French producers for his new projects.

Kieślowski had been moving gradually away from documentary observations and documentary techniques by adding metaphysical elements and relying on visual associations. In his Polish-French co-productions, beginning in 1991 with *Podwójne życie Weroniki* (*La Double Vie de Véronique*; *The Double Life of Véronique*), the realistic, often uncomplimentary vision of Poland – a realm of drab landscapes populated by grey characters that are dwarfed by the political system – gives way to dazzling photography, as if taken from glossy illustrated journals. Individuals struggling with themselves replace earlier recognisable characters struggling with communist reality. The unglamorous female characters from Kieślowski's previous films, often portrayed as narrow-minded and not understanding the aspirations of the male protagonists, are replaced by glamorous foreign characters. From being almost always on the margin of Kieślowski's stories, and often not deserving of the viewer's sympathy, they move to the centre of his films. They are young, beautiful and tirelessly dynamic.

Unlike Kieślowski's earlier works, his films made in the 1990s become visually refined to the point of being ornate. The camera does not reveal, as in his early films, but intrudes, and calls attention to itself through the symbolic, 'unnatural' use of colours, camera angles and lighting. The same can be said about Zbigniew Preisner's music which sometimes takes over the films. Kieślowski's change of direction can be described as follows: from functional to 'expressionistic' photography, from unobtrusive soundtrack to overwhelming musical score, from ordinary characters in everyday situations to literary characters set in a designer's world, from the particular to the general, from outer to inner reality and from realism to 'artiness'. A director of detailed realistic observations becomes a director of metaphysical experiences.

In her insightful essay, 'The Double Life of Kieślowski', Maria Kornatowska writes that in Kieślowski's last films 'his now poetic heroines, the embodiment of oversensitivity and emotionality, are moving in a vacuum, moving above the earth ... psychologically trembling heroines living inauthentic lives in a diminished reality'.[8] Kornatowska suggests that Kieślowski's lack of knowledge of the French language and French social and cultural contexts may be partly to blame for the above-mentioned portrayal. Although this explanation is sound, the stylistic elements of 'later Kieślowski' can undoubtedly be found in his earlier narrative films. For example, in *Decalogue* Polish reality is suggested rather than shown, sketched rather than developed. 'Early Kieślowski' pays more attention to social observations than to the private sphere; the private lives of manager Stefan Bednarz in *The Scar* or amateur film-maker Filip Mosz in *Camera Buff* are not developed sufficiently, and this results in a portrayal of women (wives in particular) bordering on misogyny.

Kieślowski's early films depict 1970s Polish 'glamour': an uncanny landscape consisting of factories, smoke-filled conference rooms and managerial offices, rundown streets leading to shabby, claustrophobic flats with television sets nestling in the impersonal, almost identical apartment buildings (*bloki*), locally produced cars and vodka served during all gatherings. A mood of melancholy dominates the screen. Rarely is there a sunny day in the summer or a nice snowy day in winter, as if the director is afraid that these seasons may project a different, more optimistic mood incompatible with the oppressive reality. In this cheap, depressing world, characters are portrayed as powerless victims of their environment. Lovemaking scenes are graphic and unattractive, like the reality that surrounds the lovers. Asked why they are so unappealing, Kieślowski comments that they are 'seen by a person who suddenly opened the door'.[9] In *No End*, for example, the sexual encounter between Urszula and the English-speaking tourist is, as if to make it more depressing, accompanied by Preisner's funeral music. In 1987 Kieślowski claimed, 'in my films erotic scenes always will look the way they look'.[10] Crude nudity and lovemaking scenes that are deprived of eroticism in earlier films (*Blind Chance* and *No End* in particular) are replaced by the new tone in *The Double Life of Véronique* which captivates the viewer with the sexual appeal of its young female protagonist, photogenic nudity and glossy lovemaking scenes.[11] To put it more bluntly, in Kieślowski's new films, colourful postcards from Kraków, Paris and Geneva replace the portrayal of the unrefined Polish reality of the 1970s.

Kieślowski's last films belong to the domain of European art cinema that occupies a different cultural and economic space (the commercialism of Hollywood versus serious 'artistic messages' of art cinema) and is primarily addressed to sophisticated viewers. Theoretical analyses of art cinema by

David Bordwell in 1979[12] and, two years later, by Steve Neale[13] introduced several distinctions between art cinema and commercial cinema and offered a model which remains essentially unchallenged today.

According to Bordwell, art cinema refers to films with a novelistic form and thematics; with its unique history, formal conventions and methods of distribution, it is different from the Hollywood mode of making films.[14] Bordwell asserts that, in spite of numerous differences, many common thematic and stylistic features enable us to distinguish art cinema as a distinct critical and theoretical construct. Unlike Hollywood films with their cause-effect narrative strategy, art films are episodic and their open structure almost 'invites' viewers to experience a very personal form of reception. The stress is placed on authorial expressiveness.

Bordwell goes further and lists typical thematic obsessions permeating art cinema: ambiguity, openness, sensitive protagonists wandering aimlessly on the screen, sometimes even disappearing from it (for example, *L'Avventura*, Michelangelo Antonioni, 1960), the protagonist's psychology as more important than action ('it is a cinema of psychological effects in search of their causes')[15], the presence of dreams, fantasies and memories from childhood, and the use of flashforward to stress the authorial character of the film. Bordwell adds that 'in the classic detective tale ... the puzzle is one of *story*: who did it? how? why? In the art cinema, the puzzle is one of plot: who is telling this story? how is this story being told? why is this story being told this way?'[16]

The author is the source of meaning in art cinema, almost the main protagonist in this type of cinema. The authorial presence can be detected by every film buff, every educated viewer; it prompts the viewer to look at a single film within the context of the directorial *oeuvre* (citations, allusions, autobiographical motifs and familiar characters reappearing in a number of films). Since in many examples of art cinema there are no internationally recognised stars (for example in the cinema of Kieślowski, with the exception of Juliette Binoche and Jean-Louis Trintignant), the persona of the director/auteur organises the filmic text and usually remains the only point of reference for the viewer. The spectator identifies with the author of the film more than with the characters populating the cinematic screen.

Perhaps the single most important feature of art cinema, however, is its ambiguity.[17] The viewer watching an art film faces a mystery; the meaning of the film is barely signalled and the multiplicity of 'art techniques' directs the viewer's attention to the work and its author, relegating to secondary importance questions customarily posed while watching a mainstream narrative film. A number of film-makers, including Kieślowski, do not stick to one particular form of authorial expression; at various stages of their careers they apply different narrative and stylistic devices, or they do it interchangeably. Therefore, one can debate the distinction between the 'early' realist and 'mature' metaphysical Kieślowski.

The Double Life of Véronique: Doppelgängers and Puppeteers

One film (*La Double Vie de Véronique*): two nations (Poland and France); two directors (Alexandre and Kieślowski): two Véroniques; three artists (Weronika's father, Véronique's father and Weronika/Véronique): three viewers (I, Thou and the 'Included Third'); many post-nationalist films: many myths of identity.

– James Winchell[18]

Kieślowski often returns to characters and stories from his earlier films. In his first film made outside Poland, *The Double Life of Véronique*, he develops the character of a young female singer who appears in *Decalogue 9*. She sings Bach and Mahler in addition to her favourite Van den Budenmayer – the fictitious eighteenth-century Dutch composer (Zbigniew Preisner's creation), introduced for the first time in that part of *Decalogue*, whose music features prominently in later Kieślowski films. Pressured by her mother, the young singer undergoes heart surgery in order to continue her singing career, although she seems to prefer a quiet family life ('I want to live. That's enough for me.'). After the operation on her heart, she proclaims to the operating surgeon: 'I know that I'm someone else … I want to sing and I want a lot of people to hear me sing.'

The predicament of the young singer is on the margin of the main story of *Decalogue 9* and acts only 'as a sort of window, as a contingency for the main character', as Kieślowski explains.[19] It finds, however, its continuation in *The Double Life of Véronique*, another story about the ethical choice between artistic vocation, which may lead to death, and quiet family life. In this film, Kieślowski not only builds the whole story around aspiring singer(s), but also continues to employ Van den Budenmayer's music extensively, which is performed by Elżbieta Towarnicka, a Polish opera singer who also lends her angelic voice to the young singer in *Decalogue 9*.

The Double Life of Véronique, produced with the participation of Kieślowski's regular contributors including Krzysztof Piesiewicz (co-scriptwriter), Sławomir Idziak (cinematography) and Zbigniew Preisner (music), is a rare 'art film' dealing with the subject of doubleness.[20] The film revolves around the story of two young women, Weronika in Poland and Véronique in France, both memorably played by Irène Jacob (b. 1966, winner of the Best Actress award at Cannes),[21] who do not know each other but whose lives have a number of mysterious parallels. The film's pre-credit scenes, set in 1968, introduce a two-year-old Polish girl, Weronika, and her French counterpart, Véronique, listening to the off-screen comments of their mothers. In the first scene, the Polish mother shows her child the blue sky with stars on a winter night. Another scene takes the viewer to France where another mother shows her child a leaf that appeared in spring, and is seen through a magnifying glass. The film credits that follow are interrupted by two enigmatic and distorted images which will appear later in the first, Polish part of the film – the barely readable flashforwards of Weronika on Kraków's Market Square.

The Polish part, opening in 1990, is shorter, compact and more dynamic. Its protagonist, Weronika, lives for the art of singing as if unaware of what is going on around her. After the credits, she is portrayed singing outdoors in a female choir. Despite some heavy rain, and unlike her friends who immediately seek shelter, Weronika continues singing alone until the last note, almost ecstatically, looking upward toward the sky and pouring rain. Although Weronika is surrounded by loving people, including her father (Władysław Kowalski), lover Antek (Jerzy Gudejko) and aunt (Halina Gryglaszewska), she is willing to sacrifice everything for her singing career despite her serious heart condition. The symptoms of the illness occur during an audition before the conductress of a choir (Kalina Jędrusik) and the choir director and composer (Aleksander Bardini[22]), and later, during a walk through a park. After winning the singing competition, Weronika becomes a soloist at the gala performance of the Kraków Philharmonic. During a brilliant performance featuring Van den Budenmayer's music, her voice suddenly loses its pitch which signals the forthcoming heart attack. She collapses on the stage (which is shown with the use of subjective camera) and is pronounced dead. The Polish part of the film ends with the scene of Weronika's funeral, with another unsettling point of view shot, this time from inside the glass-covered coffin indicating that, perhaps, Weronika is not gone. This shot reminds the viewer of a similar scene in Carl Theodor Dreyer's classic *Vampyr* (1932) with the earth thrown into the grave (and onto the camera) by some mourners. The dirt is piled on the coffin until the screen becomes dark.

The story of Weronika dissolves into the story of Véronique in the second part of the film. The camera cuts to France and portrays Véronique during a passionate lovemaking scene. Suddenly she becomes grief-stricken as her alter ego is being buried. Later she tells her father that she unexpectedly feels very alone in the world, which reminds the viewer of an earlier, similar comment by Weronika who reveals to her father that she feels as if she is no longer alone

Irène Jacob (Weronika) and Jerzy Gudejko (Antek) in *The Double Life of Véronique* (1991)

in the world, although she cannot know about the existence of Véronique. Their paths cross briefly only once, during a political disturbance in Kraków's Market Square, when Weronika notices her double among the French tourists hastily boarding a bus.

The French Véronique, who works as a primary school music teacher, is unaware of Weronika's existence yet, thanks to the mysterious link between the two women, she learns from Weronika's experiences and 'mistakes'. Despite the objections of her elderly music mentor, she gives up singing lessons because she instinctively fears that it may lead to her death. During a school performance she notices a masterful puppeteer and children's writer, Alexandre Fabbri (Philippe Volter), who performs a story with puppets about the death of an attractive ballerina and her re-birth as a butterfly. Later, Alexandre sends the intrigued Véronique some mysterious letters with items alluding to Weronika, and a tape with noises recorded at the Gare Saint-Lazare station where he waits for her. Their initial meeting, however, brings Véronique only disappointment; she feels used by him for the purpose of conducting 'a psychological experiment' for his new book project. Subsequently, after consummating their brief love affair, thanks to Alexandre, Véronique learns about the existence of Polish Weronika from looking at a photograph unwittingly taken during her trip to Kraków. She also discovers the similarity between herself and the two dolls made by her lover. Although Alexandre explains that he uses two dolls because 'one might be damaged' during the performance, the frightened Véronique leaves his apartment and drives to the house of her father (Claude Duneton). This ending, as Kieślowski explains, is a logical conclusion to the film, since for Europeans 'going back to the family home represents a certain value which exists in our tradition, in our history and also in our culture'.[23]

Kieślowski's film was made with two slightly different endings designed for European and American audiences. The original version ends with Véronique standing in front of her father's house outside of Paris and touching a tree, while her father, who realises that she is outside, works with timber inside his studio. After the American premiere at the 1991 New York Film Festival, Kieślowski decided to make the ending more explicit.[24] Thus, in the American version, Véronique rushes to hug her father, who stands in front of the house and calls her. The camera portrays their warm embrace and then depicts the same scene from inside the house, through a window. The film ends with two images of Véronique hugging her father thus, once again, doubling the whole experience.[25] The forceful and ethereal music composed by Zbigniew Preisner, fragments of which appeared throughout the film, bursts into the scene.

The element of chance is once again, after *Blind Chance*, a driving force in *The Double Life of Véronique*. As in *Blind Chance* and *Decalogue*, characters reappear in other distinct parts of the film. Like Filip in *Camera Buff*, the protagonist(s) must choose between pursuing a demanding vocation and a safer family life. Annette Insdorf writes that *The Double Life of Véronique*'s 'central question seems to be blatantly metaphysical: can there be – in God's spectacle, which includes individual "damage" – a double who prepares us for survival? Or might some of us be the double who is setting the stage for another to live more wisely?'[26] Simon Winchell puts it in a similar manner: 'The film's eventual drama therefore derives from Véronique's ability to learn from Weronika's unhappy and seemingly doomed experience.'[27]

The theme of doubleness and doubling permeates the film's narrative that consists of two parts in two national languages and introduces two similar female protagonists (perhaps one with another life). The film focuses on the parallel existences of the Polish Weronika and the French Véronique. Both are born on the same day, have striking physical similarities, analogous gestures (for example, each uses a golden ring to rub her eyelid) and beautiful voices. They also share an intense devotion for singing but their musical careers are jeopardised by acute heart problems. Both women are also motherless and are caring about their affectionate fathers, and are portrayed as sensual, passionate lovers, although emotionally distanced from their men. The perceptive viewer may also discover a number of small details that enhance the sense of a double life, among them the figure of an old, hunched-over woman seen twice in two parts of the film (when Weronika prepares in her apartment for the concert and during Véronique's class). Other features include, among others, the same hotel room numbers (287) in Kraków and Clermont-Ferrand, the same woman who looks disapprovingly at Weronika during the audition (and is seen among the mourners at the cemetery) and later, in the French part, who is surprised to see Weronika's double – Véronique. The mysterious link between the two young women is also expressed by Alexandre who works on a children's story called 'The Double Life of…'. In addition, he sends Véronique a shoelace, which resembles the lace of the portfolio that Weronika played with while singing during her audition. The shoelace, according to Kieślowski, alludes to the protagonist's heart condition (the line on the electrocardiogram), which perhaps becomes obvious only after reading the director's comments.[28]

The Double Life of Véronique is the story about two coinciding paths, the conviction that there is 'another self', that one is not 'alone in the world', as Weronika tells her father. With its fascination with the world of doubles, Kieślowski's narrative borrows heavily from the nineteenth-century stories about telepathic bonds, metempsychosis and Doppelgängers (ghostly doubles). German Romantic writers, such as E. T. A. Hoffman and several Russian 'Hoffmanists' contributed to this 'genre' extensively.[29] Although used by some writers for comedic effects, the most interesting literary works focus on the darker side of Doppelgängers. According to lore, Doppelgängers can cause the physical person to die if they are seen. It is also believed that they appear to steal souls and take their place in life. Perhaps this is the reason why Weronika dies soon after noticing Véronique – the harbinger of death – getting onto a tourist bus on Kraków's medieval Market Square. It is also probably why Véronique immediately feels overwhelmed by sadness when she discovers the photograph of Weronika. The film is not, however, a simple play on the theme of doubling or an exercise for viewers to pick up such elements. Kieślowski's film defies any simple interpretation.

Véronique's (Weronika's?) 'double life' is intensified by Sławomir Idziak's remarkable cinematography and Zbigniew Preisner's poignant score. The film's cinematography, although it calls attention to itself, is at the service of the story with its reliance on yellowish filters which help to create warmth and a sense of otherworldliness and fuzzy images and landscapes that generate a dreamlike atmosphere. The film features an abundance of point-of-view shots, upside-down images (for example Weronika's onstage death, images seen by Weronika as a child) and mirror images (such as Alexandre's performance viewed by Véronique in a mirror) – the extensive use of mirrors not only multiplies space but also makes the whole film a spectacle of ambiguity. *The Double Life of Véronique* is also defined by the extensive use of distorted images through windows (when Weronika travels by train to Kraków), images from behind massive doors with tiny glass ornaments (when Alexandre searches for Véronique who is hiding at the entrance to an apartment building), shots through a magnifying glass (the scene with a two-year-old Véronique) and blurred images seen through a transparent toy ball (during Weronika's journey to Kraków when she sees the 'upside-down church'). Another impressive shot portrays Weronika after the rehearsal, with dust slowly falling onto her face. The 'art film atmosphere' is also emphasised by the wealth of unusual camera angles, the most memorable of which is perhaps the point of view of Weronika at the *Planty* park in Kraków when she suffers heart problems, kneels in pain and notices the slowly approaching male exhibitionist who exposes himself and passes silently.

The visual doubling also has its sound equivalent. The same 'Van den Budenmayer's song', incorporating lyrics from Dante's *Divina Commedia*, which Weronika sang so brilliantly during her Kraków performance, is repeated off-key in the French part by Véronique's schoolchildren, and it becomes the main musical motif of the 'French part' of the film. Preisner's powerful music occasionally overtakes the screen, which seems justified by the film's theme. It enhances the inexplicable link between the two women and the otherworldly atmosphere of the film.

Kieślowski's Polish-French co-productions, starting with *The Double Life of Véronique*, are often read allegorically by critics as commentaries on the relationship between Poland and Western Europe. Polish critic Maciej Pawlicki in his report from the 1991 Cannes Film Festival provides a parallel between the death of Weronika and the demise of the communist Polish People's Republic. The surviving, more pragmatic French Véronique yearns for her absent-minded, confident and energetic missing double. Pawlicki calls Kieślowski's film 'a sad film on the occasion of Europe's unification'.[30] Film critics in Poland usually stress that Véronique, in broader terms Western Europe, learns from Weronika's (Poland's) mistakes and is able to change the course of events. Weronika warns Véronique with her unreturned gaze in Kraków. The Polish title of Kieślowski's film, *Podwójne życie Weroniki* (*The Double Life of Weronika*), clearly stresses the Polish perspective. This is Weronika's, not Véronique's, double life, her second ('French') chance, her film. Apart from the strange 'Dreyerian shot' from inside the coffin, this type of reasoning is also supported by an unusual overhead shot when Weronika collapses onstage which indicates that, perhaps, her spirit is leaving her body. After all, Kieślowski seems to suggest that this is the story of rebirth: Weronika is introduced in the winter (symbolising death) and Véronique in spring (representing re-birth), which also indicates that Weronika's experiences precede those of her French double; Alexandre's marionette show introduces a symbolic story about a ballerina who dies and is reborn as a butterfly; the brownish autumnal colours of the 'Polish part' of the film are contrasted with the sunlit 'French part'.

This slow-paced enigma, beautifully crafted and governed by a sense of mystery, appears to be almost the essence of 'European art cinema' due to its personal character, sensuality, ambiguity, subjective camera, self-referentiality and to the fact that it is saturated with art film clichés. Kieślowski reveals: 'I play on pure emotions in *Véronique* because it's a film about emotions and nothing else. There's no action in it.'[31] His episodic film, full of unexplained occurrences and 'concerned with the luminous, the numinous and the ominous',[32] relies heavily on magnification, enigmatic doubling and symbolism. Its elliptical narrative construction, which is mysterious to the point of teasing the spectator, resists any explicit interpretation. The film's energy and breadth does not allow it, however, to be another 'fairly conventional box of ontological tricks, recycling traditional metafictional paradoxes'.[33]

Kieślowski's formalist exercise is exquisite and frustrating, mesmerising and ostentatious. It probably did to art films in the 1990s what Sergio Leone's spaghetti westerns did to the western in the 1960s – the accumulation and intensification of features characteristic of the 'genre'. The accumulation of symbolic associations and other art cinema qualities in *The Double Life of Véronique* prompted Gaylyn Studlar to remark that it looks almost like 'a virtual parody of all the established stereotypes of Continental film-making associated with an earlier generation of film-makers, such as Ingmar Bergman and Alain Resnais'.[34]

For Kieślowski, this film also marks a radical departure from his early filmic essays to polished international and apolitical co-productions. This is a turn toward privacy and 'calm', a retreat from the pressure of politics that is openly manifested in the Polish part of the film. Politics, always present although not necessarily openly discussed in Kieślowski's earlier films, is completely relegated to the background in *The Double Life of Véronique*. For example, Weronika does not notice a huge socialist-realist statue (of Marx/Lenin?) being towed away on a truck signalling, perhaps, the fall of communism. She also casually whistles the 'Internationale' over the phone to her friend after arriving in Kraków. In another scene, after the rehearsal, as Weronika stares at her double among the tourists in Kraków's Market Square, she seems totally unaware of the political demonstration, police trucks and the riot police (ZOMO) surrounding her and ready to attack. Weronika is as free from politics as is the film, to the astonishment of many Polish film critics. One of them, Tadeusz Lubelski, bitterly comments that during the Kraków riot scene Kieślowski virtually ignores the protagonists of some of his early films – the young demonstrating activists. Here they perform only a negative role: they prevent the meeting between Weronika and Véronique.[35]

It is difficult now not to read the film through the context of Kieślowski's much-heralded 'early retirement' and his untimely death at the peak of his artistic powers. For example, Slavoj Žižek comments that the film is 'clearly allegorical: it contains a reference to Kieślowski himself. Was not his choice that of Polish Weronika – aware of his heart condition, he chose art/vocation (not singing, but film-making), and then died of a sudden heart attack?'[36] Indeed, there are several traits in Kieślowski's biography that support this claim: the director's heart problems, his early retirement from film-making (Véronique does the same with singing) and finally, his 'double life': Polish (serious art, realism, social concern) and French (art-house, metaphysical, lacking a base).[37] The puppeteer Alexander, who charms and exploits Véronique, can be, perhaps, viewed as a self-referential likeness of another puppeteer/manipulator – the film's director.

The Double Life of Véronique can be also viewed as a film about Kieślowski's move to France and the sense of betrayal felt by some Polish film critics. Perhaps, as Tadeusz Lubelski points out, this is a film about Kieślowski's 'disappointment with Poland', about his 'unrequited love for Poland'.[38] A similar tone can be found in several reviews, beginning with Maciej Pawlicki's report from the 1991 Cannes Film Festival, where the film had its premiere. Discussing Weronika's death, Pawlicki writes that this symbolises Kieślowski's 'farewell to a Poland that no longer exists'.[39] An expert on Polish cinema and Kieślowski, Paul Coates, writes the following: 'For all its beauty and virtuosity, *The Double Life of Véronique* is debilitatingly decorative. As such it surely reflects Kieślowski's uncertainty concerning both the Polish identity and his own, as the remnants of People's Poland atrophy.' He also adds, 'If the double life is also that of Kieślowski himself, could it be that he, too, is abusing his talent?'[40]

Film critics in Poland, who stressed that the film 'marks the return of Polish cinema to puzzling questions, mystery and poetry',[41] generally praised *The Double Life of Véronique*. Some of them, however, were troubled by the film's 'superficial metaphysics', alleged banality and Kieślowski's escape from the realistic, even harsh, portrayal of everyday phenomena in favour of existential enigma.[42] Nonetheless, Polish reviewers almost unanimously emphasised the formal beauty of the film.

Interestingly, Krzysztof Zanussi, who is credited as the art director of *The Double Life of Véronique*, directed in 1992 a multinational production, *Dotknięcie ręki (The Silent Touch*, 1992, Poland/UK/Denmark) that shares some similarities with Kieślowski's film. *The Silent Touch* tells a story about a young musicologist from Kraków (Lothaire Bluteau) who has a dream about an unknown musical masterpiece. He writes down its basic tones and travels abroad to an old eccentric composer (Max von Sydow), once famous and worldly, now living in seclusion, to convince him to write the piece. The composer has been silent for almost forty years, withdrawn from musical life. The young messenger from Poland has to awaken him from artistic inertia, to awaken his sexuality, to enable him to compose the work of his life. Its Faustian references aside, Zanussi reverses the story of Kieślowski and Piesiewicz: the Polish messenger brings the Western composer back to life with his instinctive metaphysical knowledge. The likeness to *The Double Life of Véronique* is also furthered by the presence of Aleksander Bardini in the role of a Music Professor in Kraków and the importance of the striking musical score composed by one of the most distinguished Polish composers, Wojciech Kilar.

The Three Colours Trilogy: The Long Films About Love

> Kieślowski seems to be abandoning tales of fictitious characters, much in the same way he had once abandoned the documentary for fiction … attempting to render inexpressible, agnostic states concerning not just one character, but interpersonal, intersubjective states…
>
> – Tadeusz Sobolewski[43]

Kieślowski's *Three Colours* trilogy, *Trois couleurs: bleu* (*Three Colours: Blue*, 1993), *Trois couleurs: blanc* (*Three Colours: White*, 1994) and *Trois couleurs: rouge* (*Three Colours: Red*, 1994), a major cinematic achievement of the 1990s, is a trilogy inspired by the French tricolour flag and the central notions of the French revolution, *liberté, égalité* and *fraternité*. In spite of these political connotations, Kieślowski does not seem to be particularly interested in politics or social problems; instead, once again, he continues transcendental and metaphysical issues and deals with protagonists facing moral dilemmas with their individual quests for the three values embodied in the French flag. This is not so much a trilogy about liberty, equality and fraternity but, as Tony Rayns has said, 'a trilogy about love in the 1990s'.[44] Other critics describe it differently, for example a trilogy about fate or 'a trilogy preoccupied with themes of death, loss and trauma'.[45]

The trilogy premiered at major European film festivals: *Blue* in Venice in September of 1993, *White* in Berlin in February 1994 and *Red* in Cannes in May 1994 – an important fact, because it shows the aspirations of Kieślowski and his French producer, Marin Karmitz. The films won numerous awards, including the Golden Lion at the Venice International Film Festival for *Blue* (jointly with Robert Altman's *Short Cuts*). At the same festival, the Best Actress award was given to Juliette Binoche and the Best Photography award to Sławomir Idziak. *White* received the Silver Bear award at the Berlin Film Festival (Best Director category). Although *Red* received no award at the Cannes International Film Festival (the grand prize, the *Palme d'Or*, was given to Quentin Tarantino for his *Pulp Fiction* (1994)), it received numerous other awards, including three Academy Award nominations in 1995 (direction, screenplay, cinematography), four BAFTA nominations (direction, screenplay, actress, non-English language film), the Grand Prix at the Vancouver International Film Festival and the Los Angeles and New York Film Critics' awards for Best Foreign Film.

The French-Polish-Swiss production, with the action set in France, Poland and Switzerland respectively, is financed by director-turned-producer Marin Karmitz, whose credits as a film producer before the trilogy include films directed by Jean-Luc Godard, Claude Chabrol and Louis Malle. In 1993 and 1994, apart from working with Kieślowski, Karmitz produced more films by the film-makers from 'the other Europe', such as Czech Jiři Menzel and Romanian Lucian Pintilie. Critics often stress the cosmopolitan character of the trilogy ('Four languages were spoken on the set – Polish, English, French and German – with permanent simultaneous translation', recalls Karmitz)[46], its 'European spirit', two languages spoken on the screen, and Polish, French and Swiss actors and crew involved. The immensity of the project and, as a consequence, the problems involved in its production, certainly later contributed to Kieślowski's fatigue and the publicly-announced decision to retire from film-making.

Although carefully designed as a trilogy and released as such within a short span of time, the three films can be viewed separately, as Kieślowski indicated on several occasions. The films' dominant colours, which attract so much critical attention, are, however, treated by Kieślowski quite pragmatically. According to the director, 'If a different country had provided the finance – Germany, for instance – and I had made it as a German film, then yellow would have taken the place of blue and one would have had "yellow, red and black".'[47]

Film critics usually apply the term 'trilogy' a posteriori to films made earlier by great auteurs and linked thematically and (rarely) stylistically. For example, Western critics often discuss Andrzej Wajda's 'war trilogy': *A Generation*, *Kanał* (*Kanal*, 1957) and *Ashes and Diamonds*;[48] and István Szabo's 'Central European trilogy': *Mephisto* (1981), *Redl Ezredes* (*Colonel Redl*, 1985) and *Hanussen* (1988). To group films into 'series' is also the auteurial/marketing strategy used consciously by some directors, for example Eric Rohmer, who produces a series of films under labels such as *Contes moraux* and *Contes des quatre saisons*.

As always, Kieślowski surrounds himself with the same group of collaborators. Apart from co-scriptwriter Piesiewicz and composer Preisner, he also works with his earlier cinematographers: Sławomir Idziak (*Blue*), Edward Kłosiński (*White*) and Piotr Sobociński (*Red*). In a typically unselfish manner, he acknowledges their great contributions not only as cinematographers but also as 'script consultants'. In addition, he acknowledges as 'script consultants' the help of his friends, distinguished Polish film-makers Agnieszka Holland and Edward Żebrowski,[49] with whom he worked closely together on earlier projects but whose contributions were not previously credited. Kieślowski also chose Jacques Witta, the editor who worked with him on *The Double Life of Véronique*.

Given the fact that, in true auteurial fashion, Kieślowski works with the same collaborators-friends, it comes as no surprise that the trilogy is ostensibly self-reflexive and self-referential. As in *Decalogue* and *The Double Life of Véronique*, characters appear and reappear; 'Van den Budenmayer's music' is quoted extensively. Kieślowski remarks that these interconnections are 'for the pleasure of some cinephiles who like to find points of reference from one film to another'.[50] The director employs many chance scenes with no apparent link to the story, rejects causal narrative and peoples his films with familiar supporting characters, for example elderly ladies in *Blue* and *Red* and an old man in *White* slowly crossing the street and struggling at the recycling bin, perhaps reminding the protagonists of the fragility of life. The same tendency toward mannerism is evident in the cinematography and *mise-en-scène*, including the extensive use of the films' key colours to stress each main theme and the reliance on mirror images, filters and views through windows and doors. Kieślowski produces films for cine-buffs; there are more questions than answers in his cinema and everything here is geared toward mystery.

Tadeusz Szczepański comments, 'Kieślowski ingeniously multiplies subtle refrains, parallelisms, counterpoints, correspondences, symmetries, echoes and mirror effects not only on the level of narrative threads, situations, characters or props in the roles of *res dramatica*, but also in *mise-en-scène*, use of colour, sound and, of course, music.'[51] Another Polish scholar, Grażyna Stachówna, lists recurrent motifs in the trilogy that also refer to Kieślowski's earlier films: 'colours, slogans of the French Revolution, blind chance, Van den Budenmayer, voyeurism and eavesdropping, an old woman with a bottle, the final cry of the protagonists, windows, beads made of glass, the two-franc coin, loneliness, jealousy, humiliation, contempt, sex and suicide'.[52]

The semantic richness of Kieślowski's trilogy is not, however, taken by all scholars and critics, Polish authors in particular, as a sign of art. Some of their expressed concerns are similar to that raised by Geoffrey Macnab in *Sight and Sound*: 'Perhaps Kieślowski is, as his supporters so ardently proclaim, the most important film-maker in Europe; but his blithe abandonment of social issues and retreat into a remote, mystical realm where personal experience is all that matters, do not augur well for the future.'[53] Although (as in the case of *The Double Life of Véronique*) Polish critics praise the visual aspect of the trilogy, they also point out its alleged emptiness, superficiality and pop-metaphysics ('metaphysics for the poor'). For example, Mariola Jankun-Dopartowa claims that *Three Colours* cannot be described within the existing boundaries of art cinema. According to her, the trilogy is somewhere between the domain of Bergman's cinema and video clip or 'pretentious European production'. She accuses Kieślowski of telling stories familiar from numerous soap operas and 'magazines for thinking women', promoting the 'religion of blind chance', abandoning his earlier film poetics and bordering on kitsch sensibility.[54] The kitschy aspect of Kieślowski's trilogy, writes Jankun-Dopartowa, involves a number of psychological and existential improbabilities that contribute to the superficially complex yet trivial depth.[55] Another critic, Tadeusz Sobolewski, who strongly supported Kieślowski's early films and the Cinema of Distrust movement in the late 1970s, speaks of 'artful calligraphic form', 'a *schmaltzy* finale' and 'a banal musical score'.[56] Furthermore, even some close Kieślowski friends and collaborators did not appreciate his rejection of the realistic description of reality.[57]

Three Colours: Blue

In *Blue* the prison is created by both emotions and memory.
– Krzysztof Kieślowski[58]

The first part of the trilogy, *Blue*, shares some noticeable thematic similarities with the earlier *No End*. Both films tell stories about mourning following the sudden death of a well-known public figure and they focus on the young and beautiful widows whose excruciating grief isolates them from the world. Also, the composer Preisner utilizes his 'funeral musical score' from *No End* during the televised memorial service in *Blue*. The latter film, however, is deprived of a concrete political context, and focuses on a purely private experience of grief.

Blue tells the story of Julie (Juliette Binoche) who endures the death of her daughter Anna and her husband Patrice, a famous French composer, in a car accident. She learns about the plight of her family while recovering after the crash in a hospital, and watches the funeral on a small television screen. After an unsuccessful suicide attempt (she steals pills from the nurse but is unable to swallow them), she tries to rebuild her life anew. The camera captures Julie's severe grief, her attempts to detach herself from her friends completely and her desire to free herself from the past and its painful associations. She says, 'I don't want any belongings, any memories. No friends, no love. Those are all traps.' Julie destroys her husband's remaining compositions, including the unfinished musical score praising European unity, *Concerto for the Unification of Europe* (ironically, at the same time Julie desperately tries to disconnect from the world). She attempts to sell a family mansion, grants large allowances to her gardener and housemaid and moves to another quarter of Paris to live an anonymous life. She takes with her only one reminder of the past life – a blue chandelier that belonged to her daughter. When she symbolically cuts her ties with the past (while watching her husband's last musical score being destroyed in a garbage truck), she achieves an illusory freedom.

The self-imposed detachment from the world – personal liberty according to the film's ruling concept – does not help Julie to achieve calm. Despite the fact that she does almost everything not to be reminded of Anna and Patrice, reality intrudes. She has to face a number of situations and people that represent the past or evoke it, such as the conversation with a female journalist who asks whether Julie, rather than her husband, wrote the 'European concerto', meeting people who knew her husband and listening to a mysterious flautist who performs Patrice's tune. Also, Julie discovers a mouse with young babies in her apartment that is conveniently located in an adults-only building. Kieślowski provides an ironic commentary on Julie's desperate attempts to be rid of the past during the following scene, set in a blue-lit swimming pool where she usually takes refuge, and during her conversation with her new neighbour and unlikely friend, the stripper Lucille (Charlotte Véry). Their conversation about killing the family of mice is interrupted by a group of young girls in swimming suits who joyously dash to the water.

Patrice's close friend and collaborator, Olivier (Benôit Régent), who is secretly in love with Julie, tries to help her. Soon after leaving hospital, she invites him to her desolate mansion, makes love to him and immediately leaves explaining, 'I appreciate what you did for me. But you see, I'm like any other woman. I sweat, I cough, I have cavities. You won't miss me.' Although she refuses to cry and show any sign of weakness, her pain is visible in the following scene when, out of desperation, she deliberately scrapes her knuckles against a stonewall. Several months later Olivier, however, tracks Julie down in a quiet Paris suburban apartment, offers his love and convinces

Juliette Binoche as Julie and Jacek Ostaszewski (the enigmatic flautist) in *Three Colours: Blue* (1993)

her to work on Patrice's unfinished concerto. When Julie accidentally learns about her husband's infidelity and discovers that his mistress Sandrine (Florence Pernel), who is working at the courts of law, is pregnant with her husband's child, she gradually embraces the life she has attempted to suppress. Perhaps the realisation that she was 'left earlier' by her husband helps Julie to come to terms with her loss? She generously offers Sandrine her chalet to raise Patrice's child and decides to work with Olivier on the unfinished symphony.

The first part of *Blue*, almost purely visual and prominently featuring the colour blue, sets the tone for the whole film. In the opening scene, during a bluish, foggy morning, the camera is placed behind the front wheel of a dark blue Alfa Romeo. The director then cuts to a close-up of Anna's hand waving a blue foil paper from the car's window. The car speeds into a tunnel with Anna on the back seat looking through the rear window at the passing lights (mostly red, white and blue) that are also reflected on her face. When the car stops for a moment, the camera reveals a mechanical problem. The shot of the fluid dripping from a pipe underneath a car (probably brake fluid) begins to build suspense. The next shot introduces a young man, perhaps a hitchhiker, standing near the side of the road. He plays with a wooden ball, attached by a string to a stick, by putting it onto the stick. The sound of the crash is heard when he succeeds and smiles victoriously. The director then cuts to the crash scene revealing the car almost 'glued to a tree' (as if crucified on a tree), a dog running madly in the area of the crash and a beach ball rolling out of the wreck. The scene of the accident is portrayed in a long-shot without providing any further details. The hitchhiker leaves his (blue) backpack and runs towards the scene. The sequence ends abruptly, leaving the viewer with a sense of mystery and confusion regarding the direction the film may take. The hitchhiker himself closely resembles the mysterious young man of the *Decalogue* series; he seems to act as a harbinger of death, a witness or, perhaps, somebody who is trying to warn. The opening segment also poses some typical Kieślowskian questions regarding the role of blind chance: what if the car had stopped and the couple had taken a hitchhiker? What if he had been a passenger?

The next segment relies heavily on extreme close-ups that sometimes last several seconds. For example, when a physician informs Julie about the death of Anna and Patrice, his reflection is seen in an extreme close-up of Julie's iris (a take achieved with a new 200mm lens). The shot indicates that things in the film are and will be seen from Julie's perspective. In the same segment, the director resorts to an extreme close-up of Julie's lips and eyes when she watches the funeral of her family on the small television screen viewed under her duvet in the hospital bed and tries very hard not to cry. Later in the film such images, achieved with the 200mm lenses as well, enhance the art-film atmosphere of *Blue*. They include, for example, an image of a lump of sugar, which slowly darkens and dissolves inside a cup of coffee, and the image of Julie's face reflected in a teaspoon.

The final montage sequence, the film's coda devoid of dialogue and strengthened by Preisner's choral music, retells important moments in Julie's life and focuses on people that helped her embrace life. The six-minute sequence, which has an almost dream-like dimension, begins when Julie finally accepts Olivier's love and goes to his apartment. The camera then focuses on Julie during the lovemaking with Olivier. The scene looks as if photographed from behind a water tank with Julie's face gently touching the glass. The way she is photographed, as some critics noted, may remind the viewer of a 'womblike space'.[59] After focusing on Julie and Olivier making love, then showing her face frontally in a close-up, the camera slowly moves upward and the screen fades to black. The unhurriedly moving (mostly to the right) camera then captures four scenes that are distinctly separated from each other by the darkness of the screen. Antoine, the hitchhiker, is shown in his room in the morning waking to the sound of his alarm clock and touching the necklace with a cross, which he stole from the scene of the accident, but which was later officially given to him by Julie. Later the camera reveals two mirror reflections of Julie's mother and then captures her in a close-up. She is portrayed closing her eyes, which perhaps serves as an indication of her imminent death, when the nurse rushes to her room (the opening of *Citizen Kane* comes to mind). After a slow-paced movement to the left, the camera then portrays Lucille's strip joint and stops with her close-up. Continuing the movement, as if finishing the full circle, the camera subsequently captures Patrice's mistress looking at the bluish flickering ultrasound image of her baby. The camera then captures an image of Julie seen in Olivier's eye, stressing the circular structure of the whole film. *Blue* ends with a close-up of Julie portrayed behind bluish glass, with tears of joy or, perhaps, relief appearing on her face (laughter through tears?). The screen darkens and then turns blue, followed by final credits.

As indicated by the film's title, the colour blue dominates the screen. Credited as the script consultant, Sławomir Idziak employs blue filters extensively and neutralises the cold colour blue by the warm amber colour. As in *A Short Film About Killing* and *The Double Life of Véronique*, Idziak favours multiple images reflected in glass or shown through glass, mirror images, images captured with a hand-held camera. More important than the dominant colour, however, is the presence of blue objects on the screen. The list is extensive and includes Anna's lollipop foil wrapper that she holds in her hand during the opening scene, the blue colour of a folder containing Patrice's personal documents that Olivier takes away from Julie, Julie's corrections in blue ink on Patrice's concerto, the 'blue room' of Anna, the blue lollipop that Julie devours and Anna's blue chandelier, among others. The swimming pool where Julie swims alone, which according to Annette Insdorf 'symbolises incomplete mourning as the space where Julie opts for physical exertion rather than emotional confrontation of loss',[60] is also blue-lit. At one point she apparently tries to commit suicide in the pool by submerging for a long time and then emerging coughing. The colour blue, apart from its immediate connotations with sadness and melancholy, clearly stands for the past. After being released from the hospital, Julie clears the blue room that belonged to Anna, in a way symbolically cutting the cord with the past. However, like the flashes of memory, the colour blue bursts onto the screen unexpectedly, strengthened by bits and pieces of the unfinished concerto. In addition to Julie's blue-lit image on the screen, the colour blue frequently reflects on her face, as if caressing her.

Almost the whole story of Julie's mourning and healing is told visually with the help of music, sound effects and effectively used blocks of silence. The dialogue is limited, dwarfed by the imagery and Zbigniew Preisner's music. As in *The Double Life of Véronique*, the striking musical score dominates the trilogy, especially *Blue*, replacing dialogue and strengthening the narrative. Indeed *Blue*, like *The Double Life of Véronique*, is in fact also about music; it bursts onto the screen whenever Olivier or Julie look at the musical notes during their collaboration on Patrice's unfinished piece devoted to the idea of Europe's unification, originally composed with an idea of performing it concurrently in the capitals of all European Union members. The film's narrative suggests that Julie co-authored that composition. Parts of the concerto appear throughout the film, and they serve (like the colour blue) as a reminder of the past. Towards the end of the film, Preisner's music explodes with the 'European Concerto', which employs St. Paul's First Letter to the Corinthians stressing the absolute love of God and the necessity for a human being to reciprocate that love:

Though I speak with the tongue of angels, if I have no love, I am become as hollow brass. Though I have the gift of prophesy, and understand all mysteries and all knowledge, and though I have enough faith to move the mightiest of mountains, if I have not love, I am nothing. Love is patient, love is kind. It bears all things, it hopes all things. Love never fails. For prophesies shall fail, tongues shall cease, knowledge will wither away. And now shall abide faith, hope and love; but the greatest of these is love. (Corinthians 13: 1–3)

Julie's true liberation comes with accepting Olivier's love and showing affection and generosity toward others.

Sound effects also play a powerful role in *Blue*: noises from the street (the street brawl) and in Julie's apartment (mice in a closet, noises on the staircase), the noise of the garbage truck crushing Patrice's musical score (as if crushing the music – the noise overtakes the music), the sound when Julie breaks the window in the hospital. The loud sounds often accompany the flashes of blue and the flashes of Patrice's concerto (for example when Julie smashes down the lid of the piano).

These flashes of blue and the bursts of the 'European Concerto' that over-take the screen from time to time emphasise the importance of memory. Near the beginning of the film Julie asks her maid Marie, 'Why are you crying?' She responds by saying, 'Because you are not. I keep thinking of them. I remember everything. How can I forget?' To be free from the past (liberty from past commitments and past memories) is illusory according to the film's logic. The enigmatic flautist reminds Julie that 'You have to always hold on to something', a sentence she probably does not hear. As if commenting on Julie's withdrawal from life, Kieślowski incorporates the scenes from a nursing home where her Alzheimer's disease-suffering mother, who confuses Julie with her sister Marie-France, kills time by endlessly watching television (she explains that she 'can see the world', while watching bungee jumping on television). The fact that she is played by Emanuelle Riva of *Hiroshima mon amour* (1959, Alain Resnais) fame, another great art film about memory, adds an additional dimension to the scene.

Kieślowski attempts to represent mental states that remain the domain of literature, a superior art according to several of his comments. In order to do so, as Richard Rushton convincingly elaborates, Kieślowski tries to invent a new cinematic language to 'open the ground of new cinematic vistas (the sugar cube receding in the coffee, the mysterious flautist). These do not seem to me to be playthings, or distractions, trivialities or seductions. On the contrary, they represent a striving towards new discoveries (of the cinema, of humanity), as strategies of destabilisation that are unnerving to the same degree as they are beautiful.'[61] To stress the importance of memories that haunt Julie, Kieślowski employs fades to black lasting several seconds before the action resumes from the moment before the blackout. *Blue* features four such blackouts, each time accompanied by the unfinished concerto composed by Patrice: while Julie watches the funeral on television; during her conversation with the hitchhiker Antoine in a coffee shop, after he mentions the crash; when Lucille notices in the swimming pool that Julie is crying; and when she learns from Olivier about her husband's mistress.

In *Blue*, Kieślowski employs the obsessions, intensity and strategies characteristic of art cinema. He also portrays a protagonist typical of art cinema: alienated, sensitive, with psychological problems and observed during an existential crisis. Like other great art cinema *auteurs*, Kieślowski is preoccupied with the exploration of his protagonist's mind. The stillness of the screen during blackouts, episodic and random incidents that are both frustrating and puzzling, action that is difficult to predict, and mysterious characters and objects that populate the screen reflect Julie's 'mindscreen', to use Bruce F. Kawin's term,[62] her mental landscape filled with painful emotions. Representative art cinema film-makers often deal with mental subjectivity and employ 'mindscreen narration'.[63] Film directors such as Werner Herzog in *Jeder für sich und Gott gegen alle* (*The Enigma of Kaspar Hauser*, 1974) and Paul Cox in *My First Wife* (1984) abruptly interrupt the linear action of their films by inserting material on Super 8 film that reflects the mental landscape of the protagonist. It is typically formed by images that are often exotic and far removed from the film's narrative; by doing so, Herzog and Cox force the viewer to focus on the new hypnotic cinematic space. Kieślowski, equally interested in depicting his character's mental condition, resorts to breaking the visual flow of the action not by the insertion of the unrelated images but by the blackness of the screen that marks the 'return of the repressed' – painful memories associated with the past that Julie attempts to suppress in the name of liberty.

Interestingly, Peter Weir's *Fearless*, which was also released in 1993, deals with another 'life after tragedy' that culminates in the protagonist's return to life. Weir introduces a successful San Francisco architect, Max (Jeff Bridges), who survives a plane crash and lives in the realm of fearlessness he felt during the crash. He also withdraws from everyday life, alienates his family and acts 'as if he was dead' (his words). Max's euphoria after surviving the plane crash prevents him from returning to earth.[64]

Like other Polish-French co-productions by Kieślowski, *Blue* features a number of references to the director himself and his films. While searching for her husband's mistress, Julie enters a courtroom at the Palais de Justice during the divorce trial between Karol and Dominique, the protagonists of the second part of the trilogy, when Karol complains about the lack of equality. Patrice incorporates 'his favourite' Van den Budenmayer's music (sung by Elżbieta Towarnicka) into his 'European Concerto'. As if to stress the link with *The Double Life of Véronique* even further, in episodic roles Kieślowski employs actors who appeared in the previous film, such as Philippe Volter (as a real estate agent) and Claude Duneton (as a physician), and includes a scene with an elderly woman struggling at the recycling bin and unnoticed by Julie who sits outside and enjoys the sun. The viewer familiar with Kieślowski's biography may also recognise the similarity between the photograph of Patrice and Kieślowski's father (reproduced in *Kieślowski on Kieślowski* on page 3). In another scene, when Julie emerges from the subway onto a busy street before seeing the real-estate agent, Kieślowski briefly appears on the screen as a bystander. When Julie moves away from the camera, Kieślowski appears in front of it as if observing Julie, with his back covering almost the whole screen.

Like Irène Jacob as Weronika and Véronique, Juliette Binoche (b. 1964) is always in the centre of the film, almost in every shot. Several film critics praised her performance, which arguably surpassed her previous accomplishments in Philip Kaufman's *The Unbearable Lightness of Being* (1988) and Louis Malle's *Damage* (1992). Geoffrey Macnab, suggesting that *Blue* has more to do with the French New Wave style than Kieślowski's realistic films made in Poland, compares it to Jean-Luc Godard's *Vivre sa vie* (*My Life to Live*, 1962) and notices the similarities between Anna Karina and Juliette Binoche. He also stresses the way Julie's sense of isolation is almost aestheticised by Kieślowski. Macnab writes, 'With its swirling classical music, sumptuous production values and *la belle* Binoche at its core, there are moments when the movie seems like an upmarket brandy commercial'.[65] He adds, however, that the film is 'rescued from the dead end of arthouse chic' by Binoche's performance and Kieślowski's sharp sense of observation.

Three Colours: White

I'm not against Polish entrepreneurialism, but people now care for nothing but money. I don't know what happened to us.

– Krzysztof Kieślowski[66]

A black comedy, *White*, the 'Polish' part of *Three Colours*, deals with the issue of equality in an unconventional way – it offers a vengeance story, a tale about getting even. Like *Blind Chance* and *The Double Life of Véronique*, *White* opens with a flashforward, in this case of a huge trunk on an airport conveyor belt. This image is inter-cut with a close-up of a man's legs walking briskly in a Chaplinesque manner. The camera then introduces the film's protagonist, Karol (played compellingly by Zbigniew Zamachowski), a prize-winning Polish hairdresser living in Paris who goes through a bitter divorce with his French wife Dominique (Julie Delpy). Karol's impotence and his inability to communicate with the bad-tempered Dominique (he only speaks broken French) end the marriage after six unconsummated months. A (white) pigeon dropping that falls from the sky on Karol's coat while he is on his way to the Palais de Justice foretells his future miseries. He is publicly humiliated at the court, deprived of his possessions, and left only with a trunk full of useless hairdressing diplomas. Also, his passport is taken away and his credit card cut in front of his eyes by a bank teller, and his bank and other assets are frozen. Desperate, Karol tries to win Dominique back, strives to make love to her, but fails. In addition, Dominique frames him for arson of their beauty salon and he has to fight with the ticket vendor in a subway station to get back his two-franc coin 'stolen' by the public phone. He is also mortified when he listens over the phone to Dominique's voice while she makes love to another man. The extent of Karol's misfortune makes him smile when he notices an old man at the recycling bin (a reference to other parts of the trilogy); perhaps he feels superior to the old man, or at least in a more favourable position.

When the anxious Karol ends up on a subway station playing on a comb a famed Polish pre-war song, *To ostatnia niedziela* (*This is Our Last Sunday*), he is noticed by a fellow Pole Mikołaj (Janusz Gajos): 'Do you live off that comb?' asks Mikołaj. The famous tango, composed by Jerzy Petersburski to the lyrics of Z. Friedwald, which reappears later in the film incorporated into Preisner's score, clearly comments on the action. Its 'suicidal lyrics' about being separated forever and hoping for the last chance (hoping for 'the last

Zbigniew Zamachowski as Karol and Janusz Gajos as Mikołaj (right) in *Three Colours: White* (1994)

Sunday') refer to Karol's state of affairs with Dominique as well as Mikołaj's personal problems. The latter, a successful professional bridge player with an excruciatingly great memory, who has lost all motivation to live, offers Karol the job of killing him, an offer he does not take up.

With the help of Mikołaj, Karol is (improbably) smuggled in his own trunk to Poland (the scene announced by the opening flashforward), where he recovers at the house owned by his brother Jurek (Jerzy Stuhr) after being beaten by airport thieves. Karol brings only two souvenirs from France: the two-franc coin and a white alabaster bust of a young woman that strongly resembles Dominique. After several weeks of helping Jurek with his hairdressing business and learning French from tapes, Karol decides to venture into the wild Polish capitalist life. He gets a job as a bodyguard of a Warsaw currency dealer (Cezary Pazura) and parades with a tear-gas pistol in front of the dealer's office. Later he outsmarts his boss and another thug, who speculate on land, by buying properties in the country where Ikea and

Hartwig are planning the development of their warehouses, and quickly amasses a fortune.

With the help of Mikołaj, Karol devises a plan to get even with his French wife (or, perhaps, to win her back). He changes his will, fakes his own death and leaves Dominique his now substantial assets. She appears in Poland to attend his funeral and claim his legacy. To her surprise, Karol waits for her after the funeral in a hotel's bed – in his own country he proves to be no longer impotent. When he leaves silently in the morning, she is arrested by the police and accused of murdering her husband. In the final scene Karol stands outside of Dominique's prison. The camera moves closer toward Dominique as if 'removing' the prison bars that separate the couple. Her gestures clearly indicate a desire to be with Karol, probably even to remarry him after her release. The film ends with a close-up of Karol's face with tears in his eyes. He knows that his is a Pyrrhic victory after realising that he still loves her. Kieślowski insists that his film offers a happy ending: 'For me the essential thing was a kind of "happy end", and the fact that between these two people, who hated each other and ought to have hated each other – her hating him and him hating her for humiliating him – love won out over hatred.'[67] As Kieślowski comments in another conversation, the film's happy ending is clear only after viewing the third part of the trilogy.[68] The conclusion to *Red*, and the whole trilogy for that matter, provides the second ending to *White*; it obviously indicates that Karol and Dominique will be together, and perhaps remarry, as Dominique tries to signal to Karol in her basic sign language.

The majority of critics discuss *White* as, to use Geoff Andrew's description, 'a droll black comedy, complete with such generic staples as missing corpses, cunning schemes and sexual humiliation'.[69] Western critics in particular also see the second part of the trilogy, like the earlier *The Double Life of Véronique*, as commenting on the ties between Poland and the West. Coates, for instance, states that *White* 'dramatises Polish fears of exclusion from Europe', and 'Karol's impotence may be that of the Pole confronting locked European doors'.[70] In the film, Karol is impotent only abroad; in Poland he is thriving in all domains – rich, full of energy, wearing designer clothes and even speaking better French. One can go further and contemplate that he gets even with Julie, as Poland gets even (united) with Western Europe. Such political interpretations of the film seem to be valid – the film includes some penetrating, humorous references to Polish 'capitalist reality' – yet this is not the tone of the majority of reviews published in Poland. By and large, *White* is discussed there as merely a 'comic interlude' within the trilogy, a disappointing film devoid of serious examination of Polish reality and filled with suspicious art-house clichés. The titles of a number of reviews published in Polish major journals are self-explanatory: 'Downwards', 'Cold', 'The Coloured Emptiness' and 'Without Colour'.[71]

With the exception of *Decalogue 10*, also starring Zamachowski and Stuhr as brothers and scriptwriter-actor Cezary Harasimowicz as a police inspector, Kieślowski never ventures into the realm of comedy. Although his pessimistic, sarcastic humour manifests itself in a number of his documentary and narrative films, an English reviewer is probably right when saying, 'Kieślowski and comedy form an uncomfortable partnership'.[72] Polish critic Tadeusz Sobolewski calls *White* a 'comedy with a lump in one's throat' and notices that the film is deprived of the precise description of Polish reality of Kieślowski's early films such as *Camera Buff* and the equally accurate description of mental reality in *Blue*.[73] Like Sobolewski, several Polish critics did not appreciate Kieślowski's move toward satire and saw it as resulting in simplifications and a sketchy picture of the new 'capitalist' Polish reality.

White paints a bleak vision of the Polish post-1989 state of affairs: a country populated by crooks, nouveaux riches, bandits pretending to be businessmen (according to Polish folk wisdom, gangsters and businessmen have a lot in common; their moralities fuse), foreign currency dealers, thieves at the airport and backward farmers. As portrayed in the film, this is a country where it is still possible to become rich overnight, where one can buy almost everything, including a Russian corpse ('Russian import') with its head crushed and impossible to identify, needed by Karol to trick the authorities. 'This is Europe now', says Karol's brother explaining the flashy neon sign 'Karol' that advertises his 'hairdressing salon' located in a dilapidated building near impersonal apartment complexes. Being a successful hair stylist with foreign experience, however, Karol does not want to work in a modest hair salon now owned by his brother. He puts the two-franc coin into 'his coffin' with the Russian corpse, thus symbolically burying his Parisian past, and begins a new entrepreneurial chapter in his life. Kieślowski's sharp satire on the new capitalist Poland includes several scenes pointing to Karol's 'capitalist behaviour', for example when he captures the satisfaction on Karol's face as he orders construction workers to knock down the wall surrounding his manor house and build a new one, only four centimetres thicker. He also refers to the powerful role played by the Catholic Church in Poland in the scene of the confrontation between Karol and his boss, who intimidates him at home. When Karol says that in his will he gave all his assets to the Church, this ends the threats ('If I die, everything goes to the Church', says Karol. 'Jesus! To the Church! We are screwed', is the response). In another scene, when Karol and Mikołaj form a business venture and rent a large office space in an office block with a view of the tallest building in Warsaw, *Pałac Kultury*

Polish capitalist reality in *Three Colours: White* (1994): Karol (Zbigniew Zamachowski) in the centre, with two 'businessmen', Grzegorz Warchoł (left) and Cezary Pazura

(The Palace of Culture), Karol comments that 'Warsaw [is] at our feet.' Built during the Stalinist period, the Palace of Culture epitomises the communist past for some (mostly older) Poles and the oppressive years deprived of political freedom.

A different scene, however, is perhaps the most indicative of Kieślowski's satiric endeavour – Karol's return to Poland inside his own trunk. The flashforward image of a trunk on a conveyor belt, which appears at the very beginning of the film, now finds its place within the narrative. The airport luggage handlers steal Karol's trunk hoping to find something valuable inside and they get only him wearing a cheap Russian wristwatch. He fights bravely with his scissors to keep the two-franc coin, but is badly beaten and left on a vast rubbish dump. 'Home at last!' – he mutters looking at the desolate land covered with early snow. The scene provides an apt illustration of a Polish idiomatic expression of 'being at home' (literally, 'on one's own junk'),[74] but more importantly, for cine-literate viewers it also supplies a reference to a scene from the Wajda's classic film, *Ashes and Diamonds*, when the protagonist Maciek (Zbigniew Cybulski) lies in convulsions in a foetal position as death overtakes him on the city garbage heap. Furthermore, another scene in *White*, when Karol shoots Mikołaj with a blank bullet in the Paris metro and catches the falling ('killed') fellow Pole into his arms, may refer to a scene from *Ashes and Diamonds* when the underground fighter Maciek and the communist leader Szczuka embrace in a grim dance of death. Citations from Wajda's classic film are common in Polish cinema. One can find the references to the two above-mentioned scenes from Wajda also in *Szamanka* (*She-Shaman*, 1996) by Andrzej Żuławski and *The Pigs 2: Last Blood* by Władysław Pasikowski, among others.

With its references to wild Polish capitalism along with its sarcastic humour, Kieślowski's *White* can be discussed together with other Polish films made at that time such as *It's Better to Be Beautiful and Rich* by Filip Bajon which offers a modern version of the Cinderella story with a distinct Polish flavour. In this film, Adrianna Biedrzyńska (who also stars in *Decalogue 4*) plays a young female weaver in a declining factory that is permanently on strike who one day discovers that she has inherited the factory. The film mocks success stories and provides an ironic commentary on the new Polish dream of becoming rich overnight. Bajon's fairy-tale meanders toward an unavoidable happy ending that implicitly pokes fun at popular films. With its bleak vision of Polish reality, Kieślowski's film also shares some similarities with Polish action films made at that time, such as Władysław Pasikowski's *Kroll* (1991) and *The Pigs* (1992).[75] These films reveal the escalation of crime that before 1989 was a rarely publicised fact (but which now makes front-page news), refer to contemporary political and criminal affairs, stress the helplessness of the Polish police and the corruption of its high-ranking officers and demonise the Russian mafia. However, unlike action films, which celebrate the machismo Polish style of their male protagonists and introduce characters bearing foreign names such as Kroll, Maurer, Wolf or Kossot, *White* offers an inconspicuous everyman (a hairdresser, albeit an award-winning one) named Karol, a name usually 'reserved' in Polish cinema for comedies such as *Och, Karol* (*Oh, Charles*, 1985) by Roman Załuski.

Karol's character owes a lot to Zbigniew Zamachowski (b. 1961), an accomplished theatrical and film actor who specialises in such ordinary characters struggling under the pressure of politics. He appeared in several Polish films made at the beginning of the 1990s, including Wajda's *Korczak* (1990) and was voted the best Polish actor in 1994 and 2001 in a popular plebiscite conducted by the magazine *Film*. His popularity was sealed in Kazimierz Kutz's films *The Turned Back* and *Pułkownik Kwiatkowski*

(*Colonel Kwiatkowski*, 1996) and later in diverse films such as the epic *Ogniem i mieczem* (*With Fire and Sword*, 1999, Jerzy Hoffman) and the gritty realistic *Cześć Tereska* (*Hi, Tessa*, 2001, Robert Gliński). With the role of Dominique, Julie Delpy (b. 1969) continues her appearances at the beginning of the 1990s in films directed by Polish film-makers – *Europa, Europa* (1991, Agnieszka Holland) and *Tragarz puchu* (*Warszawa 5703*, 1992, Janusz Kijowski). The cast of *White* also includes a group of distinguished Polish actors, including Jerzy Stuhr, Jerzy Trela (as Karol's driver Bronek), Janusz Gajos and Cezary Pazura (as Karol's boss), one of the leading actors embodying popular Polish cinema of the 1990s.

Compared to other parts of the trilogy, the photography in *White* is more naturalistic and functional, like the story itself, which is more mainstream and straightforward. Unlike the cinematographer Idziak in *Blue*, Edward Kłosiński, known for his close collaboration with Andrzej Wajda and Krzysztof Zanussi, among others,[76] employs the colour white without excess. The colour is chiefly associated with the two flashbacks (perhaps flashforwards) of the wedding: the scene that depicts Dominique dressed in white leaving an old, dark church into a sunlit town square with the hand-held camera closely following her, and the sexual union and climax during the lovemaking scene between Dominique and the miraculously 'resurrected' Karol, whilst the screen fades to black and after that into white ('you moaned louder than on the phone', Karol tells her). Several white objects in the film, such as the alabaster bust reminding Karol of Dominique, the whiteness of the frozen Vistula River when Mikołaj and Karol celebrate their return to Poland and the fair look of the blonde Dominique (her white skin) also provide subtle references to the film's title colour. Similar to the photography, Preisner's musical score, which is deprived of the usual references to Van den Budenmayer, is less overpowering and features the tango theme that stresses Karol's sense of revenge (like a male dancer in tango, Karol is clearly in charge, especially after his return to Poland), along with romantic piano music.

Apart from the image of an old man at the recycling bin, *White* provides one more explicit reference to other parts of the trilogy. Looking for Patrice's mistress Sandrine working in the courthouse, Julie from *Blue* gazes inside a courtroom where Karol bitterly complains about inequality during his divorce proceedings. References to other parts of the trilogy notwithstanding, some critics also argue that *White* contains a reference to the French New Wave Cinema in the scene featuring Brigitte Bardot's billboard poster from Jean-Luc Godard's *Le Mépris* (*Contempt*, 1963). When Karol points at Dominique's window, Mikołaj thinks that he is indicating the poster of Bardot, which is to the left of the window ('isn't she a bit over the hill?' asks

Mikołaj). This scene prompts Emma Wilson to open her chapter on *Blue* with a lengthy, three-page discussion on Kieślowski's reference to Godard's film. Arguing that Kieślowski consciously refers to the *Nouvelle Vague* (not only in *White* but also in the whole trilogy) she notices that 'Kieślowski's concern in referring to *Le Mépris* is with the memory and survival of a certain generation of film-making ... with a certain ideal of cinematic femininity, fostered and critiqued by Godard'.[77] It is difficult to agree with such reasoning. Godard was never a popular figure in Poland, largely due to the political views expressed explicitly in both his films and in many interviews. Firstly, his fascination with various leftist forms of Marxism (Trotskyism, Maoism) was certainly too much for the communist authorities as well as for the pro-party film critics who needed artists only to express and promote the party line and not to challenge it. Secondly, Godard's political views also made him an unpopular figure among the film-makers and audiences. This was a part of the 'political landscape' in Poland, in which no artist or intellectual was taken seriously if he expressed explicitly pro-communist sympathies. Such artists and intellectuals were ridiculed as those who are politically blind and cannot (or do not want) to see the practical side of communism. In a 1995 interview with Paul Coates, Kieślowski admits that he 'didn't like the fact that, in a certain sense, *Three Colours* falls under a peculiar Godardian tradition of the title', and agreed to this title because producer Karmitz liked it.[78] To conclude, given Kieślowski's background, the poster from *Le Mépris* should probably be taken literally – as a comment on the state of affairs between Karol and Dominique.

In *White*, Kieślowski also addresses the discourses on voyeurism, impotence and betrayal which he developed earlier in *Decalogue 2*, 6 (and *A Short Film About Love*) and 9. After the divorce proceedings, Karol watches Dominique's silhouette in an apartment window, notices the presence of another man with her and listens over the phone to Dominique's orgasmic moans. In Poland, where Karol lures Dominique with the prospect of a fortune from his will, he gazes at her with the opera glasses during 'his funeral', and later watches her in the prison cell. Highly critical of Kieślowski's portrayal of women in his earlier films and discussing *White* as a continuation of this depiction, Alicja Helman convincingly argues that 'for Kieślowski, sexual dominance is the decisive factor in male-female relationships. It is less a case of the natural character of the physical link between the members of a heterosexual couple than of sex as a means of exerting power over – of subjugating – the woman. The man who lacks such a power (and it need not be through impotence, as *A Short Film About Love* reminds us), becomes the woman's victim.'[79] Like Tomek, the protagonist of *A Short Film About Love*, and Roman in *Decalogue*

9, Karol suffers a humiliation at the hands of 'his woman'. His obsession with Dominique results in the staged 'death' (attempted suicides in previous films) that makes it possible for his love to be reciprocated.

Three Colours: Red

> This is a film about communication that disappears. We have better and better tools and less and less communication with each other. We only exchange information.
>   – Krzysztof Kieślowski[80]

Kieślowski's *Red*, probably the most sophisticated and widely praised part of the trilogy, tells the story of a young student and part-time fashion model living in Geneva, Valentine Dussaut (Irène Jacob), and her chance encounter with a retired judge, Joseph Kern (Jean-Louis Trintignant), who is obsessed with illegal electronic surveillance of his neighbours. Another character is also introduced, Valentine's neighbour, Auguste Bruner (Jean-Pierre Lorit), a young law student preparing for his final bar exams, whose life mirrors that of the old judge. Valentine and Auguste live in the same neighborhood surrounding *Café chez Joseph* (which is portrayed in the film as almost the centre of the universe) and their paths repeatedly cross. For example, they are seen in the same places, such as the music store and the bowling alley. During the scene at the bowling alley, when the camera moves away from Valentine to the left, passing behind red seats, it pauses on a table and portrays in a close-up shot a broken beer glass and an empty pack of Marlboros – a sign that Auguste has just left the place. Valentine and Auguste pass by not knowing each other and remain unknown to each other until the fate of destiny brings them together in the final scene of the film.

Kieślowski once commented: 'The theme of *Red* is the conditional mood – what would have happened if the Judge had been born forty years later?'[81] The 'what-if' structure of several of his earlier films is cleverly retold in *Red*, which offers a game of associations, a story of chance encounters, double chances, mystifying coincidences and destiny. When Valentine runs over a German shepherd, Rita, which belongs to the Judge, it changes her life forever. Returning the injured dog, she meets the disillusioned and misanthropic judge who seems unconcerned with the plight of Rita: 'If I ran over your daughter, would you be so indifferent?' asks the enraged Valentine; 'I have no daughter, Miss. Go away', is his supposedly heartless response. Despite this unpromising beginning, the Judge intrigues Valentine and the complex relationship that develops between them constitutes the centre of the film. Judge

Kern, who is listening to his neighbours' private phone calls, gives himself up to the police and is prosecuted for the illegal eavesdropping. When Valentine learns from the newspaper about his fate and visits him to explain that she is not responsible for leaking the information to the neighbours and the police, the Judge informs her that he thought she would come to see him after reading this information. (The scene is clearly reminiscent of the manner in which Véronique's lover, Alexandre, is conducting his 'psychological experiment' in the *Double Life of Véronique*.) Towards the end of the film, thanks to the generous and good-hearted Valentine, the embittered Judge reconnects with the world in the same way Julie in *Blue* returns to life thanks to the patient love of Olivier.

The third part of the trilogy revolves around several puzzlingly connected subplots: Valentine's personal life is juxtaposed with that of Auguste; her telephone conversations with the controlling and absent (because based in London) lover Michel and the troubled teenaged brother Marc, a heroin user, are intertwined with scenes from Auguste's relationship with a slightly older woman, Karin (Frédérique Feder), who runs a personal weather forecast service. Like the Judge several years earlier, Auguste is betrayed by his lover. The similarities between Judge Kern and his much younger alter ego, Auguste, are carefully placed in the narrative. Both men are lawyers, own dogs, experience the betrayal by unfaithful blonde lovers (both witness them making love to somebody else) and listen to music composed by Van den Budenmayer. The

Irène Jacob (Valentine) and Jean-Louis Trintignant (Judge Kern) in *Three Colours: Red* (1994)

scene with the falling textbook that opens on a page containing the answer to a future exam question also emphasises the mysterious connection between them which recalls the equally perplexing link between the Polish Weronika and the French Véronique in *The Double Life of Véronique*. As portrayed in the film, Auguste's life echoes that of the Judge; he seems to be the Judge's alter ego. Perhaps the Judge creates himself once again in searching for his 'second life', his 'second chance'.

As with other films by Kieślowski, in *Red* moments of good luck come with a heavy price and serve as ominous signs of terrible things to come. Possibly, that is why Valentine treats winning some money from the 'one-armed-bandit' as a calamitous signal: 'That's a bad sign', the bartender at the *Café chez Joseph* tells her after seeing her winning combination. In another scene, resembling the scene with the hitchhiker in *Blue*, when Auguste goes to Karin only to discover her in bed with another man, the camera portrays his car from inside the café then pans to the right to reveal the winning (red) combination on the slot-machine.

Like other parts of the trilogy, Kieślowski opens *Red* with an almost psychedelic speeded-up sequence filmed with an extensive use of Steadicam. The camera traces a phone call, in a way following an electronic impulse, beginning with a hand dialling the number, then the cord, the plug socket and bundles of wires, before the cable plunges into the English Channel where it resembles a sea monster and rapidly emerges on the other side, never reaching the destination. The red pulsating beep of a busy phone begins to form the background for the film's title and Kieślowski's and Piesiewicz's names credited as scriptwriters. The camera moves back to the dialling hand that hangs up the phone. The photograph of Valentine on the desk of the dialling person indicates that this must be her unseen and domineering boyfriend Michel. The opening scene also introduces one of the film's major preoccupations – with the lack of real communication between people who, instead of being united, are separated from each other by modern technology. In *Red*, telephone conversations, which play such an important role in several scenes, replace human contact. *Red* features people with their phones, missed phone calls, conversations that are overheard and answering machines that respond instead of characters. Valentine talks to her jealous boyfriend in London and tries to maintain contact with her mother and brother Marc. The camera also reveals the lack of communication in seemingly working relationships. For example, Judge Kern is listening to a conversation between a mother trying to see her daughter and using tricks to lure her home. In another scene, when the angry Valentine tries to warn the neighbours of Judge Kern that he spies on the husband who is betraying his wife with a homosexual lover, she notices that the damage has been done – the husband's daughter is secretly listening to her father's conversation with the lover.

The final scene also focuses on characters that appear alienated rather than being united by the immense tragedy. The Judge witnesses on television the news about a tragic ferry accident in the English Channel, which happened due to freak weather and despite the good forecast provided by Auguste's former lover Karin. She has to pay with her life (lost without trace while yachting with her lover) not so much as a punishment for her professional mistake but for her adulterous behaviour. Valentine and Auguste are shown among the mere seven survivors out of the 1,435 ferry passengers, but despite their mysterious connection, emphasised throughout the film, the final freeze-frame with the red background suggests that they do not yet know each other – they appear together within one frame but look into different directions. In an attempt to sum up the trilogy, the film also lists additional survivors whose names include the earlier protagonists: Julie and Olivier from *Blue* as well as Karol and Dominique from *White*. Furthermore, given that the television broadcaster informs the viewers about the death of Julie's husband a year before, the events portrayed in the trilogy must have occurred within a year. Although Kieślowski is known for his particular understanding of 'happy endings' (evidenced by the last scenes of *White* and, most prominently, the depressing *No End*), it is not easy to bring together the idea of a 'happy ending' with the immensity of the tragedy. Several hundreds of passengers are dead but the chosen ones, 'our protagonists', are saved. As depicted in *Red*, the ending serves almost as a mockery of happy endings and seems to be closer to the realm of disaster genre rather than art cinema.

In this film about the power of accidental occurrences there is, however, nothing accidental as far as the narrative structure is concerned. The film's cinematographer, Piotr Sobociński, once commented:

We had shot the last scene of the film, the video 'news footage' of the ferry boat accident, several months before we began principal photography. After we had finished it, I was watching it one day on tape and I happened to hit the pause button. There was a fireman with a red jacket crossing behind Irene Jacob, who was in profile. I said to myself, 'this is a key for the film'. It occurred to us that maybe the events in the film were not so accidental; maybe the Judge had some control over the events. So we made the billboard poster in the film exactly like the stop-frame I had found on the tape. The whole film progressed in this backwards fashion. It was like a game of billiards: we already knew the final configuration of balls on the table, and we had

A scene from *Three Colours: Red* (1994): Valentine (Irène Jacob) posing for the chewing-gum poster

to work out the patterns that would get them there. When you see the billboard poster recreated in the stop-frame at the end of the film, you have the impression that nothing happened accidentally.[82]

The huge chewing-gum advertising poster with a sad-looking image of Valentine portrayed against the background of a red drape, which fills the screen several times during the film, returns at the very end when the Judge watches the report of the ferry accident. The freeze-frame of Valentine that ends the film looks almost like a replica of her carefully arranged sad pose during an elaborate studio session ('Don't smile; be sad', she is instructed by the photographer). Although red filters play a significant role in the film, it is not so much the lighting, but numerous red objects within the film that glue the film together and magnify the intricacy of the multilayered narrative: Valentine's red sweater and umbrella, Michel's jacket with which she sleeps, the chewing-gum poster, red cars on the street, Rita's red leash, red bowling balls in the bowling alley full of red colour and red ferry tickets, among other things.

As Piotr Sobociński reveals, Vermeer was his 'visual inspiration', particularly in the scenes involving the portrayal of the Judge's house with its brownish interiors.[83] Although Kieślowski finds Geneva an 'exceptionally unphotogenic' city,[84] the quiet neighbourhoods of Geneva play as important a role as the urban locations of Paris and Warsaw. The camera moves a lot, rarely rests, and is truly voyeuristic: gliding on the streets, following Valentine, even rushing after the (red) bowling ball as it rolls down a bowling lane. Sobociński also uses Technocrane shots, for example in the scene after the fashion show when the Judge recalls the story about the book that fell down from the balcony before his exam – the story that recalls Auguste's experience.

As part of Kieślowski's self-reflexive narrative strategy, a number of scenes in *Red* either recall earlier films or refer directly to them. A shot familiar from the three previous films (with an old person carrying a glass to the recycling bin) is repeated this time as well, albeit somewhat differently. Unlike former protagonists, who either passively observed the elderly man (Karol), did not notice the old woman because of their preoccupation with their own problems (Julie) or at least appeared to be willing to help the old women (Weronika and Véronique), the generous Valentine actually helps the old woman. Dave Kehr writes that that this 'simple act of kindness is the climax of the entire trilogy, the gesture that saves the world'.[85] The references to *The Double Life of Véronique*, which were indicated earlier in the text, are abundant in *Red*. Both films deal with the theme of a possible double life, parallel experiences, the ability to learn from somebody else's mistakes, and destiny. When Valentine tells the Judge in an empty theatre after the fashion show, 'I feel something important is happening around me. And it scares me', it brings memories of the dual life of Weronika and Véronique. Furthermore, several images, such as the one when the Judge and Valentine part and they put their hands against each side of his car window, are reminiscent of similar scenes from *The Double Life of Véronique* and *Blind Chance*. The two scenes portraying Valentine's participation in the physically exhausting ballet lessons are close to Kieślowski's documentary *Seven Women of Different Ages*. The self-reflexive nature of this film also owes something to Preisner's music and references to Van den Budenmayer's music. Even though the film features primarily a romantic bolero theme, Van den Budenmayer's name and music appear briefly when the camera captures the cover of the disk owned by the Judge and later when Valentine and Auguste are listening in the same record store, but unaware of each other, to Van den Budenmayer's music. The link between *Red* and earlier parts of the trilogy is also stressed by the brief incorporation of the tango motif that dominated in *White*.

Kieślowski's unexpected death on 13 March 1996 prompted several critics to look at his artistic *oeuvre* through the prism of his biography. Such a critical approach, analysing films from *The Tram* to *Three Colours: Red* as films about

Kieślowski, seems justified. Following the great European *auteurs* from the 1960s and 1970s, Kieślowski often stressed the semi-autobiographical nature of his films. For example, in the documentary *I'm So-So* he pronounces, 'I turn the camera on myself in all my films'. Apart from citations from earlier works and, in his 'Polish films', thinly-veiled allusions to political and social contexts, Kieślowski's films are filled with numerous biographical references. For example, his protagonists experience acute heart problems (the lawyer Zyro in *No End* and Weronika in *The Double Life of Véronique* die unexpectedly of heart attacks); live without parents (Filip in *Camera Buff*, Tomek in *A Short Film About Killing*; the death of the father in *Blind Chance*, the motherless protagonists in *The Double Life of Véronique*); and die unexpectedly (Paweł in *Decalogue 1*, Julie's family in *Blue*). The puzzling openings of *Three Colours: Red* and other parts of the trilogy, which are later incorporated into the narrative, find their predecessors in earlier films: the image of a hawk in *Camera Buff*, the puzzling close-up at the beginning of *Blind Chance* and several openings in *Decalogue*. Kieślowski's observations are always detailed, realistic (with a documentary flavour) and often incorporating supposedly unrelated episodes (like the memorable scene with the two jugglers observed by Witek in *Blind Chance*).

For a number of Polish critics, Kieślowski seems to be the true hero in his films. Tadeusz Sobolewski writes that in spite of Kieślowski's often declared agnosticism, his films are imbued with strong religious overtones. For instance, the Judge in *Three Colours: Red* 'becomes simultaneously the figure of Kieślowski and the Lord God as imagined by common folk'.[86] Another Polish critic, Piotr Wojciechowski, notices that Judge Kern is 'somewhat God, somewhat Kieślowski himself'.[87] The Judge certainly is portrayed almost as a God-like manipulative figure, perhaps the film director himself. When Valentine hesitates on whether to go to England, the Judge tells her 'Leave. It is your destiny.' He can also predict the future. 'You were fifty years old and you were happy' he tells Valentine, recounting his dream after the fashion show and indicating that maybe she is the woman he never met. 'Who are you?' asks the bewildered Valentine, to which he responds: 'A retired judge.'

The Judge is another puppeteer overhearing people's conversations and meddling in their lives; he is an embittered and lonely character who retired earlier due to personal disappointments in order to live a secluded life, and the one who oversees the break up of the relationship between Auguste and Karin to pair his alter ego with Valentine. Given Kieślowski's reclusive artistic persona, his early retirement from film-making caused by some professional disappointments and moral dilemmas at work and the nature of film-making in general, the parallels between the Judge and Kieślowski seem reasonable. Comparing the Judge to film-makers, Dave Kehr writes the following: 'Trintignant invests the Judge with much of Kieślowski's own flinty contrariness, and it isn't hard to imagine the solitary smoker of Kieślowski's retirement occupying a house just like the Judge's, sitting just as quietly amid the clutter of a lifetime'.[88] The performance of Jean-Louis Trintignant (b. 1930), an actor very popular in Poland (and elsewhere) after the success of Roger Vadim's *Et Dieu créa la femme* (*And God Created Woman*, 1956) and, in particular, Claude Lelouch's *Un homme et une femme* (*Man and a Woman*, 1965), adds another dimension to the film.

AFTERWORD

With all his films, consistently moving away from the external, Krzysztof Kieślowski was moving toward the land of no return. He reached its limits and the limits of the cinematic medium. He stopped talking, and I was left with a multitude of questions.

– Piotr Lis[1]

During his last public appearance on 24 February 1996, Kieślowski commented on the reasons behind his self-imposed retirement from film-making that had been officially announced earlier, during the making of *Three Colours* trilogy:

I stopped making films for a number of reasons. I think that one of the reasons was that I was tired. I made a number of films in a short period of time, perhaps too many. There was undoubtedly a lot of bitterness involved and the feeling that I tried too hard and never achieved what I really wanted. Apart from that, I started to live in a fictional world that I imagined, and was artificial. I ceased participating in real life and started in the one that I invented either alone or with my colleague [Krzysztof] Piesiewicz. And since it happened from film to film, essentially without a break, to be honest, I lost the feeling that I was communicating with the world. I drove myself into some fictitious world; I removed myself from those near and dear to me because fictitious problems started to become extremely important ... Then I started to think that enough is enough.[2]

Before his death on 13 March 1996, despite his much-heralded retirement from film-making, Kieślowski was embarking on a new project with his long-time collaborator Krzysztof Piesiewicz. They started working on another trilogy of films titled *Raj* (*Paradise*), *Piekło* (*Hell*) and *Czyściec* (*Purgatory*). The script of *Paradise*, the last film written together by Kieślowski and Piesiewicz, was published after Kieślowski's death;[3] Piesiewicz wrote the other parts of the trilogy later.[4] In 2001 *Paradise* was directed by Tom Tykwer, titled *Heaven* (Italy/Germany/USA) and premiered at the 2002 Berlin Film Festival. The film tells the story of a young Englishwoman, Philippa (Cate Blanchett), working as a schoolteacher in Turin, Italy. After several failed attempts at contacting police about a well-connected local drug baron, who disguises himself as a respected businessman but is responsible for the death of her husband and some of her students, Philippa decides to take the law into her own hands and punish him. In the Hitchcockian opening sequence Philippa plants a homemade bomb in the drug dealer's office but the bomb ends up killing four innocent people and leaves the drug trafficker unharmed. She is devastated after learning how her good intentions turned bad. As a result of her action, the police accuse Philippa of political terrorism. With the help of a young policeman Filippo (Giovanni Ribisi), who serves as the translator during her interrogation, she escapes to the countryside where the police eventually surround the two doomed lovers.

Heaven polarised film critics who, by and large, discussed the degree of fidelity to the spirit of Kieślowski's cinema and considered Tykwer almost as a director working on behalf of Kieślowski. Although Tykwer's film has several recognisable elements of Kieślowski's last works (slow pace, art-film atmosphere, ambiguous ending, lyricism, hypnotic photography and a story about deadly choices), it does not duplicate the earlier experience.

In the 1990s Kieślowski also acted as artistic supervisor on several short films made at the Łódź Film School. They include *Pańcia* (*Missy*, 1995), directed by Iwona Siekierzyńska; *Przed zmierzchem* (*Before the Sunset*, 1995), directed by Grzegorz Zgliński; and *Późne popołudnie* (*Late Afternoon*, 1996), made by Gilles Renard. In addition, a number of films made in Poland in the mid-1990s seem to owe their inspiration to Kieślowski's cinema. They include, for example, a series of television films produced by Krzysztof Zanussi, *Opowieści weekendowe* (*Weekend Stories*, 1996–97), close in spirit to *Decalogue*.

Although Kieślowski's films are unique in the Polish context, one may see a continuation of his cinema in recent films directed by one of his favourite actors, Jerzy Stuhr: *Historie miłosne* (*Love Stories*, 1997), *Tydzień z życia mężczyzny* (*A Week in the Life of a Man*, 1999), *Duże zwierzę* (*The Big Animal*, 2000) and the most recent *Pogoda na jutro* (*Tomorrow's Weather*, 2003). The spirit of Kieślowski is undoubtedly present in the 1997 winner of the Festival of Polish Films, *Love Stories*: he helped with the script and the film is dedicated to him. Stuhr presents four parallel stories with four different protagonists (all played by Stuhr): a university teacher, a priest, an army officer and a convicted thief. They have to choose between love and career, between the complications that love might introduce into their lives and the boredom of a stability that is often illusory. Stuhr employs an 'art-film atmosphere', down-to-earth characters facing moral choices and mysterious, otherworldly figures like the 'Master-Pollster' (played by Jerzy Nowak) who questions the four protagonists about the true nature of their choices. *Love Stories* resembles a morality play permeated with the very metaphysical ingredients that are so characteristic of Kieślowski's last films.

In *A Week in the Life of a Man*, Jerzy Stuhr once again casts himself as a public prosecutor, Adam Borowski, eager to prosecute others yet equally guilty in his private life. He has an extramarital affair, attempts to avoid paying taxes and does not understand his wife's (Gosia Dobrowolska) urge to adopt a child. Stuhr stresses the contrast between the public and private spheres of life and subtly criticises the emerging post-communist middle class in Poland by the ironic use of a line from *Hamlet*, sung in a song by Wojciech Kilar. Borowski belongs to a choir that rehearses 'What a piece of work is a man' several times in the course of the film, an ironic comment on the duality of the main protagonist.

Stuhr's *The Big Animal* is adapted from a script written by Kieślowski in 1973 and based on a short story *Wielbłąd* (*A Camel*), published by dissident writer Kazimierz Orłoś. Due to communist censorship, Kieślowski had to abandon the script. After Kieślowski's death, the respected Polish School director Janusz Morgenstern found the script in Wiesbaden (Germany) and gave it to Stuhr, who edited and modernised it. *The Big Animal* tells the story of a simple office worker (played by Stuhr) who, despite problems with his neighbours and the authorities, takes care of a camel that had been abandoned by a wandering circus. The camel clearly serves as a poetic metaphor for tolerance and personal freedom in Stuhr's realistic observations of small-town mentality.

The forthcoming years most likely will bring more films made in the spirit of Kieślowski, thanks to the collaboration between scriptwriter Krzysztof

Piesiewicz and film director Michał Rosa (b. 1963), known for his early realistic works such as the medium-length *Gorący czwartek* (*Hot Thursday*, 1993) and the feature *Farba* (*Paint*, 1997). In 2001, Rosa directed *Cisza* (*Silence*, 2001), which was well received by the judges at the 2001 Festival of Polish Films in Gdynia.[5] According to Piesiewicz, *Silence* begins an ambitious eight-part series of feature films called *Naznaczeni* (*Predestined*), which 'attempt to synthesise the last twenty years in Polish history'.[6] Several Polish papers also reported in May 2001 that Kieślowski's *Camera Buff* would find its continuation: Stanisław Latek, who earlier worked with Kieślowski as an assistant on *White* and *Blue* and on *Red* as the director of the second unit, is directing *Camera Buff 2*.

Krzysztof Kieślowski's importance continues to manifest itself not only in cinematic ways: high schools in Warsaw, Łódź and Mieroszów (where he lived as a child) have been named after him. The Faculty of Radio and Television at the Silesian University in Katowice (*Wydział Radia i Telewizji Uniwersytetu Śląskiego*, known as the Katowice Film School), where Kieślowski taught from 1979 to 1982, is also named after him. Furthermore, Kieślowski's Polish friends and collaborators established the 'Krzysztof Kieślowski Award' for those artists who continue his creative ideas. The award was given for the first time to Iréne Jacob at the 2002 Festival of the Art of Cinematography 'Camerimage' in Łódź. Similar awards also exist elsewhere: for example, French producer Marin Karmitz established Prix Kieślowski in 1998 – an annual international competition for young film-makers. Kieślowski's place in the pantheon of great European cinematic auteurs seems to be assured.

NOTES

PREFACE

1 'We were quite a poor family. My father was a civil engineer, my mother an office clerk. My father had tuberculosis and for twelve years after the Second World War he was dying of it. He'd go to sanatoria and since we wanted to be near him – my mum, that is, and the two of us, me and my sister – we'd follow him.' Danusia Stok (ed.), *Kieślowski on Kieślowski* (London: Faber and Faber, 1993), 2–5.

2 Mariola Jankun-Dopartowa, 'Fałszywa inicjacja bohatera. Młode kino lat siedemdziesiątych wobec założeń programowych Młodej Kultury', in Mariola Jankun-Dopartowa and Mirosław Przylipiak (eds), *Człowiek z ekranu: Z antropologii postaci filmowej* (Kraków: Arcana, 1996), 108. See the chapter on 'Camouflage and Rough Treatment: The Cinema of Distrust, the Solidarity Period and Afterwards' in my *Polish National Cinema* (Oxford/ New York: Berghahn Books, 2002), 146–75.

3 For a fuller discussion of Wajda's position in such central debates see John Orr and Elżbieta Ostrowska (eds), *The Cinema of Andrzej Wajda: The Art of Irony and Defiance*, (London: Wallflower Press, 2004).

4 Tadeusz Sobolewski, 'Peace and Rebellion: Some Remarks on the Creative Output of Krzysztof Kieślowski', in Ewelina Nurczyńska-Fidelska and Zbigniew Batko (eds), *Polish Cinema in Ten Takes* (Łódź: Łódzkie Towarzystwo Naukowe, 1995), 124.

5 Ibid., 125.

6 Krzysztof Kieślowski, 'In Depth Rather Than Breadth', *Polish Perspectives* 24, no. 6–7 (1981), 67.

7 Mirosław Przylipiak writes about the reception of Kieślowski's films in Poland: 'Filmy fabularne Krzysztofa Kieślowskiego w zwierciadle polskiej krytyki filmowej', in Tadeusz Lubelski (ed.), *Kino Krzysztofa Kieślowskiego* (Kraków: Universitas, 1997), 213–47; also Przylipiak's 'Monter i studentka', *Kino* 3 (1997), 6–9; 50.

8 Sobolewski, 'Peace and Rebellion', 126.

9 Paul Schrader quoted in Thomas Elsaesser, 'Putting on a Show: The European Art Movie', *Sight and Sound* 4, no. 4 (1994), 22.

10 Kieślowski's staging of Tadeusz Różewicz's play is now available in Poland on VHS and distributed with other prominent works under the label 'The Golden One Hundred Works of Television Theatre'. Różewicz, one of the most innovative of Polish writers, wrote *The Card Index* in 1960.

1 Krzysztof Kieślowski, 'In Depth Rather Than Breadth', *Polish Perspectives* 24, no. 6–7 (1981), 68. The English translation of Kieślowski's text, 'Głęboko zamiast szeroko', *Dialog* 1 (1981), 109–11.

2 Starting in 1961, the Documentary Film Studio in Warsaw has also produced mainstream narrative films. This was reflected in the 1980s in the studio's name being changed to *Wytwórnia Filmów Dokumentalnych i Fabularnych* (Documentary and Narrative Film Studio).

3 Karabasz's *Sunday Musicians* belongs to the canon of Polish documentary films. It received awards at, among others, the Venice International Short and Documentary Film Festival (First Prize, 1960) and the Oberhausen International Festival of Short Films (Grand Prix, 1961).

4 Jadwiga Głowa, 'How Do Polish Documentary Film-makers Maintain Their Identity?', in Wiesław Godzic (ed.), *Aspects of Audiovisual Popular Culture in Norway and Poland* (Kraków: Jagiellonian University Press, 1999), 69.

5 See important studies published in recent years in Poland: Mikołaj Jazdon, 'Czarne filmy posiwiały: "Czarna seria" polskiego dokumentu 1956–1958', in Małgorzata Hendrykowska (ed.), *Widziane po latach: Analizy i interpretacje filmu polskiego* (Poznań: Wydawnictwo Poznańskiego Towarzystwa Przyjaciół Nauk, 2000), 43–66; and Jolanta Lemann, '"Czarna seria" polskiego dokumentu – kreatorzy i aktorzy', in Ewelina Nurczyńska-Fidelska and Bronisława Stolarska (eds), *'Szkoła Polska' – Powroty* (Łódź: Łódź University Press, 1998), 145–63.

6 An eminent Polish film historian, Jerzy Toeplitz (1909–95), was the head of the Łódź Film School from 1957 to 1968. From 1973 to 1979 he acted as the director of the Australian Film, Television and Radio School in Sydney.

7 Stanisław Zawiśliński (ed.), *Kieślowski* (Warsaw: Skorpion, 1998), 36.

8 Krzysztof Kieślowski, *Film dokumentalny a rzeczywistość* (Łódź: Łódź Film School, 1968). Fragments published as 'Dramaturgia rzeczywistości' (The Dramaturgy of Reality), in *Film na Świecie* 3–4 (1992), 7–9.

9 Kieślowski's theoretical work *Documentary Cinema and Reality* was evaluated as 'good' and his two diploma films received the highest grade: 'very good'. The examining committee unanimously granted Kieślowski a Master's degree with the 'very good' grade. The document is at the Łódź Film School. Reprinted in Zawiśliński, *Kieślowski*, 44.

10 Jerzy Bossak's comment on the role and specificity of documentary cinema ['Rola i specyfika filmu dokumentalnego'], his answer to the poll conducted by *Kwartalnik Filmowy* 2 (1965), 26.

11 Kieślowski, 'In Depth Rather Than Breadth', 67–70.

12 Kazimierz Karabasz, *Bez fikcji – z notatek filmowego dokumentalisty* (Warsaw: Wydawnictwa Artystyczne i Filmowe, 1985), 148.

13 Kieślowski, 'In Depth Rather Than Breadth', 71.

14 Discussed in Wojciech Kałużyński, 'Krzysztofa Kieślowskiego "opowiadanie rzeczywistością"', in Tadeusz Lubelski (ed.), *Kino Krzysztofa Kieślowskiego* (Kraków: Universitas, 1997), 22.

15 Hanna Krall, 'Zrobiłem i mam' [interview with Krzysztof Kieślowski], *Polityka* 5 (1979). Quoted from its reprinted version in Lubelski, *Kino Krzysztofa Kieślowskiego*, 271.

16 Krzysztof Wierzbicki, *I'm So-So* (1995, television film, Denmark).

17 Kieślowski, 'In Depth Rather Than Breadth', 68.

18 See my discussion on Third Polish Cinema in *Polish National Cinema* (New York/Oxford: Berghahn Books, 2002), 125–34.

19 For example Jerzy Skolimowski made *Rysopis* (*Identification Marks: None*, 1965), *Walkower* (*Walkover*, 1965), *Bariera* (*The Barrier*, 1966) and *Ręce do góry* (*Hands Up*, 1967, released in 1985). Krzysztof Zanussi started with a series of television films and then directed *Struktura kryształu* (*The Structure of Crystals*, 1969).

20 Mirosław Przylipiak, 'Polish Documentary Film after 1989', in Janina Falkowska and Marek Haltof (eds), *The New Polish Cinema* (London: Flicks Books, 2003), 144–6.

21 Discussed in details by Mirosław Przylipiak in his book, *Poetyka kina dokumentalnego*

(Gdańsk: Wydawnictwo Uniwersytetu Gdańskiego, 2000), 185–93.

22 Tadeusz Sobolewski, '100 lat kina w Polsce: 1974–1976', *Kino* 5 (1999), 52.

23 Andrzej Mellin's documentary, *Szajbus – Film o Wojtku Wiszniewskim* (*Lunatic – The Film About Wojciech Wiszniewski*, 1985), provides an insight into the life and work of Wiszniewski, one of the most innovative of Polish documentary film-makers.

24 Annette Insdorf writes, 'In his frustration, the young man can be seen as an embryonic version of the awkward voyeur Tomek in *A Short Film about Love*', *Double Lives, Second Chances: The Cinema of Krzysztof Kieślowski* (New York: Hyperion Books, 1999), 11.

25 Kieślowski mentions Marek Piwowski's *Muchołuk* (*Fly-swat*, 1967) as a good example. See Danusia Stok (ed.), *Kieślowski on Kieślowski* (London: Faber and Faber, 1993), 51. To this I would like to add Krystyna Gryczełowska's classic documentary, *Nasze znajome z Łodzi* (*Our Friends from Łódź*, 1972), which deals with the harsh working conditions of female textile-workers in Łódź.

26 See *Film* 7 (1996), 10.

27 Stok, *Kieślowski on Kieślowski*, 44.

28 See Jadwiga Anna Łużyńska, 'Fenomen Krzysztofa Kieślowskiego', *Iluzjon: Kwartalnik Filmowy* 1–4 (1995), 16. The 1794 national insurrection (known as *Powstanie Kościuszkowskie* – The Kościuszko Insurrection), which followed the 1793 second partition of Poland, ended in defeat by a combined Russian and Prussian army. As a consequence, Poland was partitioned for the third time in 1795 and disappeared from the map.

29 Paul Coates, 'Kieślowski and the crisis of documentary', in Paul Coates (ed.), *Lucid Dreams: The Films of Krzysztof Kieślowski* (London: Flicks Books, 1999), 38.

30 Similar issues are raised in a later documentary, *Wszyscy tu do mnie przyjdziecie* (*You All Come to Me*, 1981), by Tomasz Lengren. He introduces an ex-communist apparatchik who left the Central Committee of the Communist Party in 1956 and has become the director of the cemetery. In his new work this man applies the same totalitarian politics (for example, keeping an eye on hierarchy even after death) and phraseology (communist newspeak).

31 Karabasz, *Bez fikcji*, 90.

32 Stok, *Kieślowski on Kieślowski*, 79.

33 Ibid., 81; 86.

34 In his conversations with Danusia Stok, Kieślowski says that his family stayed in Sokołowsko three times due to his father's treatment in a TB sanatorium. Ibid., 15.

35 Ibid., 64.

36 The original television version of *First Love* lasted 55 minutes. The 30-minute version was prepared for the Festival of Short Films in Kraków. Tadeusz Lubelski, 'The Sequel Will be Shown without Him…: Interview with Jacek Petrycki, a cameraman of *First Love*', in Bożena Janicka and Andrzej Kołodyński (eds), *Chełmska 21. 50 lat Wytwórni Filmów Dokumentalnych i Fabularnych w Warszawie* (Warsaw: WFDiF, 2000), 167. The film was awarded the Grand Prix ('Złoty Lajkonik') at the 1974 National Short Film Festival in Kraków and the Special Jury Award at the 1974 International Short Film Festival in Kraków.

37 Lubelski, 'The Sequel Will be Shown without Him…', 166.

38 Stok, *Kieślowski on Kieślowski*, 64.

39 Lubelski, 'The Sequel Will be Shown without Him…', 167.

40 Stok, *Kieślowski on Kieślowski*, 68.

41 Ibid., 60.

42 Mikołaj Jazdon, *Dokumenty Kieślowskiego* (Poznań: Wydawnictwo Poznańskie, 2002), 111.

43 In a recent study on Kieślowski's documentaries, Mikołaj Jazdon quotes the editor of the film, Lidia Zonn, who reveals that the answer in the original version of the film was 'militiaman'. The censor ordered it removed from the film. Jazdon, *Dokumenty Kieślowskiego*, 164.

44 Stok, *Kieślowski on Kieślowski*, 75.

45 One of the Cinema of Distrust films is even titled in a similar manner: *Jak żyć?* (*How Are We to Live?*), directed by Marcel Łoziński, made in 1977, premiered in 1981.

46 Zygmunt Kałużyński, 'Jak skompromitowałem się w Krakowie', *Polityka* 24 (1971). Quoted from Jazdon, *Dokumenty Kieślowskiego*, 61–3. According to Jazdon, Kieślowski admitted

in 1996 that the title, *Talking Heads*, refers to his polemics with Kałużyński in the weekly *Polityka*. Furthermore, writes Jazdon, Kieślowski originally wanted to dedicate his film to the critic (p. 73).

47 Interestingly, in 1979 Kazimierz Karabasz commented on the importance of human faces in his book *Cierpliwe oko* (*The Patient Eye*) (Warsaw: Wydawnictwa Artystyczne i Filmowe, 1979), 65.

48 Stok, *Kieślowski on Kieślowski*, 86.

49 Coates, 'Kieślowski and the crisis of documentary', 40.

50 Jazdon, *Dokumenty Kieślowskiego*, 90–1.

CHAPTER TWO

1 Krzysztof Kieślowski's interview, published in the Polish weekly *Polityka* (no. 4, 1979). Quoted from Małgorzata Hendrykowska, *Kronika kinematografii polskiej 1895–1997* (Poznań: Ars Nova, 1999), 366.

2 I discuss the Cinema of Distrust in more detail in *Polish National Cinema* (New York/Oxford: Berghahn Books, 2002).

3 Julian Kornhauser and Adam Zagajewski, *Świat nie przedstawiony* (Kraków: Wydawnictwo Literackie, 1974).

4 The term 'Young Culture' (*Młoda kultura*) refers to the title of a Kraków periodical.

5 Adam Zagajewski, 'Rzeczywistość nie przedstawiona w powojennej literaturze polskiej', in Kornhauser and Zagajewski, *Świat nie przedstawiony*, 32.

6 Ibid. 43–4. The translation is quoted from Clare Cavanagh, 'Lyrical Ethics: The Poetry of Adam Zagajewski', *Slavic Review* 59, no. 1 (2000), 5.

7 Tadeusz Lubelski, 'A Difficult Return to Freedom Cinema', in Janina Falkowska and Marek Haltof (eds), *The New Polish Cinema* (London: Flicks Books, 2003), 27.

8 Michał Głowiński describes the weak foundations of the communist system in his seminal works and analyses the use of language – the Orwellian 'newspeak'. See, for example, Głowiński's *Nowomowa po polsku* (Warsaw: OPEN, 1990); *Rytuał i demagogia: trzynaście szkiców o sztuce zdegradowanej* (Warsaw: OPEN, 1992), and *Peereliada: komentarze do słów 1976–1981* (Warsaw: Państwowy Instytut Wydawniczy, 1993).

9 Tadeusz Sobolewski, 'Wyzwoliłam się: mówi Agnieszka Holland', *Kino* 12 (1992), 8.

10 Sobolewski, 'Wyzwoliłam się', 8.

11 Krzysztof Kieślowski, 'Czy mam prawo ryzykować', *Polska* 5 (1976), 69.

12 Since 1955, the film industry in Poland was based on a film units (*Zespoły Filmowe*) system. Each film unit was composed of film directors, scriptwriters, and producers, and was supervised by an artistic director, with the help of a literary director and a production manager. See my *Polish National Cinema*, 77.

13 Stanisław Różewicz (b. 1924) started his career in 1954 with *Trudna miłość* (*Difficult Love*). In the 1950s and the 1960s he directed a number of classic Polish films, mostly dealing with World War Two, such as *Trzy kobiety* (*Three Women*, 1957), *Wolne miasto* (*Free City*, 1958), *Świadectwo urodzenia* (*The Birth Certificate*, 1961) and *Westerplatte* (1967).

14 Kieślowski's *Pedestrian Subway* marks the real beginning of Andrzej Seweryn's impressive acting career in film (earlier he appeared, often not credited, only in episodic roles). Seweryn (b. 1946) belongs to the most accomplished Polish theatrical and film actors. Teresa Budzisz-Krzyżanowska (b. 1942) appears later in an episodic role in Kieślowski's *Three Colours: White*.

15 Juliusz Machulski (b. 1955) is known as a director of several popular films. He started his successful career at the beginning of the 1980s with *Vabank* (*Va Banque*, 1982), its sequel *Va Banque II* (1985) and *Seksmisja* (*Sex Mission*, 1984), and continued later with *Déjà Vu* (1989, a Polish-Soviet coproduction) and *Girl Guide* (1995). His recent box-office successes include *Kiler* (1997) and its 1999 sequel *Kiler-ów 2-óch* (*Kiler 2*). During the making of *Personnel*, Machulski was a student of film directing at the Łódź Film School. Since 1988, he has been the head of the film studio Zebra and a producer of a number of films, including works directed by Jerzy Stuhr.

16 In the 1970s, Tomasz Zygadło (b. 1947) made documentary films such as *Szkoła podstawowa*

(*Elementary School*, 1971) and *Mikrofon dla wszystkich* (*Microphone for Everybody*, 1976) and feature films such as *Rebus* (1977) and *Ćma* (*Moth*, 1980).

17 Danusia Stok (ed.), *Kieślowski on Kieślowski* (London: Faber and Faber, 1993), 96.

18 In the mid 1970s, Michał Tarkowski (who appears in Kieślowski's film as the tailor Sowa) played honest characters trying to do their best despite the overwhelming pressure of politics, for example in Wajda's *Man of Marble* and Kieślowski's next film, *The Scar*.

19 Tadeusz Lubelski, 'From Personnel to *No End*: Kieślowski's political feature films', in Paul Coates (ed.), *Lucid Dreams: The Films of Krzysztof Kieślowski* (London: Flicks Books, 1999), 60.

20 Hanna Krall, 'Zrobiłem i mam' [interview with Krzysztof Kieślowski], *Polityka* 4 (1979). Quoted from the reprinted version in Tadeusz Lubelski (ed.), *Kino Krzysztofa Kieślowskiego* (Kraków: Universitas, 1997), 272. Apart from Tomasz Zygadło, *Personnel* also features actor-director Tomasz Lengren as the opportunistic chief tailor Romek. Lengren (b. 1945) appears also as an actor in the leading role in Piotr Andrejew's *Klincz* (*Clinch*, 1979). In the 1980s he directed the medium-length *Choinka strachu* (*The Christmas Tree of Fear*, 1982, released in 1989) and the full-length *Tanie pieniądze* (*Cheap Money*, 1986).

21 In his conversations with Danusia Stok, Kieślowski says, 'When I made documentaries which were short and compact, I'd always have an enormous amount of material which I liked a lot but which I had to throw out. This material was only interesting when it was on screen for quite a long time; gossip, for example, and various observations about people's behaviour ... I thought that I'd use this sort of material in *Personnel* as a dramatic device.' Stok, *Kieślowski on Kieślowski*, 97.

22 Ibid., 96–7.

23 Andrzej Munk (1921–61) was a leading director of the Polish School generation known for such classic films as *Człowiek na torze* (*Man on the Track*, 1957), *Eroica* (1958), *Zezowate szczęście* (*Bad Luck*, aka *Cockeyed Luck*, 1960) and the incomplete *Pasażerka* (*The Passenger*, 1963) which had its premiere on the second anniversary of the tragically-deceased director.

24 Stok, *Kieślowski on Kieślowski*, 99. Although so critical about his film, Kieślowski also produced a six-minute documentary, *Klaps* (*Slate*), consisting of out-takes from *The Scar*.

25 Paul Coates, '"The inner life is the only thing that interests me"': a conversation with Krzysztof Kieślowski,' in Coates, *Lucid Dreams*, 165.

26 Agnieszka Holland (b. 1948) later directed a number of films in Poland, Germany, France and the United States. Her Polish films include *Aktorzy prowincjonalni* (*Provincial Actors*, 1979), *Gorączka* (*Fever*, 1981) and *Kobieta samotna* (*A Woman Alone*, 1981, released in 1988), among others. In Germany she made *Angry Harvest* (1985) and *Europa, Europa* (1991), and in France *To Kill a Priest* (1988), *Olivier, Olivier* (1992) and *Total Eclipse* (1995, French-British coproduction). Her Hollywood films include *Secret Garden* (1993), *Washington Square* (1997), *The Third Miracle* (1999) and *Shot in the Heart* (2001). Her most recent film, *Julia wraca do domu* (*Julie Walking Home*), a Canadian-German-Polish coproduction, was released in 2003.

27 The film credits acknowledge only that the film 'is based on Lech Borski's novel'. The script by Kieślowski appeared in *Dialog* 4 (1977), 34–52.

28 See Piotr Litka, 'Najważniejszy jest dialog' [interview with Jerzy Stuhr], *Kino* 12 (1999): 22–4.

29 Krzysztof Kieślowski, 'No Heroics, Please' [interview with Kieślowski], *Sight and Sound* 50, no. 2 (1981), 90.

30 Stanisław Zawiśliński (ed.), *Kieślowski* (Warsaw: Skorpion, 1998), 152.

31 Kieślowski employs excerpts from the award-winning documentary film by Zbigniew Raplewski, *Araby* (*Arab Horses*, 1963).

32 Tadeusz Szczepański, 'Drzewo, które jest' [interview with Krzysztof Kieślowski and Krzysztof Piesiewicz], *Film na Świecie* 385 (1991), 12. The image of horses was carefully planned by Kieślowski and appeared in the published script. Krzysztof Kieślowski, 'Spokój', *Dialog* 4 (1977), 34–52.

33 Mirosław Winiarczyk, '*Spokój*, czyli o Solidarności', *Ekran* 3 (1980), 11.

34 An extensive overview concerning the reception of *Camera Buff* (and other films by Kieślowski until *No End*) in Poland is provided by Mirosław Przylipiak in his invaluable text: 'Filmy fabularne Krzysztofa Kieślowskiego w zwierciadle polskiej krytyki filmowej', in

Tadeusz Lubelski (ed.), *Kino Krzysztofa Kieślowskiego* (Kraków: Universitas, 1997), 213–47.

35 Krzysztof Kieślowski, 'Amator', *Dialog* 4 (1978), 84–105.

36 Jerzy Płażewski, *Historia filmu dla każdego* (Warsaw: Wydawnictwa Artystyczne i Filmowe, first edition 1967). This is the standard film history book in Poland.

37 Stok, *Kieślowski on Kieślowski*, 112.

38 Jerzy Stuhr's comment in Zawiśliński, *Kieślowski*, 139.

39 Jan F. Lewandowski, 'Społeczne kłopoty człowieka z kamerą', *Dziennik Zachodni* 14 (18 January 1980), 4.

40 Paul Coates, *The Story of the Lost Reflection: The Alienation of the Image in Western and Polish Cinema* (London: Verso, 1985), 45.

41 Krzysztof T. Toeplitz, '*Amator* czyli moralność sztuki', *Miesięcznik Literacki* 12 (1979), 83.

42 Jadwiga Anna Łużyńska, 'Fenomen Krzysztofa Kieślowskiego', *Iluzjon: Kwartalnik Filmowy* 1–4 (1995), 42.

43 Providing another ironic twist, Kieślowski names Filip's understanding supervisor, played by Jerzy Nowak, Marian Osuch.

44 Stok, *Kieślowski on Kieślowski*, 65.

45 Ibid., 208.

46 Ibid., 110. The documentary film produced in 1999 by Polish Television and directed by one of Kieślowski's close collaborators, Krzysztof Wierzbicki, *Kieślowski i jego Amator* (*Kieślowski and his Camera Buff*), pays attention to the real-life situations and characters that shaped Kieślowski's film. It introduces cine-buffs such as Franciszek Dzida, Jan Dzida and Józef Brzóska, among others, members of the Amateur Film-making Club 'Klaps' in Chybie (Southern Poland).

47 Alicja Helman, 'Women in Kieślowski's late films', in Coates, *Lucid Dreams*, 117.

48 Stok, *Kieślowski on Kieślowski*, 115–16.

49 Ibid., 116.

50 Viewers familiar with Polish cinema may, however, recognise several actors, such as Tadeusz Bartosik, Michał Szewczyk and Paweł Nowisz, who appeared in supporting or episodic roles in a number of popular Polish films.

51 Stok, *Kieślowski on Kieślowski*, 119.

52 Kieślowski, 'In Depth Rather Than Breadth', 69–70.

CHAPTER THREE

1 Krzysztof Kieślowski, 'No heroics, please', *Sight and Sound* 50, no. 2 (1981), 90.

2 Discussed in more detail in my *Polish National Cinema* (New York/Oxford: Berghahn Books, 2002), 164–71. The next three paragraphs use some portions from *Polish National Cinema*.

3 Gary Mead, 'Volksfilm for the 1980s: Prospects for Polish Cinema after Martial Law', *Sight and Sound* 52, no. 4 (1983), 231.

4 Waldemar Krzystek, 'Było sobie kino', *Kino* 12 (1995), 8.

5 Jerzy Płażewski, 'Film zagraniczny w Polsce', in Edward Zajiček (ed.), *Encyklopedia kultury polskiej XX wieku* (Warsaw: Instytut Kultury, Komitet Kinematografii, 1994), 348. As an example of the situation, Płażewski points out that between 1982 and 1989 Poland imported only six films from Italy (p. 349).

6 Danusia Stok (ed.), *Kieślowski on Kieślowski* (London: Faber and Faber, 1993), 39.

7 Precisely, the Radio and Television Faculty at the University of Silesia in Katowice (Wydział Radia i Telewizji Uniwersytetu Śląskiego w Katowicach). In 2001, the School was named after Krzysztof Kieślowski.

8 Discussed in detail in Piotr Wasilewski's book, *Świadectwa metryk* (Kraków: Powiększenie, 1990).

9 Tadeusz Sobolewski, '*Przypadek* – postscriptum', *Kino* 6 (1987), 8.

10 Krzysztof Kieślowski, 'Przypadek', *Dialog* 5 (1981), 7–25.

11 Stok, *Kieślowski on Kieślowski*, 113.

12 Two prominent Polish film critics, Tadeusz Lubelski and Tadeusz Sobolewski, write that *Blind Chance* was inspired by Krzysztof Zanussi's television film *Hipoteza* (*The Hypothesis*, 1972). I can see more similarities, however, between *Blind Chance* and Zanussi's other philosophical

essays such as *Illumination* (1973). Tadeusz Sobolewski, 'Gra z życiem', *Tygodnik Powszechny* 36 (1995), 7. Tadeusz Lubelski, 'From *Personnel* to *No End*: Kieślowski's Political Feature Films', in Paul Coates (ed.), *Lucid Dreams: The Films of Krzysztof Kieślowski* (London: Flicks Books, 1999), 67.

13 The Poznań events of 1956 are the subject of Filip Bajon's historical reconstruction, *Poznań 56* (*Street Boys*, 1996).

14 Although the three variants of Witek's life are treated as equally important in the film (despite their different lengths), Kieślowski admits in interviews that the third story, or the 'third Witek' is the closest to his beliefs. See Maria Marszałek, 'O mnie, o tobie, o wszystkich' [interview with Kieślowski], *Kino* 8 (1987), 10. Kieślowski expressed a similar opinion at the press conference at Cannes where his film was shown outside of the competition. See Stanisław Wyszomirski's report from Cannes in *Ekspres Wieczorny* 91 (1987), 2.

15 Marszałek, 'O mnie, o tobie, o wszystkich', 10.

16 Maciej Pawlicki, 'Wishful thinking: *Przypadek*', *Kino* 6 (1987), 6.

17 Sobolewski, '*Przypadek* - postscriptum', 9.

18 Konrad J. Zarębski (ed.), '*Przypadek*', *Filmowy Serwis Prasowy* 5 (1987), 17

19 *The Catalogue of the XIX Festival of Polish Feature Films in Gdynia*, 78–9. In the 1990s Linda became another generational actor who followed two acting personalities known for their roles in Andrzej Wajda's films: Zbigniew Cybulski and Daniel Olbrychski. Like his predecessors, and unlike the majority of Polish actors, he is known exclusively for his filmic roles. Linda is also a film and theatre director; in 1989 he made his first feature film, *Seszele* (*Seychelles*), which was well received by young audiences, and in 2001 he directed *Sezon na leszcza* (*The Sucker Season*).

20 Tadeusz Lubelski, 'Bogie, na jakiego zasłużyliśmy', *Kino* 7–8 (1994), 41.

21 Sobolewski, '*Przypadek* – postscriptum', 11.

22 Pawlicki, 'Wishful thinking', 7.

23 Quoted from Stanisław Zawiśliński (ed.), *Kieślowski* (Warsaw: Skorpion, 1998), 67.

24 Krzysztof Kłopotowski, 'Rozsądny bezpartyjny', *Przegląd Powszechny* 5 (1987). Quoted from Mirosław Przylipiak, 'Filmy fabularne Krzysztofa Kieślowskiego w zwierciadle polskiej krytyki filmowej', in Tadeusz Lubelski (ed.), *Kino Krzysztofa Kieślowskiego* (Kraków: Universitas, 1997), 241.

25 Marcin Sułkowski, 'Witek, nic nie musisz', *Res Publika* 4 (1987), 39.

26 Ibid., 42.

27 Slavoj Žižek, *The Fright of Real Tears: Krzysztof Kieślowski between Theory and Post-Theory* (London: British Film Institute, 2001), 81.

28 Marszałek, 'O mnie, o tobie, o wszystkich', 9.

29 Stok, *Kieślowski on Kieślowski*, 127.

30 Ibid., 134.

31 Due to this ending, the film's original title was *Happy End*, which may serve as an example of Kieślowski's bitter sense of humour. See Stok, *Kieślowski on Kieślowski*, 134.

32 Marszałek, 'O mnie, o tobie, o wszystkich', 8.

33 Paul Coates, 'Politics of Memory, Ghosts of Defeat: Kieślowski's *No End*', *The Polish Review* 33, no. 3 (1988), 345.

34 Philip Strick, '*Bez końca (No End)*', *Monthly Film Bulletin* 55, no. 650 (1988), 77.

35 Fragments of Ernest Bryll's poem in my translation.

36 Tadeusz Sobolewski, 'W samotności', *Kino* 12 (1985), 12.

37 Michel Ciment's interview with Krzysztof Piesiewicz published in *Positif* (October 1989). Quoted from the Polish translation: 'Wyzbyć sie polocentryzmu. Z Krzysztofem Piesiewiczem rozmawia Michel Ciment', *Kwartalnik Filmowy* 3/4 (1992), 23.

38 Mirosław Przylipiak gives a detailed account of the reception of *No End* in his 'Filmy fabularne Krzysztofa Kieślowskiego w zwierciadle polskiej krytyki filmowej', in Lubelski, *Kino Krzysztofa Kieślowskiego*, 213–47. Przylipiak himself wrote a critical review of *No End* in a leading Polish monthly on cinema, *Kino*, pointing out that Kieślowski artificially mixes genres and talks 'off the subject'. Mirosław Przylipiak, 'Nie na temat', *Kino* 2 (1986), 8. *No End*, however, received the Polish Federation of Cine Clubs (DKF) Award, 'Don Quixote 1985'.

39 Stok, *Kieślowski on Kieślowski*, 136.

40 Tadeusz Sobolewski, 'Peace and Rebellion', in Ewelina Nurczyńska-Fidelska and Zbigniew Batko (eds), *Polish Cinema in Ten Takes* (Łódź: Łódzkie Towarzystwo Naukowe, 1995), 133.

41 Maciej Chrzanowski, 'Bez końca', *Kultura* 9 (1985), 12; Mirosław Ratajczak, 'Bez znaczenia', *Odra* 10 (1985), 81–2. For example, Chrzanowski claims that *No End* is a 'one-dimensional picture, black-and-white, closely resembling simplified schematas of socialist realist films'. He accuses Kieślowski of 'incoherent poetics and narration' in a 'primitive film on a cognitive level, and placing itself on the border of paranoia on the intellectual level'.

42 Apart from the presence of an actor-symbol, Jerzy Radziwiłłowicz, the film relies on the performance of Grażyna Szapołowska (b. 1953), voted Best Polish Actress in 1985 and 1986 by readers of the popular weekly *Film*.

43 Zbigniew Preisner began working as a composer in 1977. First he was associated with the famous Kraków cabaret 'Piwnica Pod Baranami' (The Cellar under the Rams), and then he became better known as a film composer. *No End* is his second feature film after *Prognoza pogody* (*Weather Forecast*, Antoni Krauze, 1983). Preisner's haunting (almost overwhelming) musical scores, particularly in later Kieślowski works, have gained him international attention and popularity. He composed music for, among others, Agnieszka Holland's films such as *Europa, Europa* (1989), *Olivier, Olivier* (1991) and *The Secret Garden* (1993), Louis Malle's *Damage* (1992), Hans Peter Moland's *Aberdeen* (2000) and Wojciech Marczewski's *Weiser* (2000).

CHAPTER FOUR

1 Danusia Stok, *Kieślowski on Kieślowski* (London and Boston: Faber and Faber, 1993), 145.

2 Michel Ciment, 'Wyzbyć się polonocentryzmu', *Film na Świecie* 3–4 (1992), 25. (Originally published in *Positif*, October 1989. Quoted from the Polish translation by Witold Zakrota.)

3 Christopher Garbowski, *Krzysztof Kieślowski's Decalogue Series: The Problem of the Protagonists and Their Self-Transcendance* [sic] (Boulder: East European Monographs, 1996), 14.

4 The critical recognition and popularity of Kieślowski's *Decalogue* prompted actor-director Rafał Wieczyński to produce *Naprawdę krótki film o miłości, zabijaniu i jeszcze jednym przykazaniu* (*A Truly Short Film About Love, Killing and One More Commandment*, 1993, Polish-French production), an uneven film parodying Kieślowski's thematic preoccupations.

5 Katarzyna Jabłońska, 'Wariacje na temat Dziesięciorga Przykazań', *Kwartalnik Filmowy* 18 (1997), 157.

6 Tadeusz Szczepański, 'Drzewo, które jest' [interview with Krzysztof Kieślowski and Krzysztof Piesiewicz], *Film na Świecie* 385 (November–December 1991), 12.

7 Stok, *Kieślowski on Kieślowski*, 145.

8 Krzysztof Kieślowski, 'Introduction', in Krzysztof Kieślowski and Krzysztof Piesiewicz, *Decalogue: The Ten Commandments* [translated by Phil Cavendish and Suzannah Bluh] (London: Faber and Faber, 1991), xiv.

9 Tim Pulleine, '*Krótki Film o Miłości* (*A Short Film About Love*)', *Monthly Film Bulletin* 57, no. 676 (1990), 132.

10 Kieślowski's fascination with Bergman is discussed extensively in Tadeusz Szczepański's essay, 'Kieślowski wobec Bergmana, czyli Tam, gdzie spotykają się równoległe', in Tadeusz Lubelski (ed.), *Kino Krzysztofa Kieślowskiego* (Kraków: Universitas, 1997), 163–71. [Szczepański quotes Jannike Åhlund's interview with Bergman, 'Sista intervjun med Bergman', *Expressen* (23 November 1995).]

11 Stok, *Kieślowski on Kieślowski*, 156.

12 See interview with Lidia Zonn in Mateusz Werner, 'Wspólny rytm', *Film na Świecie* 3–4 (1992), 141.

13 Stok, *Kieślowski on Kieślowski*, 159.

14 Grzegorz Gazda, 'Nie chcę realizować formy poza świadomością reżysera' [interview with Wiesław Zdort], *Film na Świecie* 3–4 (1992), 128–9. In his conversation with Danusia Stok, Kieślowski reveals that the literary director of Studio Tor, Witold Zalewski, inspired him to think about such a character. See Stok, *Kieślowski on Kieślowski*, 158.

15 Tadeusz Sobolewski, 'Grasz to, co w sobie masz' [interview with Artur Barciś], *Kino* 2 (1990), 9.

16 Wojciech Klata (b. 1976) also appeared in the leading role in another seminal Polish film of the late 1980s, *300 mil do nieba* (*300 Miles to Heaven*, 1989), directed by Maciej Dejczer. Klata later appeared in Andrzej Wajda's *Korczak* (1990) and Steven Spielberg's *Schindler's List* (1993), among others. In 1996 he also served as Wajda's assistant during the production of *Panna Nikt* (*Miss Nobody*).

17 The published screenplay, however, provides a rational explanation for the tragedy – somebody discharges warm water into the pond and it causes the ice to melt. See Kieślowski and Piesiewicz, *Decalogue: The Ten Commandments*, 24

18 Lisa Di Bartolomeo, 'No Other Gods: Blue and Green in Kieślowski's *Dekalog I*', *Studies in Slavic Cultures* (February 2000), 54.

19 Gazda, 'Nie chcę realizować formy...', 128.

20 The image of the ice as the symbol of the Host was carefully planned by Kieślowski. See Wiesław Zdort's comment in Gazda, ibid., 129.

21 Di Bartolomeo, 'No Other Gods,' 47–59.

22 Slavoj Žižek, *The Fright of Real Tears: Krzysztof Kieślowski Between Theory and Post-Theory* (London: British Film Institute, 2001), 123.

23 Christopher Garbowski notices a problem in the film's script. When Ewa and Janusz are about to kiss in her apartment, they are unexpectedly visited by a group of carolling children. Aside from the ludicrous time (the early morning of Christmas Day), Garbowski also comments that 'carolling does not take place before the Second Day of Christmas' and that 'the custom has virtually disappeared in larger centres such as Warsaw'. See Garbowski, *Krzysztof Kieślowski's Decalogue Series*, 55.

24 Annette Insdorf, *Double Lives, Second Chances: The Cinema of Krzysztof Kieślowski* (New York: Hyperion, 1999), 85.

25 Paul Coates, 'The Curse of the Law: *The Decalogue*', in Paul Coates (ed.), *Lucid Dreams: The Films of Krzysztof Kieślowski* (London: Flicks, 1999), 100.

26 Insdorf, *Double Lives, Second Chances*, 89.

27 Francis J. Rigney, '*The Decalogue*: A Psychoanalytic Deadlock', *Film Criticism* 14, no. 3 (1990), 60.

28 Stok, *Kieślowski on Kieślowski*, 159.

29 Charles Eidsvik, '*Decalogue 5* and 6 and the two *Short Films*', in Coates, *Lucid Dreams*, 82.

30 Tadeusz Sobolewski, 'Wszyscy jesteśmy mordercami', *Kino* 8 (1988), 10.

31 Christopher Garbowski, 'Krzysztof Kieślowski's *Decalogue*: Presenting Religious Topics on Television', *The Polish Review* 37, no. 3 (1992), 330.

32 Ibid, 330.

33 Paul Coates, 'Anatomy of a Murder: *A Short Film About Killing*', *Sight and Sound* 58, no. 1 (1988/1989), 63.

34 Stok, *Kieślowski on Kieślowski*, 170.

35 Eidsvik, '*Decalogue 5* and 6 and the two *Short Films*', 86.

36 Stok, *Kieślowski on Kieślowski*, 169.

37 Žižek, *The Fright of Real Tears*, 115.

38 Rigney, '*The Decalogue*: A Psychoanalytic Deadlock', 63.

39 Alicja Helman, 'Women in Kieślowski's late films' [translated from the Polish by Paul Coates], in Coates, *Lucid Dreams*, 124.

40 Paul Coates, 'The Curse of the Law: *The Decalogue*', in Coates, *Lucid Dreams*, 106.

41 See my discussion in *Polish National Cinema* (Oxford/New York: Berghahn Books, 2002), chapter 10 on 'National Memory, the Holocaust and Images of the Jew in Postwar Polish Films', 222–42.

42 Jan Błoński, 'Biedni Polacy patrzą na getto', *Tygodnik Powszechny* (11 January 1987), 1; 4. For a translation of Błoński's essay and the discussion it initiated in Poland, see Anthony Polonsky (ed.), *My Brother's Keeper? Recent Polish Debates on the Holocaust* (London and New York: Routledge, 1990).

43 Rigney, '*The Decalogue*: A Psychoanalytic Deadlock', 66.

44 Insdorf, *Double Lives, Second Chances*, 114. Slavoj Žižek also labels this part the 'most Hitch-cockian of all of Kieślowski's films' in *The Fright of Real Tears*, 117.

1 Tadeusz Sobolewski, 'Ponad podziałami' [interview with Krzysztof Piesiewicz], *Kino* 6 (1994), 10.
2 See my discussion in *Polish National Cinema* (Oxford and New York: Berghahn Books, 2002), 176–83. In the following five paragraphs I use some portions from that book.
3 See Krzysztof Zanussi's comment, 'Obrona kosmopolityzmu', *Kino* 2 (1992), 16–18.
4 Danusia Stok (ed.), *Kieślowski on Kieślowski* (London and Boston: Faber and Faber, 1993), 151–2.
5 Ibid., 204.
6 See Wanda Wertenstein and Jerzy Płażewski, 'Współprodukcje: hydra czy szansa', *Kino* 6 (1993), 6–9.
7 See, for example, Kazimierz Kutz's comment, 'Przestaliśmy istnieć' [fragment of a discussion: 'Co z polskim kinem?'], *Kino* 11 (1992), 21.
8 Maria Kornatowska, 'Podwójne życie Krzysztofa Kieślowskiego', in Tadeusz Lubelski (ed.), *Kino Krzysztofa Kieślowskiego* (Kraków: Universitas, 1997), 120.
9 Maria Marszałek, 'O mnie, o tobie, o wszystkich' [interview with Krzysztof Kieślowski], *Kino* 8 (1987), 8.
10 Ibid., 8.
11 For example, the video covers are graced with the pictures of female characters from Kieślowski's films in 'artfully erotic poses'. Although Zbigniew Zamachowski is in the centre of *Three Colours: White*, the video cover features Julie Delpy.
12 David Bordwell, 'The Art Cinema as a Mode of Film Practice', *Film Criticism* 4, no. 1 (1979), 56–63.
13 Steve Neale, 'Art Cinema as Institution', *Screen* 22, no. 1 (1981), 11–39.
14 Bordwell, 'The Art Cinema as a Mode of Film Practice', 56.
15 Ibid., 58.
16 Ibid., 60.
17 See Robert Self, 'Systems of Ambiguity in the Art Cinema', *Film Criticism* 4 (1979), 74–80.
18 James Winchell, 'Metaphysics of Post-Nationalism: La Double Vie de Krzysztof Kieślowski', *Contemporary French Civilization* 22, no. 2 (1998), 261.
19 Stok, *Kieślowski on Kieślowski*, 177.
20 Slavoj Žižek notices however that several recent films, for example *Hilary and Jackie* (1998, Anand Tucker), deal with the 'ethical choice between mission and life'. Tucker's film introduces two brilliant musical prodigies, Jackie and Hilary. Although later Jackie has an international career, she yearns for the apparently simpler life led by her sister who marries a fellow musician and starts a family. The film, according to Žižek, deals with the death of Jackie, who opted for 'mission', and the fate of her understanding sister, who chose 'life'. See Slavoj Žižek, *The Fright of Real Tears: Krzysztof Kieślowski between Theory and Post-Theory* (London: British Film Institute, 2001), 139.
21 For Iréne Jacob, this was a breakthrough role. Earlier she appeared only in brief episodes, for example in Louis Malle's *Au revoir les enfants* (*Goodbye Children*, 1987).
22 Aleksander Bardini (educator, actor, stage director and theatre manager) repeated his screen image known to millions of Polish television viewers. He was chiefly known for his extremely popular television programs with musically talented amateurs.
23 Stok, *Kieślowski on Kieślowski*, 7.
24 Since there are a number of (sometimes conflicting) interpretations of that scene, it is worth presenting Kieślowski's own explanation: 'I think that this tree is a simple thing. This is something that existed when she was small, when her mother was small, and something that will exist when her daughter is small. This tree is; it exists. Something permanent, certain. Art is not certain. One never knows how this is going to end. The fate of Weronika is a good example here. Love can be fulfilled or not. That person will be either worthy or not worthy of this love. There may be somebody who will exploit feelings, love and naïvety. The tree, however, will always be there. This is the place one can touch with the complete assurance that, if touched, this will be the same bark which has more or less the same shape, the same smell, and the same touch it had two hundred years ago, and will have in two hundred years. This is something

lasting, permanent and solid. It has to be touched from time to time; we have to return periodically to the place where we feel assured that something we see truly exists, that it is.' Tadeusz Szczepański, 'Drzewo, które jest' [interview with Krzysztof Kieślowski and Krzysztof Piesiewicz], *Film na Świecie* 385 (November–December 1991), 15.

25 Kieślowski originally also intended to screen a number of different versions of the ending to make the film even more puzzling. His idea, which never materialised, was to screen various endings in different movie theatres. See Stok, *Kieślowski on Kieślowski*, 187–8. The screenplay of *The Double Life of Véronique*, titled 'Chórzystka' (The Choir Singer) and published in 1990 in the Polish monthly *Dialog*, ends with a universalising metaphor. The camera portrays from outside Alexandre and Véronique together at night in an apartment. Then the camera moves toward neighboring windows, showing other people during their everyday routines, and then portrays nearby houses and streets. Krzysztof Kieślowski and Krzysztof Piesiewicz, 'Chórzystka', *Dialog* 12 (1990), 39. The idea of the final scene about Véronique returning home came from the film's cinematographer, Sławomir Idziak. See Szczepański, 'Drzewo, które jest', 15.

26 Annette Insdorf, *Double Lives, Second Chances: The Cinema of Krzysztof Kieślowski* (New York: Hyperion, 1999), 131.

27 Winchell, 'Metaphysics of Post-Nationalism', 250.

28 Stok, *Kieślowski on Kieślowski*, 185.

29 See, for example, E. T. A. Hoffman, *Tales of Hoffman*, Christopher Lazare (ed.) (New York: A. A. Wyn, 1946), 218–65; Charles Passage, *The Russian Hoffmanists* (The Hague, Mouton, 1963), 15–58.

30 Maciej Pawlicki, 'W Cannes objawienie: bracia Coen', *Film* 22 (2 June 1991), 2.

31 Stok, *Kieślowski on Kieślowski*, 189.

32 Jonathan Romney, 'The Double Life of Véronique', *Sight and Sound* 1, no. 11 (1992), 43.

33 Ibid., 43.

34 Gaylyn Studlar, 'The Double Life of Véronique', in Frank N. Magill (ed.), *Magill's Cinema Annual 1992: A Survey of the Films of 1991* (Pasadena and Englewood Cliffs: Salem Press, 1992), 120.

35 Tadeusz Lubelski, 'Podwójne życie Kieślowskiego', *Kino* 9 (1991), 5.

36 Žižek, *The Fright of Real Tears*, 137.

37 The Polish/French 'double life' of Kieślowski is stressed in the titles of some seminal texts published in Polish. For example, Maria Kornatowska, 'Podwójne życie Krzysztofa Kieślowskiego' (The Double Life of Krzysztof Kieślowski), in Tadeusz Lubelski (ed.), *Kino Krzysztofa Kieślowskiego* (Kraków: Universitas, 1997), 117–27; Tadeusz Lubelski, 'Podwójne życie Kieślowskiego' (The Double Life of Kieślowski), *Kino* 9 (1991), 2–5.

38 Lubelski, 'Podwójne życie Kieślowskiego', 5.

39 Pawlicki, 'W Cannes objawienie', 2.

40 Paul Coates, 'Metaphysical Love in Two Films by Krzysztof Kieślowski', *The Polish Review* 37, no. 3 (1992), 343.

41 Maciej Pawlicki, 'Podwójne życie Weroniki', *Film* 51/52 (20–27 December 1992), 45.

42 The reception of *The Double Life of Véronique* is discussed thoroughly by Mirosław Przylipiak in his 'Krótkie filmy, Dekalog oraz Podwójne życie Weroniki Krzysztofa Kieślowskiego w zwierciadle polskiej krytyki filmowej', *Kwartalnik Filmowy* 24, no. 84 (1998), 133–71.

43 Tadeusz Sobolewski, 'Peace and Rebellion: Some Remarks on the Creative Output of Krzysztof Kieślowski', in Ewelina Nurczyńska-Fidelska and Zbigniew Batko (eds), *Polish Cinema in Ten Takes* (Łódź: Łódzkie Towarzystwo Naukowe, 1995), 123.

44 Tony Rayns, 'Glowing in the Dark', *Sight and Sound* 4, no. 6 (1994), 10.

45 Tammy Clewell, 'The Shades of Modern Mourning in *Three Colours* Trilogy', *Literature/Film Quarterly* 28, no. 3 (2000), 203.

46 Serge Mensonge, 'Three Colours: Blue, White and Red. Kieślowski and Friends' [interviews] *Cinema Papers* 99 (1994), 32.

47 Paul Coates, '"The inner life is the only thing that interests me": a conversation with Krzysztof Kieślowski', in Paul Coates (ed.), *Lucid Dreams: The Films of Krzysztof Kieślowski* (London: Flicks Books, 1999), 170.

48 Interestingly, Polish critics almost never discuss Wajda's *A Generation*, *Kanal* and *Ashes and*

Diamonds as forming a 'war trilogy'.

49 Edward Żebrowski (b. 1935) directed a number of films including *Ocalenie* (*Deliverance*, 1972), *Szpital Przemienienia* (*The Hospital of Transfiguration*, 1979) and *W biały dzień* (*In Broad Daylight*, 1981). He is also known as the co-scriptwriter of several films directed by Krzysztof Zanussi.

50 Mensonge, '*Three Colours: Blue, White* and *Red*', 30.

51 Tadeusz Szczepański, 'Kieślowski wobec Begmana', in Lubelski, *Kino Krzysztofa Kieślowskiego*, 165.

52 Grażyna Stachówna, '*Trzy kolory*: wariacje na jeden temat', in Lubelski, *Kino Krzysztofa Kieślowskiego*, 102.

53 Geoffrey Macnab, '*Trois Couleurs: Blue* (*Three Colours: Blue*)', *Sight and Sound* 3, no. 11 (1993), 55.

54 Mariola Jankun-Dopartowa, 'Trójkolorowy transparent: Vive le chaos!', *Kino* 6 (1995), 4–7.

55 Ibid., 6.

56 Sobolewski, 'Peace and Rebellion', 135.

57 See, for example, Jacek Petrycki, 'Kiedy jeszcze lubiliśmy rejestrować świat', in Lubelski, *Kino Krzysztofa Kieślowskiego*, 177–85.

58 Stok, *Kieślowski on Kieślowski*, 215.

59 See, for example, Paul Coates, 'Kieślowski and the Antipolitics of Color: A Reading of the "Three Colors" Trilogy', *Cinema Journal* 41, no. 2 (2002), 50. Coates comments, 'most of the figures are naked or near-naked, reinforcing a sense of womblike space and vulnerability'.

60 Insdorf, *Double Lives, Second Chances*, 144.

61 Richard Rushton, 'Reading *Three Colours: Blue*', *Senses of Cinema* 10 (2000), www.sensesofcinema.com/contents/00/10/blue.html.

62 Bruce F. Kawin, *Mindscreen, Godard and First-Person Film* (Princeton: Princeton University Press, 1978).

63 Avrom Fleishman's term from his *Narrated Films: Storytelling Situations in Cinema History* (Baltimore: Johns Hopkins University Press, 1992), 173.

64 For more discussion on Peter Weir's film see the chapter 'The Days After: *Fearless*', in my book *Peter Weir: When Cultures Collide* (New York: Twayne, 1996), 121–8.

65 Macnab, '*Three Colours: Blue*', 55.

66 Tony Ryans, 'Glowing in the Dark', *Sight and Sound* 4, no. 6 (1994), 9.

67 Coates, '"The inner life is the only thing that interests me"', 172.

68 Stok, *Kieślowski on Kieślowski*, 217.

69 Geoff Andrew, *The 'Three Colours' Trilogy* (London: BFI, 1998), 38.

70 Paul Coates, 'The Sense of Ending: Reflections on Kieślowski's Trilogy', *Film Quarterly* 50, no. 2 (1996–97), 23–4.

71 Tadeusz Sobolewski, 'Równanie w dół: *Trzy kolory: Biały*' (Downwards: *Three Colours: White*), *Kino* 2 (1994), 10–11; Piotr Lis, 'Chłód' (Cold), *Kino* 6 (1994), 16; Mateusz Werner, 'Kolorowa pustka' (The Coloured Emptiness), *Film* 8 (1994), 72–3; Piotr Mucharski, 'Bez koloru' (Without Colour), *Tygodnik Powszechny* (27 March 1994), 11.

72 Philip Strick, '*Trois Couleurs: Blanc* (*Three Colours: White*)', *Sight and Sound* 4, no. 6 (1994), 63.

73 Sobolewski, 'Równanie w dół', 11.

74 Translated from idiomatic Polish: 'na własnych śmieciach' or 'na swoich śmieciach'.

75 I discuss Polish action cinema at length in a chapter on 'Polish Films with an American Accent' in my *Polish National Cinema*, 243–58.

76 Edward Kłosiński photographed Wajda's seminal films such as *Man of Marble* and *Man of Iron* (he started his career as a camera operator in 1970 on Wajda's *Birchwood*), and a number of Zanussi's films, including *Illumination* and *Camouflage*. He also worked as a cinematographer on such canonical Polish films as Feliks Falk's *Top Dog* and Janusz Zaorski's *The Mother of Kings*.

77 Emma Wilson, *Memory and Survival: The French Cinema of Krzysztof Kieślowski* (Oxford: European Humanities Research Centre, University of Oxford, 2000), 60.

78 Coates, 'The inner life', 170.

79 Alicja Helman, 'Women in Kieślowski's late films' [translated from the Polish by Paul Coates],

in Coates, *Lucid Dreams*, 124–5.

80 Tadeusz Sobolewski, 'Żyliśmy tam wszyscy' [interview with Krzysztof Kieślowski], *Kino* 7–8 (1994), 23.

81 Stok, *Kieślowski on Kieślowski*, 218.

82 Stephen Pizzello, 'Piotr Sobociński: *Red*', *American Cinematographer* 76, no. 6 (1995), 71–2. Before working with Kieślowski on *Decalogue* 3 and 9, Piotr Sobociński (the son of the distinguished Polish cinematographer Witold Sobociński) was chiefly known for his collaboration with Filip Bajon. After *Red* he worked as a cinematographer on *Ransom* (Ron Howard, 1996), *Marvin's Room* (Jerry Zaks, 1996), *Hearts in Atlantis* (Scott Hicks, 2001) and *Angel Eyes* (Luis Mandoki, 2001), among others.

83 Ibid., 70.

84 Stok, *Kieślowski on Kieślowski*, 223.

85 Dave Kehr, 'To Save the World: Kieślowski's *Three Colours* Trilogy', *Film Comment*, no. 6 (1994), 18.

86 Sobolewski, 'Peace and Rebellion', 136.

87 Piotr Wojciechowski, 'Orzeł, reszka, Kieślowski i Pan Bóg', *Film* 7 (1994), 49.

88 Kehr, 'To Save the World', 20.

AFTERWORD

1 Piotr Lis, 'Summa', *Kino* 7–8 (1994), 28.

2 Marek Hendrykowski and Mikołaj Jazdon (eds), 'Fragmenty spotkania z Krzysztofem Kieślowskim (24 February 1996)', *Kino* 5 (1996), 11–12.

3 Krzysztof Kieślowski and Krzysztof Piesiewicz, 'Raj', *Dialog* 3 (1997), 5–33.

4 Krzysztof Piesiewicz, 'Piekło', *Dialog* 5 (1997), 5–31.

5 *Silence* received the Best Director Award (for Michał Rosa) and the Best Actress Award (for Kinga Preis; shared with Ewa Kasprzyk for *Bellissima*). The main award, the Golden Lions, was given to the outstanding *Cześć Tereska* (*Hi, Tessa*, 2001), directed by Robert Gliński.

6 Konrad J. Zarębski, 'Zatrzymać się w ciszy' [interview with Krzysztof Piesiewicz], *Kino* 10 (2001), 21 and Konrad J. Zarębski, 'Ciągłość' [interview with Michał Rosa], *Kino* 10 (2001), 23.

FILMOGRAPHY

[Based on data from the films' credits and various published Polish and English sources. All films produced in Poland, unless indicated otherwise.]

1966

Tramwaj (The Tram)
35mm, black and white, short film, 5 mins
Director   Krzysztof Kieślowski
Script   Krzysztof Kieślowski
Photography   Zdzisław Kaczmarek
Art Direction   Wanda Jakubowska, Kazimierz Konrad
Production   Łódź Film School
Cast   Jerzy Braszka, Maria Janiec

Urząd (The Office)
35mm, black and white, documentary, 6 mins
Director   Krzysztof Kieślowski
Script   Krzysztof Kieślowski
Photography   Lechosław Trzęsowski
Editing   Janina Grosicka
Sound   Marta Stankiewicz
Art Direction   Jerzy Bossak, Kazimierz Karabasz, Kurt Weber
Production   Łódź Film School

1967
Koncert życzeń (Concert of Requests)
35mm, black and white, short film, 17 mins
Director   Krzysztof Kieślowski
Script   Krzysztof Kieślowski
Photography   Lechosław Trzęsowski
Editing   Janina Grosicka
Production   Łódź Film School
Cast   Jerzy Fedorowicz, Andrzej Titkow, Ewa Konarska, Waldemar
                  Korzeniowski, Roman Talarczyk, Ryszard Dembiński

1968
Zdjęcie (The Photograph)
16mm, black and white, documentary, 32 mins
Director   Krzysztof Kieślowski
Photography   Marek Jóźwiak, Wojciech Jastrzębowski
Editing   Jolanta Wilczak
Sound   Włodzimierz Wojtyś, Marek Jóźwik
Production   Polish Television

1969
Z miasta Łodzi (From the City of Łódź)
35mm, black and white, documentary, 17 mins
Director   Krzysztof Kieślowski
Script   Krzysztof Kieślowski
Photography   Janusz Kreczmarski, Piotr Kwiatkowski, Stanisław Niedbalski
Editing   Elżbieta Kurkowska, Lidia Zonn
Sound   Krystyna Pohorecka, Ryszard Sulewski
Production   WFD (Documentary Film Production Studio)

1970
Byłem żołnierzem (I Was a Soldier)
35mm, black and white, documentary, 16 mins
Director   Krzysztof Kieślowski
Script   Krzysztof Kieślowski and Ryszard Zgórecki
Photography   Stanisław Niedbalski
Editing   Walentyna Wojciechowska
Sound   Jan Strojecki
Production   Czołówka Film Studio

Fabryka (Factory)
35mm, black and white, documentary, 17 mins
Director   Krzysztof Kieślowski
Photography   Stanisław Niedbalski, Jacek Tworek
Editing   Maria Leszczyńska
Sound   Małgorzata Jaworska
Production   WFD (Documentary Film Production Studio)

1971
Przed rajdem (Before the Rally)
35mm, black and white/colour, documentary, 15 mins
Director   Krzysztof Kieślowski
Script   Krzysztof Kieślowski
Photography   Piotr Kwiatkowski, Jacek Petrycki
Editing   Lidia Zonn
Sound   Małgorzata Jaworska
Production   WFD (Documentary Film Production Studio)

1972

Refren (Refrain)
35mm, black and white, documentary, 10 mins
Director   Krzysztof Kieślowski
Script   Krzysztof Kieślowski
Photography   Witold Stok
Editing   Maryla Czolnik
Sound   Małgorzata Jaworska, Michał Żarnecki
Production   WFD (Documentary Film Production Studio)

Między Wrocławiem a Zieloną Górą (Between Wrocław and Zielona Góra)
35mm, colour, promotional documentary, 19 mins
Director   Krzysztof Kieślowski
Photography   Jacek Petrycki
Editing   Lidia Zonn
Sound   Andrzej Bohdanowicz
Production   WFD (Documentary Film Production Studio); commissioned by the Lubin
                  Copper Mine

Podstawy BHP w kopalni miedzi (The Principles of Safety and Hygiene in a Copper Mine)
35mm, colour, instructional documentary, 21 mins
Director   Krzysztof Kieślowski
Photography   Jacek Petrycki
Editor   Lidia Zonn
Sound   Andrzej Bohdanowicz
Production   WFD (Documentary Film Production Studio); commissioned by the Lubin
                  Copper Mine

Robotnicy '71: nic o nas bez nas (Workers '71: Nothing About Us Without Us)
16mm, black and white, documentary, 47 mins
Directors   Krzysztof Kieślowski, Tomasz Zygadło, Wojciech Wiszniewski, Paweł
                  Kędzierski, Tadeusz Walendowski
Photography   Witold Stok, Stanisław Mroziuk, Jacek Petrycki
Sound   Jacek Szymański, Alina Hojnacka
Editing   Lidia Zonn, Maryla Czolnik, Joanna Dorożyńska, Daniela Cieplińska
Production   WFD (Documentary Film Production Studio)

1973

Murarz (Bricklayer, released in 1981)
35mm, black and white, documentary, 18 mins
Director   Krzysztof Kieślowski
Photography   Witold Stok
Editing   Lidia Zonn
Sound   Małgorzata Jaworska
Production   WFD (Documentary Film Production Studio)

Przejście podziemne (Pedestrian Subway)
35mm, black and white, short film, 30 mins
Director   Krzysztof Kieślowski
Script   Krzysztof Kieślowski and Ireneusz Iredyński
Photography   Sławomir Idziak
Editing   Elżbieta Kurkowska
Sound   Małgorzata Jaworska
Production   Tor film studio
Cast   Teresa Budzisz-Krzyżanowska (Lena), Andrzej Seweryn (Michał),
                  Anna Jaraczówna, Zygmunt Maciejewski, Janusz Skalski, Jan Orsza-
                  Łukaszewicz

1974

Prześwietlenie (X-Ray)
35mm, colour, documentary, 13 mins
Director   Krzysztof Kieślowski
Photography   Jacek Petrycki
Editing   Lidia Zonn
Sound   Michał Żarnecki
Production   WFD (Documentary Film Production Studio)

Pierwsza miłość (First Love)
16mm, colour, documentary, 30 mins
Director   Krzysztof Kieślowski
Photography   Jacek Petrycki
Editing   Lidia Zonn
Sound   Małgorzata Jaworska and Michał Żarnecki
Production   Polish Television
Awards   Grand Prix ('Złoty Lajkonik') at the 1974 National Short Film Festival in
                      Kraców; Special Jury Award at the 1974 International Short Film Festival
                      in Kraców

1975

Życiorys (Curriculum Vitae)
35mm, black and white, docudrama, 45 mins
Director   Krzysztof Kieślowski
Script   Krzysztof Kieślowski, Janusz Fastyn
Photography   Jacek Petrycki, Tadeusz Rusinek
Editing   Lidia Zonn
Sound   Spas Christow
Production   WFD (Documentary Film Production Studio)

Personel (Personnel, aka Personel Subsidiaries)
16mm, colour, drama 72 mins
Director   Krzysztof Kieślowski
Script   Krzysztof Kieślowski
Photography   Witold Stok
Editing   Lidia Zonn
Sound   Michał Żarnecki
Set Design   Tadeusz Kosarewicz
Production   Tor film studio, Polish Television
Cast   Juliusz Machulski (Romek Januchta), Michał Tarkowski (Sowa), Tomasz
                      Lengren (Romek), Włodzimierz Boruński (technical director), Irena
                      Lorentowicz (designer), Andrzej Siedlecki (opera singer), Tomasz Zygadło
                      (party activist), Janusz Skalski (head of department), Krystyna Wachełko
                      (girl on the train), Ludwik Mika (opera director), Helena Kowalczyk
                      (Romek's aunt, not credited), Wilhelm Kłonowski, Jan Torończak, Jan
                      Zieliński, Edward Ciosek, Henryk Sawicki, Krzysztof Sitarski, Waldemar
                      Karst
Awards   Award of the Catholic Film Mission at the 1975 Mannheim Film Festival;
                      Grand Prix in the category of television productions and Journalists Award
                      at the 1975 Festival of Polish Films in Gdańsk

1976

Szpital (Hospital)
35mm, black and white, documentary, 21 mins
Director   Krzysztof Kieślowski
Photography   Jacek Petrycki
Editing   Lidia Zonn

Sound	Michał Żarnecki, Małgorzata Moszczeńska
Production	WFD (Documentary Film Production Studio)
Awards	Grand Prix ('Złoty Smok') at the 1977 International Short Film Festival in Kraców

Blizna (*The Scar*)
35mm, colour, drama, 104 mins

Director	Krzysztof Kieślowski
Script	Krzysztof Kieślowski. Based on Romuald Karaś's story
Photography	Sławomir Idziak
Editing	Krystyna Górnicka
Set Design	Andrzej Płocki
Music	Stanisław Radwan
Sound	Michał Żarnecki
Production	Tor film studio
Cast	Franciszek Pieczka (director Stefan Bednarz), Jerzy Stuhr (Bednarz's assistant), Mariusz Dmochowski (head of the local council), Jan Skotnicki (Stanisław Lech), Stanisław Igar (minister), Halina Winiarska (Bednarz's wife), Joanna Orzeszkowska (Ewa, Bednarz's daughter), Michał Tarkowski (television journalist), Agnieszka Holland (Bednarz's secretary), Stanisław Michalski, Asia Lamtiugina, Małgorzata Leśniewska, Andrzej Skupień, Ryszard Bacciarelli, Henryk Hunko, Tomasz Zygadło (not credited)
Awards	Special Jury Award and Best Actor Award for Franciszek Pieczka at the 1976 Festival of Polish Films in Gdańsk

Klaps (*Slate*)
35mm, colour, compilation film (out-takes from *The Scar*), 6 mins

Director	Krzysztof Kieślowski
Photography	Sławomir Idziak
Editing	Eugeniusz Dmitroca
Sound	Michał Żarnecki

Spokój (*The Calm*, released in 1980)
16mm, colour, drama, 82 mins

Director	Krzysztof Kieślowski
Script	Krzysztof Kieślowski. Based on Lech Borski's story
Dialogue	Krzysztof Kieślowski, Jerzy Stuhr
Photography	Jacek Petrycki
Editing	Maryla Szymańska
Set Design	Rafał Waltenberger
Sound	Wiesław Jurgała
Music	Piotr Figiel
Production	Polish Television, Poltel
Cast	Jerzy Stuhr (Antoni Gralak), Danuta Ruksza (wife), Izabella Olszewska (landlady), Jerzy Trela (manager), Jerzy Fedorowicz, Michał Szulkiewicz, Elżbieta Karkoszka, Jan Niziński, Feliks Szajnert, Stefan Mienicki, Ryszard Palik, Marian Cebulski, Edward Dobrzański, Jan Adamski
Awards	Special Award at the Festival of Polish Films in Gdańsk in 1981

1977
Nie wiem (*I Don't Know*, released in 1981)
35mm, black and white, documentary, 46 mins

Director	Krzysztof Kieślowski
Script	Krzysztof Kieślowski
Photography	Jacek Petrycki
Editing	Lidia Zonn
Sound	Michał Żarnecki
Production	WFD (Documentary Film Production Studio)

Z punktu widzenia nocnego portiera (*From the Point of View of the Night Porter*)
35mm, colour, documentary, 17 mins
Director   Krzysztof Kieślowski
Script   Krzysztof Kieślowski
Photography   Witold Stok
Editor   Lidia Zonn
Sound   Wiesława Dembińska, Michał Żarnecki
Music   Wojciech Kilar
Production   WFD (Documentary Film Production Studio)
Awards   Grand Prix ('Złoty Lajkonik') at the 1979 National Short Film Festival in
                Kraców; FIPRESCI Award at the 1979 International Short Film Festival in
                Kraców; Jury Prize at the 1979 International Short and Documentary Film
                Festival in Lille

1978
Siedem kobiet w różnym wieku (*Seven Women of Different Ages*)
16mm, black and white, documentary, 16 mins
Director   Krzysztof Kieślowski
Photography   Witold Stok
Editing   Alina Siemińska, Lidia Zonn
Sound   Michał Żarnecki
Production   WFD (Documentary Film Production Studio)
Awards   Grand Prix ('Złoty Lajkonik') at the 1979 National Short Film Festival in
                Kraców (jointly with *From the Point of View of the Night Porter*)

1979
Amator (*Camera Buff*)
35mm, colour, feature, 117 mins
Director   Krzysztof Kieślowski
Script   Krzysztof Kieślowski
Dialogue   Krzysztof Kieślowski and Jerzy Stuhr
Photography   Jacek Petrycki
Editing   Halina Nawrocka
Set Design   Rafał Waltenberger
Sound   Michał Żarnecki
Music   Krzysztof Knittel
Production   Tor film studio
Cast   Jerzy Stuhr (Filip Mosz), Małgorzata Ząbkowska (Irena Mosz), Tadeusz
                Bradecki (Witek Jachowicz, Filip's friend), Jerzy Nowak (Stanisław
                Osuch), Ewa Pokas (Anna Włodarczyk), Stefan Czyżewski (Factory
                Manager Halski), Marek Litewka (Piotr Krawczyk), Krzysztof Zanussi
                (himself), Andrzej Jurga (himself), Bogusław Sobczuk (Kędzierski,
                television official), Tadeusz Sobolewski (himself, not credited), Tadeusz
                Huk (physician), Teresa Szmigielówna (herself), Alicja Bienicewicz,
                Tadeusz Rzepka, Andrzej Warchał, Aleksandra Kisielewska, Roman
                Stankiewicz, Jolanta Brzezińska, Jacek Turalik
Awards   Grand Prix at the 1979 Festival of Polish Films in Gdańsk ('Gdańsk
                Golden Lions'); Grand Prix at the 1980 Chicago Film Festival ('Golden
                Hugo'); Gold Medal and FIPRESCI Award at the 1979 Moscow Film
                Festival; International Evangelical Prize at the 1980 Berlin Film Festival

1980
Dworzec (*Station*)
35mm, black and white, documentary, 13 mins
Director   Krzysztof Kieślowski
Photography   Witold Stok
Editing   Lidia Zonn

| Sound | Michał Żarnecki |
| Production | WFD (Documentary Film Production Studio) |

Gadające głowy (*Talking Heads*)
35mm, black and white, documentary, 16 mins
Director	Krzysztof Kieślowski
Photography	Jacek Petrycki, Piotr Kwiatkowski
Editing	Alina Siemińska
Sound	Michał Żarnecki
Production	WFD (Documentary Film Production Studio)

1981
Przypadek (*Blind Chance*, released in 1987)
35mm, colour, feature, 122 mins
Director	Krzysztof Kieślowski
Script	Krzysztof Kieślowski
Photography	Krzysztof Pakulski
Editing	Elżbieta Kurkowska
Set Design	Rafał Waltenberger
Sound	Michał Żarnecki
Music	Wojciech Kilar
Production	Tor film studio
Cast	Bogusław Linda (Witek Długosz), Tadeusz Łomnicki (Werner), Bogusława Pawelec (Czuszka), Zbigniew Zapasiewicz (Adam), Jacek Borkowski (Marek), Adam Ferency (Father Stefan), Jacek Sas-Uhrynowski (Daniel), Marzena Trybała (Werka), Irena Byrska (Aunt), Monika Goździk (Olga), Zbigniew Hübner (dean), Jerzy Stuhr (party activist, not credited), Bogdan Niewinowski (Witek's father, not credited), Stefania Iwińska (oppositional activist, not credited), Jerzy Moes (secret police officer), Borys Marynowski (Jacek), Krzysztof Kalczyński (Werka's husband), Bohdan Ejmont (not credited), Ludwik Pak, Edward Rauch, Krzysztof Zaleski, Mirosław Siedler
Awards	Best Screenplay Award (Kieślowski) and Best Actor Award (Linda) at the 1987 Festival of Polish Films in Gdynia

Krótki dzień pracy (*Short Working Day*, TV premiere in 1996)
35mm, colour, feature, 79 mins
Director	Krzysztof Kieślowski
Script	Krzysztof Kieślowski, Hanna Krall. Based on Krall's report
Photography	Krzysztof Pakulski
Editing	Elżbieta Kurkowska
Set Design	Rafał Waltenberger
Sound	Michał Żarnecki
Music	Jan Kanty Pawluśkiewicz
Production	Tor film studio for Polish Television
Cast	Wacław Ulewicz (First Party Secretary), Tadeusz Bartosik (Deputy Party Secretary), Lech Grzmociński (commander of militia), Elżbieta Kijowska (secretary), Marek Kępiński (party bureaucrat), Paweł Nowisz (Henio, driver), Michał Szewczyk (militia captain, not credited), Mirosław Siedler (KOR activist), Barbara Dziekan, Marian Gańcza, Wojciech Pilarski, Zbigniew Bielski, Jan Konieczny, Tadeusz Płuciennik.

1985
Bez końca (*No End*)
35 mm, colour, feature, 197 mins
| Director | Krzysztof Kieślowski |
| Script | Krzysztof Kieślowski |

Photography	Jacek Petrycki
Editing	Krystyna Rutkowska
Sound	Michał Żarnecki
Music	Zbigniew Preisner
Production	Tor film studio
Cast	Grażyna Szapołowska (Urszula Zyro), Jerzy Radziwiłłowicz (Antoni Zyro), Aleksander Bardini (lawyer Labrador), Maria Pakulnis (Joanna Stach), Artur Barciś (Dariusz Stach), Michał Bajor (Miecio, apprentice lawyer), Marek Kondrat (Tomek, Zyro's friend), Tadeusz Bradecki (hypnotist), Daniel Webb (American tourist), Krzysztof Krzemiński (Jacek Zyro), Jerzy Kamas (judge), Jan Tesarz (Joanna's father), Marzena Trybała (Marta, Zyro's friend), Adam Ferency ('Rumcajs'), Andrzej Szalawski (lawyer), Elżbieta Kilarska (Antek's mother), Hanna Dunowska-Hunek (Justyna), Katarzyna Figura (hypnotist's secretary, not credited)

1988

Siedem dni w tygodniu (Seven Days a Week)
35mm, colour, documentary, 18 mins

Director	Krzysztof Kieślowski
Photography	Jacek Petrycki
Editing	Dorota Warduszkiewicz
Sound	Michał Żarnecki
Production	City Life Foundation, Rotterdam, The Netherlands

Krótki film o zabijaniu (A Short Film About Killing)
35mm, colour, feature, 85 mins

Director	Krzysztof Kieślowski
Script	Krzysztof Kieślowski, Krzysztof Piesiewicz
Photography	Sławomir Idziak
Editing	Ewa Smal
Set Design	Halina Dobrowolska
Sound	Małgorzata Jaworska
Music	Zbigniew Preisner
Production	Tor film studio, Polish Television
Cast	Mirosław Baka (Jacek Lazar), Krzysztof Globisz (Piotr Balicki), Jan Tesarz (taxi driver), Aleksander Bednarz (executioner), Zdzisław Tobiasz (judge), Jerzy Zass (prison warden), Maciej Maciejewski (prosecutor), Artur Barciś (young man), Zbigniew Zapasiewicz (bar examiner), Barbara Dziekan (cinema theatre employee), Krystyna Janda (Dorota), Olgierd Łukaszewicz (Andrzej), Maciej Szary, Zbigniew Borek, Iwona Głębicka, Elżbieta Helman, Zdzisław Rychter, Andrzej Masztalerz, Władysław Byrdy (assistant to the executioner)
Awards	Grand Prix ('Gdańsk Golden Lions') at the 1988 Festival of Polish Films in Gdańsk (jointly with *A Short Film About Love*); Best European Film: Féliks '88; Jury Award and FIPRESCI award at the 1988 Cannes Film Festival

Krótki film o miłości (A Short Film About Love)
35mm, colour, feature, 87 mins

Director	Krzysztof Kieślowski
Script	Krzysztof Kieślowski, Krzysztof Piesiewicz
Photography	Witold Adamek
Editing	Ewa Smal
Set Designer	Halina Dobrowolska
Sound	Nikodem Wołk-Łaniewski
Music	Zbigniew Preisner
Production	Tor film studio

Cast	Olaf Lubaszenko (Tomek), Grażyna Szapołowska (Magda), Stefania Iwińska (Tomek's landlady), Stanisław Gawlik (postman), Artur Barciś (elegant young man), Piotr Machalica (Roman), Rafał Imbro, Jan Piechociński, Małgorzata Rożniatowska (post office head), Jarosława Michalewska (cashier), Mirosława Chojnacka, Krzysztof Koperski
Awards	Grand Prix ('Gdańsk Golden Lions') at the 1988 Festival of Polish Films in Gdańsk (jointly with *A Short Film About Killing*; also Best Actress award for Szapołowska, Best Supporting Actress for Iwińska, and 'Silver Lion' for screenplay for Kieślowski and Piesiewicz at the same festival); Special Jury Award and FIPRESCI award at the 1988 San Sebastian Film Festival; Best Director at the 1989 'Stars of Tomorrow' Festival in Geneva

Dekalog 1 (Decalogue 1)
35mm, colour, TV drama, 53 mins

Director	Krzysztof Kieślowski
Script	Krzysztof Kieślowski, Krzysztof Piesiewicz
Photography	Wiesław Zdort
Editing	Ewa Smal
Set Designer	Halina Dobrowolska
Sound	Małgorzata Jaworska
Music	Zbigniew Preisner
Production	Ryszard Chutkowski for Polish Television
Cast	Henryk Baranowski (Krzysztof), Wojciech Klata (Paweł), Maja Komorowska (Aunt Irena), Maria Gładkowska (English teacher), Ewa Kania (Ewa), Artur Barciś (the mysterious man), Maciej Borniński, Agnieszka Brustman (chess master), Aleksandra Kisielewska, Aleksandra Majsiuk (Ola), Magda Sroga-Mikołajczyk (journalist), Anna Smal-Romańska, Maciej Sławiński (director), Piotr Wyrzykowski

Dekalog 2 (Decalogue 2)
35mm, colour, TV drama, 58 mins

Director	Krzysztof Kieślowski
Script	Krzysztof Kieślowski, Krzysztof Piesiewicz
Photography	Edward Kłosiński
Editing	Ewa Smal
Set Designer	Halina Dobrowolska
Sound	Małgorzata Jaworska
Music	Zbigniew Preisner
Production	Ryszard Chutkowski for Polish Television
Cast	Krystyna Janda (Dorota Geller), Aleksander Bardini (chief surgeon), Olgierd Łukaszewicz (Andrzej Geller), Artur Barciś (hospital worker), Stanisław Gawlik (postman), Krzysztof Kumor (gynaecologist), Maciej Szary, Krystyna Bigelmajer (secretary), Jerzy Fedorowicz (Janek), Ewa Ekwińska (Ms. Basia), Piotr Siejka (physician), Piotr Fronczewski (the voice of Dorota's lover)

Dekalog 3 (Decalogue 3)
35mm, colour, TV drama, 55 mins

Director	Krzysztof Kieślowski
Script	Krzysztof Kieślowski, Krzysztof Piesiewicz
Photography	Piotr Sobociński
Editing	Ewa Smal
Set Designer	Halina Dobrowolska
Sound	Nikodem Wołk-Łaniewski
Music	Zbigniew Preisner
Production	Ryszard Chutkowski for Polish Television
Cast	Daniel Olbrychski (Janusz), Maria Pakulnis (Ewa), Joanna Szczepkowska

(Janusz's wife), Artur Barciś (tram driver), Krystyna Drochocka (aunt), Dorota Stalińska (train station surveillant), Krzysztof Kumor (physician), Henryk Baranowski (Krzysztof), Jacek Kałucki, Zygmunt Fok, Maria Krawczyk, Jerzy Zygmunt Nowak, Piotr Rzymyszkiewicz, Włodzimierz Rzeczycki

Dekalog 4 (Decalogue 4)
35mm, colour, TV drama, 55 mins
Director   Krzysztof Kieślowski
Script   Krzysztof Kieślowski, Krzysztof Piesiewicz
Photography   Krzysztof Pakulski
Editing   Ewa Smal
Set Designer   Halina Dobrowolska
Sound   Małgorzata Jaworska
Music   Zbigniew Preisner
Production   Ryszard Chutkowski for Polish Television
Cast   Adrianna Biedrzyńska (Anka), Janusz Gajos (Michał), Artur Barciś (man with a kayak), Adam Hanuszkiewicz (drama professor), Aleksander Bardini (chief surgeon), Jan Tesarz (taxi driver), Andrzej Blumenfeld (Michał's friend), Igor Śmiałowski, Tomasz Kozłowicz (Jarek), Elżbieta Kilarska (Jarek's mother), Helena Norowicz

Dekalog 5 (Decalogue 5)
35mm, colour, TV drama, 57 mins
Television version of *A Short Film About Killing*

Dekalog 6 (Decalogue 6)
35mm, colour, TV drama, 58 mins
Television version of *A Short Film About Love*

Dekalog 7 (Decalogue 7)
35mm, colour, TV drama, 55 mins
Director   Krzysztof Kieślowski
Script   Krzysztof Kieślowski, Krzysztof Piesiewicz
Photography   Dariusz Kuc
Editing   Ewa Smal
Set Designer   Halina Dobrowolska
Sound   Nikodem Wołk-Łaniewski
Music   Zbigniew Preisner
Production   Ryszard Chutkowski for Polish Television
Cast   Anna Polony (Ewa), Maja Barełkowska (Majka), Bogusław Linda (Wojtek), Władysław Kowalski (Stefan), Katarzyna Piwowarczyk (Ania), Bożena Dykiel (railway clerk), Stefania Błońska, Dariusz Jabłoński, Artur Barciś (young man), Jan Mayzel (Grzegorz), Mirosława Maludzińska, Ewa Radzikowska, Wanda Wróblewska

Dekalog 8 (Decalogue 8)
35mm, colour, TV drama, 55 mins
Director   Krzysztof Kieślowski
Script   Krzysztof Kieślowski, Krzysztof Piesiewicz
Photography   Andrzej Jaroszewicz
Editing   Ewa Smal
Set Designer   Halina Dobrowolska
Sound   Wiesława Dembińska
Music   Zbigniew Preisner
Production   Ryszard Chutkowski for Polish Television
Cast   Maria Kościałkowska (Zofia), Teresa Marczewska (Elżbieta), Artur Barciś

(young man at the lecture), Marian Opania (dean), Bronisław Pawlik (Zofia's neighbour), Tadeusz Łomnicki (tailor), Wojciech Asiński (student), Marek Kępiński, Janusz Mond, Krzysztof Rojek, Ewa Skibińska, Wojciech Sanejko, Jerzy Schejbal, Jacek Strzemżalski, Anna Zagórska

Dekalog 9 (Decalogue 9)
35mm, colour, TV drama, 58 mins
Director   Krzysztof Kieślowski
Script   Krzysztof Kieślowski, Krzysztof Piesiewicz
Photography   Piotr Sobociński
Editing   Ewa Smal
Set Designer   Halina Dobrowolska
Sound   Nikodem Wołk-Łaniewski
Music   Zbigniew Preisner
Production   Ryszard Chutkowski for Polish Television
Cast   Ewa Błaszczyk (Hanka), Piotr Machalica (Roman), Jan Jankowski
                    (Mariusz), Artur Barciś (cyclist), Jerzy Trela (Mikołaj), Jolanta Piętek-
                    Górecka (Ola), Katarzyna Piwowarczyk (Ania), Małgorzata Boratyńska,
                    Renata Berger, Janusz Cywiński, Jolanta Cichoń, Dariusz Przychoda

Dekalog 10 (Decalogue 10)
35mm, colour, TV drama, 57 mins
Director   Krzysztof Kieślowski
Script   Krzysztof Kieślowski, Krzysztof Piesiewicz
Photography   Jacek Bławut
Editing   Ewa Smal
Set Designer   Halina Dobrowolska
Sound   Nikodem Wołk-Łaniewski
Music   Zbigniew Preisner
Production   Ryszard Chutkowski for Polish Television
Cast   Jerzy Stuhr (Jerzy), Zbigniew Zamachowski (Artur), Henryk Bista
                     (shopkeeper), Maciej Stuhr (Piotrek), Cezary Harasimowicz (police
                     officer), Jerzy Turek (stamp collector), Olaf Lubaszenko (Tomek), Elżbieta
                     Panas (Jerzy's wife), Anna Gornostaj, Henryk Majcherek (stamp collector),
                     Grzegorz Warchoł (Bromski), Dariusz Kozakiewicz

1991
Podwójne życie Weroniki/La Double Vie de Véronique (The Double Life of Véronique)
35mm, colour, feature, 98 mins (France/Poland)
Director   Krzysztof Kieślowski
Script   Krzysztof Kieślowski, Krzysztof Piesiewicz
Photography   Sławomir Idziak
Editing   Jacques Witta
Set Designer   Patrice Mercier
Sound   Edith Vassard, Michèle Catonne
Music   Zbigniew Preisner
Production   Leonardo de la Fuente; Tor film studio, Sideral Productions, Canal Plus
Cast   Irène Jacob (Weronika/Véronique) [dubbed into Polish by Anna
                     Gornostaj], Philippe Volter (Alexandre Fabbri), Aleksander Bardini
                     (orchestra conductor), Władysław Kowalski (Weronika's father), Jerzy
                     Gudejko (Antek), Halina Gryglaszewska (aunt), Kalina Jędrusik (choir
                     conductor), Sandrine Dumas (Catherine), Louis Ducreus (professor),
                     Claude Duneton (Véronique's father), Lorraine Evanoff (Claude),
                     Guillaume de Tonquedoc (Serge), Gilles Gaston-Dreyfus (Jean-Pierre),
                     Thierry de Carbonnieres (professor), Chantal Neuwirth (receptionist),
                     Alain Frerot (postman), Bogusława Szubert, Jan Sterniński, Youssef
                     Hamid, Philippe Campos, Jacques Potin, Nicole Pinaud, Beat Malczewska,

	Barbara Szałapak, Jacek Wójcicki
Awards	FIPRESCI award, Ecumenical Jury Prize and Best Actress award for Irène Jacob at the 1991 Cannes Film Festival

1993

Trois couleurs: bleu (Three Colours: Blue)
35mm, colour, feature, 98 mins (France/Poland)

Director	Krzysztof Kieślowski
Script	Krzysztof Kieślowski, Krzysztof Piesiewicz
Photography	Sławomir Idziak
Editing	Jacques Witta
Set Designer	Claude Lenoir
Sound	Jean-Claude Laureux, Claire Bez, Bertrand Lanclos
Music	Zbigniew Preisner
Production	Marin Karmitz; MK2 SA/CED Productions, France 3 Cinema, CAB Productions, Tor film studio
Cast	Juliette Binoche (Julie Vignon), Benôit Régent (Olivier), Florence Pernel (Sandrine), Charlotte Véry (Lucille), Hélene Vincent (journalist), Emmanuelle Riva (mother), Philippe Volter (real estate agent), Claude Duneton (doctor), Hugues Quester (Patrice), Jacek Ostaszewski (the flautist), Florence Vignon (copyist), Yann Regouet (Antoine), Zbigniew Zamachowski (Karol, Karol), Julie Delpy (Dominique), Isabelle Sadoyan (maid), Pierre Forget (gardener), Daniel Martin, Catherine Therouenne, Alain Ollivier, Philippe Manesse, Idit Cebula, Jacques Disses
Awards	Golden Lion at the 1993 Venice Film Festival

1994

Trois couleurs: blanc (Three Colours: White)
35mm, colour, feature, 92 mins (France/Poland)

Director	Krzysztof Kieślowski
Script	Krzysztof Kieślowski, Krzysztof Piesiewicz
Photography	Edward Kłosiński
Editing	Urszula Lesiak
Set Designer	Claude Lenoir
Sound	Jean-Claude Laureux
Music	Zbigniew Preisner
Production	Marin Karmitz; France 3 Cinema, MK2 Productions, Film Studio Tor, CAB Productions, Canal+
Cast	Zbigniew Zamachowski (Karol Karol), Julie Delpy (Dominique Vidal), Janusz Gajos (Mikołaj), Jerzy Stuhr (Jurek), Cezary Pazura (businessman), Grzegorz Warchoł (businessman), Jerzy Nowak (farmer), Aleksander Bardini (lawyer), Jerzy Trela (Bronek, Karol's driver), Cezary Harasim-owicz (police officer), Michel Lisowski (interpreter), Marzena Trybała (real estate agent), Teresa Budzisz-Krzyżanowska (Ms. Jadwiga), Piotr Machalica, Philippe Morier-Genoud (French judge), Barbara Dziekan (Ms. Ewa), Yannick Evely (subway ticket vendor), Francis Coffinet (bank clerk), Jacques Disses (Dominique's lawyer), Krystyna Bigelmajer, Stan Latek, Jerzy Dominik, Zdzisław Rychter, Juliette Binoche
Awards	Silver Bear at the 1994 Berlin Film Festival

Trois couleurs: rouge (Three Colours: Red)
35mm, colour, feature, 99 mins (France-Poland-Switzerland)

Director	Krzysztof Kieślowski
Script	Krzysztof Kieślowski, Krzysztof Piesiewicz
Photography	Piotr Sobociński
Editing	Jacques Witta
Set Designer	Claude Lenoir

Sound	Jean-Claude Laureux
Music	Zbigniew Preisner
Production	Marin Karmitz; France 3 Cinema, MK2 Productions, Film Studio Tor, CAB Productions, CanalPlus
Cast	Irène Jacob (Valentine Dussaut), Jean-Louis Trintignant (Judge Joseph Kern), Jean-Pierre Lorit (Auguste Bruner), Frédérique Feder (Karin), Samuel Lebihan (photographer), Marion Stalens (veterinary surgeon), Teco Celio (barman), Bernard Escalon (record dealer), Jean Schlegel (neighbour), Zbigniew Zamachowski (Karol Karol), Julie Delpy (Dominique), Juliette Binoche (Julie), Elżbieta Jasińska, Paul Vermeulen, Jean-Marie Daunas, Roland Carey
Awards	Three Academy Award nominations (photography, script, direction); four BAFTA nominations, including direction and script); LA and New York Critics' Circle Awards for Best Foreign Film in 1994; Grand Prix at the 1994 Vancouver Film Festival

BIBLIOGRAPHY

The following bibliography lists only the most important sources, particularly those published in English and Polish in recent years. An excellent, almost forty-page, detailed bibliography is compiled by Paul Coates in his editorial work, *Lucid Dreams: The Films of Krzysztof Kieślowski*.

Films on Kieślowski

Wierzbicki, Krzysztof. *I'm So-So*. 1995 (television film, Denmark, 55 minutes).
____ *Kieślowski i jego Amator*. 1999 (television film, Poland, 25 minutes).

Screenplays by Kieślowski

Kieślowski, Krzysztof. 'Amator'. *Dialog 4* (1978), 84–105.
____ *Duże zwierzę. Scenariusz na podstawie opowiadania Kazimierza Orłosia Wielbłąd*. Introduction and editing by Jerzy Stuhr. Kraków: Znak, 2000.
____ 'Przypadek'. *Dialog 5* (1981), 7–25.
____ *Przypadek i inne teksty* [edited by Hanna Krall]. Kraków: Znak, 1998 [contains screenplays of *Personnel*, *Calm*, *Camera Buff* and *Blind Chance*]
____ 'Spokój'. *Dialog 4* (1977), 34–52.
Kieślowski, Krzysztof and Hanna Krall. 'Widok z okna na pierwszym piętrze' [screenplay of *Short Working Day*]. *Dialog 7* (1981), 5–21.
Kieślowski, Krzysztof and Krzysztof Piesiewicz. *Decalogue: The Ten Commandments* [translated by Phil Cavendish and Suzannah Bluh]. London: Faber and Faber, 1991.
____ 'Chórzystka' [screenplay of *The Double Life of Véronique*]. *Dialog 12* (1990), 5–39.
____ 'Raj'. *Dialog 3* (1997), 5–33.
____ *Three Colours Trilogy: Blue, White, Red* [translated by Danusia Stok]. London: Faber and Faber, 1998.

Books on Kieślowski

Amiel, Vincent. *Kieślowski*. Paris: Rivages/Cinéma, 1995.

____ (ed.) *Krzysztof Kieślowski*. Paris: Editions Jean-Michèle Place, 1997.

Andrew, Geoff. *The 'Three Colours' Trilogy*. London: British Film Institute, 1998.

Campan, Véronique. *Dix brèves histoires d'image: Le Décalogue de Krzysztof Kieślowski*. Paris: Presses de la Sorbonne Nouvelles, 1993.

Carluccio, Giulia, Sara Cortelazzo and Dario Tomasi (eds) *Krzysztof Kieślowski*. Turin: Scriptorium, 1995.

Coates, Paul (ed.) *Lucid Dreams: The Films of Krzysztof Kieślowski*. London: Flicks Books, 1999.

Furdal Małgorzata and Roberto Turigliatto (eds) *Kieślowski*. Torino: Museo Nazionale del Cinema, 1989.

Garbowski, Christopher. *Krzysztof Kieślowski's Decalogue Series: The Problem of the Protagonists and Their Self-Transcendance* [sic]. Boulder: East European Monographs, 1996 [distributed by Columbia University Press in New York].

Insdorf, Annette. *Double Lives, Second Chances: The Cinema of Krzysztof Kieślowski*. New York: Hyperion, 1999.

Jazdon, Mikołaj. *Dokumenty Kieślowskiego*. Poznań: Wydawnictwo Poznańskie, 2002.

Lubelski, Tadeusz (ed.) *Kino Krzysztofa Kieślowskiego*. Kraków: Universitas, 1997.

Maurer, Monika. *Krzysztof Kieślowski* (The Pocket Essential). North Pomfret: Trafalgar Square Publishing, 2000.

Murri, Serafino. *Krzysztof Kieślowski*. Rome: Il Castoro Cinema Press, 1996.

Pagnon, Gérard. *L'Itineraire de Krzysztof Kieślowski* [Etudes Cinematographiques] Paris: 1994.

Stok, Danusia (ed. and trans.) *Kieślowski on Kieślowski*. London, Boston: Faber and Faber, 1993.

Wilson, Emma. *Memory and Survival: The French Cinema of Krzysztof Kieślowski*. Oxford: European Humanities Research Centre, University of Oxford, 2000.

Zawiśliński, Stanisław (ed.) *Kieślowski bez końca*. Warsaw: Skorpion, 1994.

____ *Kieślowski* [photo album]. Warsaw: Skorpion, 1998.

Žižek, Slavoj. *The Fright of Real Tears: Krzysztof Kieślowski between Theory and Post-Theory*. London: British Film Institute, 2001.

Books with References to Kieślowski

Bren, Frank. *World Cinema 1: Poland*. London: Flicks Books, 1986.

Dabert, Dobrochna. *Kino moralnego niepokoju: Wokół wybranych problemów poetyki i etyki*. Poznań: Wydawnictwo Naukowe Uniwersytetu im. Adama Mickiewicza, 2003.

Falkowska, Janina and Marek Haltof (eds) *The New Polish Cinema*. London: Flicks Books, 2003.

Haltof Marek. *Polish National Cinema*. New York/Oxford: Berghahn Books, 2002.

Hendrykowska, Małgorzata. *Kronika kinematografii polskiej 1895–1997*. Poznań: Ars Nova, 1999.

Iordanova, Dina. *Cinema of the Other Europe: The Industry and Artistry of East Central European Film*. London: Wallflower Press, 2003.

Janicka Bożena and Andrzej Kołodyński, eds. *Chełmska 21. 50 lat Wytwórni Filmów Dokumentalnych i Fabularnych w Warszawie*. Warsaw: WFDiF, 2000 [in Polish and in English].

Jankun-Dopartowa, Mariola and Mirosław Przylipiak (eds) *Człowiek z ekranu. Z antropologii postaci filmowej*. Kraków: Arcana, 1996.

Karabasz, Kazimierz. *Bez fikcji: z notatek filmowego dokumentalisty*. Warsaw: Wydawnictwa Artystyczne i Filmowe, 1985.

Michałek, Bolesław and Frank Turaj. *The Modern Cinema of Poland*. Bloomington: Indiana University Press, 1988.

Nurczyńska-Fidelska, Ewelina and Zbigniew Batko (eds) *Polish Cinema in Ten Takes*. Łódź:

Łódzkie Towarzystwo Naukowe, 1995.

Orr, John. *Contemporary Cinema*. Edinburgh: Edinburgh University Press, 1998.

Petrie, Graham and Ruth Dwyer (eds) *Before the Wall Came Down: Soviet and East European Film-makers Working in the West*. New York: University Press of America, 1990.

Przylipiak, Mirosław. *Poetyka kina dokumentalnego*. Gdańsk: Wydawnictwo Uniwersytetu Gdańskiego, 2000.

Book Chapters, Articles, Interviews and Film Reviews

Baugh, Lloyd. 'Cinematographic Variations on the Christ-Event: Three Film Texts by Krzysztof Kieślowski. Part One: *A Short Film about Love*', *Gregorianum* 84, 3 (2003), 551–83.

Benedyktowicz, Zbigniew. 'Długi film o miłości' [on *Three Colours: Blue*]. Kwartalnik Filmowy 4 (1993/1994), 107–12.

Bolewski, Jacek. 'Odmiana życia przez przypadki. Śladami Krzysztofa Kieślowskiego', *Więź* 42, 1 (1999), 35–52.

Cavendish, Phil. 'Kieślowski's *Decalogue*', *Sight and Sound* 59, 3 (1990), 162–5.

Clevell, Tammy. 'The Shades of Modern Mourning in *Three Colours* Trilogy', *Literature/Film Quarterly* 28, 3 (2000), 203–9.

Coates, Paul. 'Anatomy of a Murder: *A Short Film About Killing*', *Sight and Sound* 58, 1 (1988/89), 63–4.

_____ 'The Curse of the Law: *The Decalogue*', *Lucid Dreams: The Films of Krzysztof Kieślowski*, ed. Paul Coates (London: Flicks Books, 1999), 94–115.

_____ 'Exile and Identity: Kieślowski and His Contemporaries', *Before the Wall Came Down: Soviet and East European Film-makers Working in the West*, eds Graham Petrie and Ruth Dwyer (New York: University Press of America, 1990), 103–14.

_____ 'Kieślowski and the Antipolitics of Colour: A Reading of the "Three Colours" Trilogy', *Cinema Journal* 41, 2 (2002), 41–66.

_____ 'Kieślowski and the Crisis of Documentary', *Lucid Dreams: The Films of Krzysztof Kieślowski*, ed. Paul Coates (London: Flicks Books, 1999), 32–53.

_____ 'Kieślowski, Goethe i kolor, który zmienił Świat', *Kwartalnik Filmowy* 24 (1998), 98–104.

_____ 'Metaphysical Love in Two Films by Krzysztof Kieślowski', *The Polish Review* 37, 3 (1992), 135–44.

_____ 'Politics of Memory, Ghosts of Defeat: Kieślowski's *No End*', *The Polish Review* 33, 3 (1988), 343–6.

_____ 'The Sense of Ending: Reflections on Kieślowski's Trilogy', *Film Quarterly* 50, 2 (1996–97), 19–26.

Cunneen, Joseph. '"Being Alive is a Gift": Krzysztof Kieślowski's *The Decalogue*', *Spiritus: A Journal of Christian Spirituality* 1, 1 (2001), 79–85.

Di Bartolomeo, Lisa. 'No Other Gods: Blue and Green in Kieślowski's *Dekalog 1*', *Studies in Slavic Cultures* (February 2000), 47–59.

Dobson, Julia. 'Nationality, Authenticity, Reflexivity: Kieślowski's *Trois couleurs: Bleu* (1993), *Blanc* (1993) and *Rouge* (1994)', *French Cinema in the 1990s. Continuity and Difference*, ed. Phil Powrie (Oxford: Oxford University Press, 1999), 234–45.

Eidsvik, Charles. 'Kieślowski's "Short Films"', *Film Quarterly* 44, 1 (1990), 50–5.

Falkowska, Janina. '*The Double Life of Véronique* and *Three Colours*: An Escape from Politics?' *Lucid Dreams: The Films of Krzysztof Kieślowski*, ed. Paul Coates (London: Flicks Books, 1999), 136–59.

_____ '"The Political" in the Films of Andrzej Wajda and Krzysztof Kieślowski', *Cinema Journal* 34, 2 (1995), 37–50.

Film na Świecie 388/389, 3-4 (1992). Polish film journal. Special issue on Kieślowski.

Garbowski, Christopher. 'Kieślowski's Seeing I/Eye', *The Polish Review* 40, 1 (1995), 53–60.

_____ 'Krzysztof Kieślowski's *Decalogue*: Presenting Religious Topics on Television', *The Polish Review* 37, 3 (1992), 327–34.

____ 'Przestrzeń, czas i bohater', *Kwartalnik Filmowy* 24 (1998), 29–54.

Gazda Janusz. 'Zimny kolor wolności' [on *Three Colours: Blue*]. *Kwartalnik Filmowy* 4 (1993/94), 89–105.

Haltof, Marek. 'A Fistful of Dollars: Polish Cinema After 1989 Freedom Shock', *Film Quarterly* 48, 3 (1995), 15–25.

____ 'Everything for Sale: Polish National Cinema after 1989', *Canadian Slavonic Papers* 39, 1 (1997), 137–52.

____ 'Krzysztof Kieślowski: European Art Film and National Context', *A World of Slavic Literatures: Essays in Comparative Slavic Studies in Honor of Edward Możejko*, ed. Paul D. Morris (Bloomington, Indiana: Slavica, 2002), 79–89.

____ 'Screening the Unrepresented World: Kieślowski's Early Film-Essays (*Personnel*, *The Scar* and *The Calm*)', *The Polish Review* 48, 4 (2003), 463–79.

Helman, Alicja. 'Women in Kieślowski's Late Films', *Lucid Dreams: The Films of Krzysztof Kieślowski*, ed. Paul Coates (London: Flicks Books, 1999), 116–35.

Horoszczak, Adam. '*Amator* – czyli optymizm utraconych złudzeń', *Kino* 9 (1979), 15–18.

Insdorf, Annette. 'Cinematic Poetry: An Affectionate Look at Krzysztof Kieślowski's *Three Colors: White*', *Film Comment* 33, 2 (1997), 46–9.

Jabłońska, Katarzyna. 'Wariacje na temat Dziesięciorga Przykazań', *Kwartalnik Filmowy* 18 (1997), 154–78.

James, Nick. 'Kind of Blue', *Sight and Sound* 12, 4 (2002), 34–6.

Janicka, Bożena. 'Kamień czy szkiełko' [on *Three Colours: White*], *Kino* 2 (1994), 8–10.

Jankun-Dopartowa, Mariola. 'Trójkolorowy transparent: Vive le chaos!' [on *Three Colours* trilogy], *Kino* 6 (1995), 4–7.

Jazdon, Mikołaj. '*Personel* – credo artystyczne Krzysztofa Kieślowskiego', *Poloniści o filmie*, ed. Marek Hendrykowski (Poznań: Wydawnictwo WiS, 1997), 151–61.

Kaplińska, Anna. 'Status ontologiczny filmu dokumentalnego na przykładzie twórczości Krzysztofa Kieślowskiego', *Kwartalnik Filmowy* 24, 84 (1998), 6–28.

Keates, Jonathan. 'Heartburn: *A Short Film About Love*', *Sight and Sound* 59, 2 (1990), 132.

Kehr, Dave. 'To Save the World. Kieślowski's *Three Colours* Trilogy', *Film Comment* 30, 6 (1994), 10–20.

Kemp, Philip. '*Three Colours: Red*', *Sight and Sound* 4, 11 (1994), 54–5.

Klawans, Stuart. '*Three Colours: Red*', *The Nation* (12 December 1994), 738–40.

Kibourn, R.J.A. 'Toward a Non-Euclidean Cinema: Kieślowski and Literature', *Canadian Journal of Film Studies* 6, 2 (1997), 34–50.

Kieślowski, Krzysztof. 'In Depth Rather Than Breadth', *Polish Perspectives* 24, 6–7 (1981), 67–71.

Kline, Jefferson T. 'Seeing Red: Kieślowski and the Uncanny', *The Psychoanalytic Review* 83, 3 (1996), 435–43.

Kornatowska, Maria. 'W czerwieni' [on *Three Colours: Red*], *Kino* 7–8 (1994), 28–9.

Krzemiński, Ireneusz. 'Dekalog, Kieślowski i Bóg', *Dialog* 7 (1990), 123–7.

Kujundžič, Dragan, 'Rozszczepione spojrzenia, inskrypcje, scenotafia: o Kieślowskiego filmowaniu żałoby', trans. Jacek Mydla. *Er(r)go* 5 (2002), 83–104.

Kulig, Agnieszka. 'Etyka w filmach Krzysztofa Kieślowskiego', *Kwartalnik Filmowy* 29–30 (2000), 53–8.

Kwartalnik Filmowy 24 (1998) [Poland]. Special issue on Kieślowski.

Łapińska, Magdalena. 'Opowieść o artyście, motylu i lustrze', *Kwartalnik Filmowy* 24 (1998), 66–84.

Lefanu, Mark. '*Camera Buff*', *Monthly Film Bulletin* 49, 577 (1982), 23–4.

Lis, Piotr. 'Summa' [on *Three Colours: Red*], *Kino* 7–8 (1994), 26–8.

Lubelski, Tadeusz. 'From *Personnel* to *No End*: Kieślowski's Political Feature Films', *Lucid Dreams: The Films of Krzysztof Kieślowski*, ed. Paul Coates (London: Flicks Books, 1999), 54–76.

____ 'The Sequel Will be Shown without Him… Interview with Jacek Petrycki, a cameraman of *First Love*', *Chełmska 21. 50 lat Wytwórni Filmów Dokumentalnych i Fabularnych w Warszawie*, eds. Bożena Janicka and Andrzej Kołodyński (Warsaw: WFDiF, 2000): 166–7.

____ 'Podwójne życie Kieślowskiego', *Kino* 9 (1991), 2–5.

Łużyńska, Jadwiga Anna. 'Fenomen Krzysztofa Kieślowskiego', *Iluzjon* 1–4 (1995), 3–56.

Macnab, Geoffrey. '*Three Colours: Blue*', *Sight and Sound* 3, 11 (1993), 54–5.

Malatyńska, Maria. 'Ćwiczenia z perspektywy (Rzecz o Krzysztofie Kieślowskim)', *Kwartalnik Filmowy* 24 (1998), 112–25.

____ 'Smutne krajobrazy', *Kino* 1 (1989), 5–7 [on *A Short Film About Love*].

Mensonge, Serge. '*Three Colours Blue, White and Red*: Krzysztof Kieślowski and Friends' [interview]. *Cinema Papers* 99 (June 1994), 26–32.

Michałek, Bolesław. 'Kieślowski: rysy odrębne', *Kino* 2 (1990), 1–3.

Michalski, Milena. '*The Double Life of Veronique*', *The Slavonic and East European Review* 72, 1 (1994), 191–2.

____ '*Three Colours: Blue*', *The Slavonic and East European Review* 72, 4 (1994), 790–1.

____ '*Three Colours: Red*', *The Slavonic and East European Review* 74, 1 (1996), 191–3.

____ '*Three Colours: White*', *The Slavonic and East European Review* 73, 3 (1995), 592–3.

Miczka, Tadeusz. '"We live in the world lacking idea on itself [sic]": Krzysztof Kieślowski's Art of Film', *Kinema* 7 (1997), 23–47.

Miler-Curtin, Anna. 'Przypadek Krzysztofa Kieślowskiego. Problem kompozycji i interpretacji', *Film: symbol i tożsamość*, ed. Jan Trzynadlowski (Wrocław: University of Wrocław Press, 1992), 179–209.

Moszcz, Gustaw. 'No heroics, please', *Sight and Sound* 50, 2 (1981), 90–1.

Paprocki, Henryk. 'Niebieski jak niebo' [on *Three Colours: Blue*], *Kwartalnik Filmowy* 4 (1993/94), 79–81.

Pawlicki, Maciej. 'Wishful Thinking', *Kino* 6 (1987), 5–7.

Perlmutter, Ruth. 'Multiple Strands and Possible Worlds', *Canadian Journal of Film Studies* 11, 2 (2002), 44–61.

____ 'Testament of the Father: Kieślowski's *The Decalogue*', *Film Criticism* 22, 2 (1997–98), 51–65.

Pizzello, Stephen. 'Piotr Sobociński: *Red*', *American Cinematographer* 76, 6 (1995), 68–74.

Płażewski, Jerzy. 'Wiecznie niezadowolony z siebie' [review of *The Scar*], *Kino* 8 (1976), 4–8.

Przylipiak, Mirosław. 'Krótkie filmy, *Dekalog* oraz *Podwójne życie Weroniki* Krzysztofa Kieślowskiego w zwierciadle polskiej krytyki filmowej', *Kwartalnik Filmowy* 24 (1998), 133–68.

____ 'Krzysztof Kieślowski – kontynuator Andrzeja Munka', *Kino* 6 (1994), 14–15.

____ 'Monter i studentka, czyli jak to naprawdę było z niszczeniem Krzysztofa Kieślowskiego przez polską prasę filmową.' *Kino* 3 (1997), 6–9; 50.

____ 'Nie na temat' [review of *No End*], *Kino* 2 (1986), 8–10.

Pulleine, Tim. '*A Short Film About Love*', *Monthly Film Bulletin* 57, 676 (1990), 131–2.

Pym, John. '*A Short Film About Killing*', *Monthly Film Bulletin* 56, 671 (1989), 371–2.

Ragland Ellie and Elizabeth Wright. '*The Double Life of Véronique*: An Inquiry into the Existence of Woman', *Psychoanalytic Psychology* 10, 3 (1993), 481–6.

Rammel, Iwona. 'Van den Budenmayer i jemu podobni. O muzyce w ostatnich filmach Kieślowskiego', *Kwartalnik Filmowy* 6 (1994), 130–40.

Rayans, Tony. 'Glowing in the Dark', *Sight and Sound* 4, 6 (1994), 8–10.

____ 'Kieślowski: Crossing Over', *Sight and Sound* 1, 11 (1992), 22–3.

Rigney, Francis J. '*The Decalogue*: A Psychoanalytic Deadlock', *Film Criticism* 14, 3 (1990), 55–71.

Romney, Jonathan. '*The Double Life of Véronique*', *Sight and Sound* 1, 11 (1992), 43.

Rubinstein, Lenny. '*Camera Buff*', *Cineaste* 11, 1 (1980–81), 37–9.

Ruppert, Peter. '*The Double Life of Véronique*', *Cineaste* 19, 2–3 (1992), 63–5.

Rushton, Richard. 'Reading *Three Colours: Blue*', *Senses of Cinema* 10 (2000), www.sensesof cinema.com/contents/00/10/blue.html

Salska-Kaca, Mirosława. 'Polski esej dokumentalny', *Film na Świecie* 351–2 (1988), 95–112.

Sobolewski, Tadeusz. 'Niepokój Kieślowskiego', *Kino* 6 (1995), 7–9.

____ 'Peace and Rebellion: Some Remarks on the Creative Output of Krzysztof Kieślowski', in *Polish Cinema in Ten Takes*, ed. Ewelina Nurczyńska-Fidelska and Zbigniew Batko (Łódź: Łódzkie Towarzystwo Naukowe, 1995), 123–37.

____ '*Przypadek* – Postscriptum', *Kino* 6 (1987), 8–11.

____ 'Równanie w dół' [on *Three Colours: White*], *Kino* 2 (1994), 10–11.

____ 'Solidarność grzesznych. *O Dekalogu* Krzysztofa Kieślowskiego', *Na Głos* 1 (1990), 91–101.

____ 'Ultimate Concerns', *Lucid Dreams: The Films of Krzysztof Kieślowski*, ed. Paul Coates (London: Flicks Books, 1999), 19–31.

Sochoń, Jan. 'Pokonać śmierć' [on *Three Colours: Blue*], *Kwartalnik Filmowy* 4 (1993/94), 83–7.

Strick, Philip. '*No End*', *Monthly Film Bulletin*, 55, 650 (1988), 76–7.

____ '*Three Colours: White*', *Sight and Sound*, 4, 6 (1994), 63–4.

Synessios, Natasha. '*A Short Film about Killing*; *A Short Film about Love*', *The Slavonic and East European Review*, 73, 2 (1995), 393–6.

Wilson, Emma. '*Three Colours: Blue*: Kieślowski, colour and the postmodern subject', *Screen* 39, 4 (1998), 349–62.

Winchell, James. 'Metaphysics of Post-Nationalism: La Double Vie de Krzysztof Kieślowski', *Contemporary French Civilization* 22, 2 (1998), 240–63.

Wojdylo, John. '*La Double Vie de Véronique*', *Cinema Papers* 93 (1993), 46–7.

Wyszyński, Zbigniew. 'Ideologia i moralistyka Krzysztofa Kieślowskiego (na przykładzie filmu *Dekalog*)', *Powiększenie* 11, 3–4 (1991), 22–32.

Zielińska, Magda. 'Krótko o 'krótkich filmach' Kieślowskiego', *Twórczość* 5 (1989), 118–21.

INDEX

2677